CRITICAL INSIGHTS

Animal Farm

CRITICAL INSIGHTS

Animal Farm

Editor
Thomas Horan
The Citadel, South Carolina

SALEM PRESS
A Division of EBSCO Information Services, Inc.
Ipswich, Massachusetts

GREY HOUSE PUBLISHING

Publisher's Cataloging-In-Publication Data
(Prepared by The Donohue Group, Inc.)

Names: Horan, Thomas, 1974- editor.
Title: Animal farm / editor, Thomas Horan, The Citadel.
Other Titles: Critical insights.
Description: [First edition]. | Ipswich, Massachusetts : Salem Press, a division
    of EBSCO Information Services, Inc. ; Amenia, NY : Grey
    House Publishing, [2018] | Includes bibliographical references
    and index.
Identifiers: ISBN 9781682179185 (hardcover)
Subjects: LCSH: Orwell, George, 1903-1950.Animal farm. | Orwell, George,
    1903-1950--Criticism and interpretation. | Totalitarianism in literature. |
    Dystopias in literature. | Anthropomorphism in literature.
Classification: LCC PR6029.R8 A633 2018 | DDC 823/.912--dc23

First Printing

Contents

Resources

About This Volume

Thomas Horan

Critical Insights: Animal Farm contextualizes the allegorical novel that established George Orwell as the greatest British satirist since Jonathan Swift. This volume considers *Animal Farm* within the author's multidisciplinary oeuvre, the complex cultural climate of its composition, and the diverse range of critical responses to the text. The first four essays, which comprise the critical contexts section of the book, cover *Animal Farm*'s literary, historical, and political importance as well as its ongoing relevance to contemporary readers, providing a foundation for further study and scholarly work.

In his essay assessing the critical reception of *Animal Farm* from the time of its publication to the present, Erik Jaccard illuminates how contradictions between Orwell's support for international socialism and his wartime embrace of popular English patriotism shape critical debate about the novel's literary and political value. Jaccard surveys critical responses to *Animal Farm*'s form and its content. He addresses how some critics lauded the skillful deployment of the age-old barnyard fable, while others excoriated the novel for its historical inaccuracy, putative disillusion, and alleged failure of political imagination. Left-wing commentators were forced to reckon with the power of the Orwell mystique and to defend socialism against a seeming indictment. Conservatives, on the other hand, attempted to promote the novel as a warning about the inherent dangers of communism and socialism generally. Jaccard concludes that continually renewing sociopolitical debates ensure that Orwell, *Animal Farm*, and the contradictions animating both will remain relevant well into the twenty-first century.

In his essay focusing on *Animal Farm*'s cultural and historical background, Bradley Hart investigates initial reactions by American writers to the publication of *Animal Farm* to explore how the book served as a sort of Rorschach test for the underlying political convictions of its stateside readers, resulting in a diverse range of early interpretations that resonate through American culture to the present day.

Gregory Brophy's critical lens essay introduces readers to critical animal studies, tracing out a surprisingly recent development in *Animal Farm*'s critical reception that interprets Orwell's animals simply as animals rather than as symbolic depictions of historical personages. Brophy casts Orwell's interpretative use of animals as yet another means of domination. This approach demands coming to terms with the spectrum of exploitative uses to which society puts animals, from the knacker and the butcher to the racket through which readers of allegory harvest fictional plots, tilled by animals, for their own anthropocentric ends.

Rafeeq McGiveron provides a revealing comparison of *Animal Farm* and *Nineteen Eighty-Four*, addressing how Orwell used very different strategies of narration to further the ever-timely warnings of his thematically similar political satires. McGiveron finds that while *Animal Farm* purports to be "a fairy story" with a deceptively simple presentation, *Nineteen Eighty-Four* provides a richer depiction of the individual's life of the mind. McGiveron considers how these contrasting approaches produce significantly different types of experiences for the reader.

The ten remaining essays provide critical readings that present a range of engaging interpretations of *Animal Farm* by perceptive scholars. In the first of these, Brian Ireland situates Orwell within the long tradition of anthropomorphism in which human traits are assigned to nonhuman objects as metaphors for the human condition. Exploring the sociopolitical ambiguity of the rats in Orwell's fable, Ireland addresses how the author's presentation of vermin in *Animal Farm* and elsewhere affects the validity of his egalitarian views.

Questioning the widespread regard for Orwell's plain style, Paige Busby argues that Orwell's desire for plain language is itself a "fairy story." For Busby, *Animal Farm* reinforces the highly complex and performative nature of language. Despite his best efforts to keep language transparent, Busby finds Orwell's prose to be like a smudged window pane, though those smudges convey a compelling story and message.

Camilo Peralta explains the influence of Mosaic Law on the Seven Commandments, devised by the animals to embody Animalism, their new belief system. His analysis reveals how the author comments on and critiques the Ten Commandments. Peralta explores Orwell's famously complicated relationship with religion, pointing out that Orwell affiliated himself with the Church of England even as he professed atheistic views.

Charity Gibson points out that unlike virtually every other dystopian novel, *Animal Farm* does not include a malcontent who actively resists the totalitarian system. Gibson asserts that because the malcontent typically functions as the protagonist, his absence leaves the audience without a character to serve as a moral compass and with no one to cheer for. By implying through his allegorical account of Soviet history that Stalin rose unopposed, Gibson argues that Orwell engages in historical revisionism.

Richard Carr's essay surveys the ways in which British parliamentarians have used *Animal Farm* from the period immediately following publication to the early twenty-first century. Carr highlights the shifting nature of Orwell's message in light of contemporary geopolitical developments, ending with a case for *Animal Farm*'s applicability to contemporary politics.

Defending Orwell from the charge of sexism by critics such as Daphne Patai, Melanie Marotta discusses how *Animal Farm* depicts women positively, contrasting Orwell's proto-feminism with the disappointing treatment of gender issues in the recent Pixar film *Zootopia* (2016). Whereas Orwell, through his depiction of the mare Clover, offers readers gender equality, *Zootopia* by comparison is dispiritingly sexist, indicating that our progress on gender issues has been sadly limited.

Josephine McQuail situates *Animal Farm* within the continuum of beast fables stretching back to antiquity. Her work elucidates the ironies of Orwell's "fable," where a society founded on utopian principles all too quickly becomes a nightmarish dystopia. McQuail shows how through the universal appeal of the beast fable, Orwell's satire can apply to almost any failed revolutionary movement, from communism to Trumpism.

Drawing on the work of prominent sociologists and political philosophers, Dario Altobelli illuminates *Animal Farm*'s subtle presentation of the violence underlying the law. Altobelli notes that even before the emergence of repressive violence in the novel, the pigs do interpretative violence to communal memory by modifying the commandments to their advantage, rendering Orwell's satire a bitter apologue on the distance that always separates justice from law, which functions as an instrument of power, domination, and oppression.

Andrew Byers sees *Animal Farm* as an early consideration of biopolitics and an analysis of how it enables and nurtures totalitarian systems. Focusing on how the pigs manipulate the bodies and activities of the farm's inhabitants, Byers interprets *Animal Farm* as a prescient depiction of how social and political power increasingly determine human life and as a forerunner of the work of such theorists as Hannah Arendt and Michel Foucault.

Finally, Robert Evans analyzes Orwell's frequent use of comedy and humor in *Animal Farm*, pointing out how in key places—especially in the novel's first half—the book is genuinely funny. Demonstrating how Orwell employs comedy to help highlight, by contrast, the tragedies to come, Evans shows how by lulling both readers and characters into an often lighthearted beginning, the author makes the ultimate catastrophe all the more emphatic and painful.

The various interpretations of *Animal Farm* presented in these insightful essays showcase the richness, complexity, and pertinence of this classic dystopian satire.

On *Animal Farm*

Thomas Horan

Although the totalitarian regime it satirized fell decades ago, George Orwell's *Animal Farm* endures as a cogent critique of various economic and sociopolitical ideologies, a commentary on human nature and dangerous habits of mind, and—above all—as great literature, sufficiently charming to please children, subtle enough to engage adults, and with moments so haunting that they leave an enduring impression on both. As Morris Dickstein notes, "*Animal Farm* went on to become one of the most widely read books of the twentieth century, selling upwards of twenty million copies" (134).

In oft-quoted lines from his preface to the Ukrainian edition of the novel, Orwell discusses how he came to write *Animal Farm*:

> On my return from Spain I thought of exposing the Soviet myth in a story that could be easily understood by almost anyone and which could be easily translated into other languages. However, the actual details of the story did not come to me for some time until one day (I was then living in a small village) I saw a little boy, perhaps ten years old, driving a huge cart-horse along a narrow path, whipping it whenever it tried to turn. It struck me that if only such animals became aware of their strength we should have no power over them, and that men exploit animals in much the same way as the rich exploit the proletariat. (179)

Here we see that while using events from Soviet history as a template, Orwell's satire is an analysis of classism, the economic exploitation underlying it, and the utopian impulse to overcome this dehumanizing and destructive tendency. When he arrived in Barcelona in late 1936, Orwell believed he had found a community that the proletarians productively and democratically controlled, a community that he was prepared to take up arms to defend: "Practically everyone wore rough working-class clothes, or blue overalls or some variant of the militia uniform. All this was queer and moving. There was much in it that I did not understand, in some ways I did not even like it, but I recognized it immediately as a state of affairs worth fighting for. Also, I believed that things were as they appeared, that this was really a workers' State" (*Homage* 7-8). *Animal Farm* partially reflects the ways in which this egalitarian society was, ironically, undermined by many on the left: "Very similar things happened during the Spanish civil war. Then, too, the factions on the Republican side which the Russians were determined to crush were recklessly libeled in the English leftwing press, and any statement in their defence even in letter form, was refused publication" ("Proposed Preface" 164-65). *Animal Farm* is—like *Nineteen Eighty-Four*—a warning about the harm caused by ideologues in Britain and throughout the world. Long critical of nationalism, Orwell was determined to facilitate translation of *Animal Farm* by writing it in a clear, graceful style, which shows that he intended it to reach a global audience in an attempt to combat fundamental biases that harm people everywhere. In his biography of Orwell, Gordon Bowker notes that *Animal Farm* has "been translated into languages as disparate as Swahili and Serbo-Croat" (xiii). As Richard Rorty succinctly puts it: "Orwell wanted to be of use to people who were suffering" (140).

At the time of the novel's composition, the Soviet Union was misperceived as a beacon of progress, rationality, and justice to many oppressed peoples. Orwell understood that this veneration of Stalinism would ultimately harm the cause of socialism, since many would be liable to conclude mistakenly that the Bolsheviks' crimes were a symptom—rather than a gross perversion—of socialism: "Indeed, in my opinion, nothing has contributed so much to the corruption of the original idea of Socialism as the belief that Russia is a Socialist country and that every act of its rulers must be excused, if not imitated. And so for the past ten years, I have been convinced that the destruction of the Soviet myth was essential if we wanted a revival of the Socialist movement" ("Preface" 179). While many conservatives misread and misappropriate both *Animal Farm* and *Nineteen Eighty-Four* as putative attacks on socialism, Orwell wrote both novels to defend and preserve the cause of democratic socialism to which he devoted the most vital years of his short life.

Nineteen Eighty-Four deservedly remains Orwell's most popular and influential book, yet *Animal Farm* illustrates many of *Nineteen Eighty-Four*'s core ideas. In *Animal Farm* we find instances of doublethink: "[W]hen the key of the store-shed was lost the whole farm was convinced that Snowball had thrown it down the well. Curiously enough they went on believing this even after the mislaid key was found under a sack of meal" (91). We also find Orwell's interest in the interdependence of language and thought, and the way totalitarian systems attempt to control both. For example, when the animals are informed that they will no longer debate and vote on issues of policy and governance, lack of language precludes the ability to understand fully what has happened: "In spite of the shock that Snowball's expulsion had given them, the animals were dismayed by this announcement. Several of them would have protested if they could have found the right arguments. Even Boxer was vaguely troubled. He set his ears back, shook his forelock several times, and tried hard to marshal his thoughts; but in the end he could not think of anything to say" (64). In *Animal Farm* we see how totalitarian systems often justify their draconian methods and perpetuate their power by promulgating fear of a powerful, unseen, omnipresent adversary, with Snowball (Trotsky) as an antecedent of *Nineteen Eighty-Four*'s Emmanuel Goldstein: "It seemed to them as though Snowball were some kind of invisible menace, pervading the air about them and menacing them with all kinds of danger" (91-92). As in *Nineteen Eighty-Four*, history and memory in *Animal Farm* are continually compromised and even eclipsed by relentless government propaganda of a superficially progressive kind. In both books, we also find a critique of H. G. Wells's notion that those with a background in science make the best sociopolitical leaders: As the duplicitous Squealer tells the other animals when the pigs hoard the milk and apples for themselves, "Milk and apples (this has been proved by Science, comrades) contain substances absolutely necessary to the well-being of a pig" (41). The tyranny of the pigs shows that erudition and training don't make leaders more just and less susceptible to corruption. Indeed, Orwell argues that just the opposite is true:

> The ordinary people in the street—partly, perhaps, because they are not sufficiently interested in ideas to be intolerant about them— still vaguely hold that "I suppose everyone's got a right to their own opinion." It is only, or at any rate it is chiefly, the literary and scientific intelligentsia, the very people who ought to be the guardians of liberty, who are beginning to despise it, in theory as well as in practice. ("Proposed Preface" 168)

While all of these concepts are more fully explored in Orwell's final novel, they feature prominently in *Animal Farm*; and, as with *Nineteen Eighty-Four*, they are at work in the English heartland, emphasizing the anti-imperialist point that there is nothing special about English culture, the English themselves, or white people for that matter: "Tolerance and decency are deeply rooted in England, but they are not indestructible, and they have to be kept alive partly by conscious effort" ("Proposed Preface" 169).

On the other hand, both *Animal Farm* and *Nineteen Eighty-Four* highlight the pride, strength, and dignity of the common people in which Orwell invests so much hope: "But if there were hardships to be borne, they were partly offset by the fact that life nowadays had a greater dignity than it had had before. . . . They found it comforting to be reminded that, after all, they were truly their own masters and that the work they did was for their own benefit" (129-30). Opposing the reductive view that most people are driven solely by materialism and personal advancement, Orwell insists that ordinary people are often motivated by nonpecuniary inclinations, such as the desire to be useful, to work hard for themselves, to be a part of larger meaningful endeavors, and to care for one another. Despite all they have, the pigs know nothing of these wholesome, sustaining joys. In tottering on their hind legs, though they see it as emblematic of their sociopolitical supremacy, the pigs become as ridiculous and unsteady as their booze-addled former master. Orwell never lost his faith in the enduring decency of the working class; in this he finds a utopian sentiment unconquered by even the bleakest totalitarianism:

"And yet the animals never gave up hope. More, they never lost, even for an instant, their sense of honour and privilege in being members of Animal Farm. . . . None of the old dreams had been abandoned. The Republic of the Animals which Old Major had foretold, when the green fields of England should be untrodden by human feet, was still believed in. Some day it was coming" (142-43). The text even implies that absent corrupt leaders, a bona fide improvement of society and perhaps even human nature may be possible. In the time immediately following the Rebellion, "Nobody stole, nobody grumbled over his rations, the quarrelling and biting and jealousy which had been normal features of life in the old days had almost disappeared. Nobody shirked—or almost nobody" (35). *Animal Farm*, despite its dispiriting conclusion, allows for the possibility of a better society under the right circumstances.

Unfortunately, such propitious conditions are absent in the story from the beginning. Humanity and ultimately the pigs represent the propertied, privileged classes. Though he does not realize it, Old Major's indictment of humankind applies just as fittingly to his own kind: "Man is the only creature that consumes without producing. He does not give milk, he does not lay eggs, he is too weak to pull the plough, he cannot run fast enough to catch rabbits. Yet he is the lord of all animals" (6). Applying Old Major's dubious criteria, which affords rights and liberties only to those who can directly produce, Jones and Napoleon are indistinguishable as rulers: "But still, neither pigs nor dogs produced any food of their own labour; and there were many of them, and their appetites were always good" (142). They are also, as Samir Elbarbary notes, alike in their brutal method of law enforcement: "It is doubly ironic that the dog, well armed with powerful physique and canine teeth, is in fact the proverbial man's best friend. As the pigs eventually turn into 'men,' tyrannical humans, this largely offers itself as a verbal pun on the proverb" (36).

In the simplistic solution Old Major puts forward, Patrick Reilly identifies a pernicious generalization more reminiscent of Hitler than Marx or Lenin: "'Only get rid of Man,' exhorts Old Major (p. 10), and then, by implication, it is clear walking to the just society:

substitute kulaks or Jews or any other single group and we have the same pernicious psychology leading to the same atrocities" (73). Old Major's grievance against humanity, unlike Hitler's and Stalin's targeting of innocent groups of people, is legitimate, yet it hardly warrants the total annihilation of humanity. Dickstein argues that even the clarity of Old Major's message—though Orwell ironically is revered for the lucidity of his prose—makes it susceptible to being condensed initially into the reductive commandments of Animalism and ultimately into a banal, repetitive chant: "When separated from actual thinking, turned into a mindless chant, the plain style shows its dark side" (141).

Richard I. Smyer points out the propagandistic nature of Old Major's disquisition, which offers a political polemic under the auspices of sharing a dream and initiates a process of indoctrination that the pigs will eventually employ to horrifying effect:

> However, worth noting about Old Major's dream is the process by which it is transformed from a glimpse of the past into a marching order directed toward the future. . . . Old Major no sooner mentions the dream than he waves it aside to make way for a political speech delivered to condition his audience to act. . . . Old Major is dogmatically "certain" that he knows the whole song of which he heard only three words in his infancy; and in inducing the animals to memorize and sing the lyrics of "Beasts of England" he is in effect conditioning them to accept the authoritarian dictates of his porcine successors. (Smyer 38-39)

By linking his dream to conditions in the distant past rather than basing his appeal solely on rational criteria, Old Major evokes a hazy nostalgia similar to Merrie England and other mythic notions of a former golden age. Given that Old Major derives a complete manifesto from a few supposedly remembered words, Smyer asserts that the prize boar may be deliberately fabricating propaganda: "We may be justified in suspecting that Old Major's secret intention of using his dream to indoctrinate the other animals for the future has led him to falsify the fragmentary nature of the original dream by imposing on it a form of certitude designed to reinforce the ideological content of the speech" (39). Old Major is undoubtedly acting with the best of intentions. However, a willful distortion of the truth for any reason, especially by a respected figure of authority, is likely to undermine both accurate memories and an investment in objectivity: "Events and circumstances both within and outside of Manor/Animal Farm conspire to instill into the animals' budding consciousness not only a distrust and possibly an abhorrence of a specific aspect of the past—their suffering under Farmer Jones—but also an indifference to the past itself" (39). As Orwell notes and fears, the past can swiftly become a figment of narrative and wishful thinking rather than the product of accurate recollections or reliable records.

Narrating from a vantage of detached neutrality, Orwell, as Dickstein observes, does not solely blame the pigs for what transpires: "When the animals invariably grow confused and go along with each twist and turn of the official line, questioning their own memories, the reader may wonder how much Orwell blames this emerging dictatorship on the threat of force, the amoral cleverness of those who manipulate public opinion, or the innocent stupidity of the masses, who are so easily cowed" (140). Instead, the author examines from a remove the societal ramifications of pervasive mendacity, self-delusion, and intellectual laziness.

From the disinterested tone of the narrative Paul Kirschner concludes that the literate, undeceived, skeptical Benjamin is a stand-in for the author himself, just as some critics and readers conflate *Nineteen Eighty-Four*'s doomed protagonist with Orwell.

> Internally, however, what matters is that Benjamin tells the animals what they cannot "read" for themselves, *as the author/narrator has been doing for us.* By usurping authorial function, Benjamin suddenly *becomes* the author—not by prudently keeping silent, but by placing sympathy before safety. He becomes "Orwell" when, through him, the "author" suddenly seems to drop his mask and show where his heart lies. (765)

Yet, unlike Benjamin, Orwell was a determined social activist for much of his adult life. Laraine Fergenson points out that he was critical of intellectual pessimists like Benjamin:

> Throughout the story, Benjamin plays the role of the uninvolved intellectual, very much the type that Orwell had criticized in his essay "Inside the Whale," in which he characterizes certain writers (chief among them Henry Miller) as committing the sin of Jonah—refusing to preach to the people of Ninevah [sic] and being encapsulated in the belly of the whale, a metaphor for the uninvolved artist or intellectual cut off from society. Benjamin the donkey, rejecting the principles of animalism because of a deep-rooted pessimism that—as Orwell often feared it might—manifested itself in political quietism, refuses to believe that life can be made better. (115-16)

This difference of opinion about Benjamin and his connection to Orwell opens the larger question of whether *Animal Farm* and its author present a pessimistic worldview.

In light of the novel's conclusion, Ramón Magráns finds the text nihilistic: "Orwell has already condemned mankind in the persons of Frederick, Jones and Pilington [sic]. Now that it is impossible to distinguish between man and beast, the whole animal kingdom is condemned; neither man nor beast can learn to govern or be governed" (397). Robert A. Lee identifies this apparent pessimism in the pigs' growing ability to police language and thought, again anticipating a central theme of *Nineteen Eighty-Four*: "The most darkly pessimistic aspect of *Animal Farm* is that the animals are unable even to recognize their new oppression, much less combat it. The difference is the control by the pigs of language; Mr. Jones controlled only action—not thought" (570). Lee's claim that Jones did not employ methods of thought control is belied by the anxiety some animals show immediately following his ejection: "Some of the animals talked of the duty of loyalty to Mr. Jones, whom they referred to as 'Master'" (15). However, this does not diminish the validity of Lee's larger point because the pigs are far more effective brainwashers than the farmer.

Feminist critic Daphne Patai traces Orwell's alleged despondency to his unacknowledged sexism. Patai demonstrates that the female animals in *Animal Farm* are "rudimentary in comparison with" their male counterparts (214), that female animals such as Clover have a moral compass but are afforded no power to effect change (206), and that the characters are rendered through "stereotypes of patriarchal power" (208). She concludes that the Rebellion fails because patriarchal norms, if unrecognized and unchallenged, undermine even the best-intentioned efforts to bring about positive change:

> It is difficult to gauge Orwell's intentions in making use of gender stereotypes in *Animal Farm*. Given the evidence of his other texts, however, it seems unlikely that the possibility of a critical, even satirical, account of gender divisions ever crossed his mind. Perhaps he simply incorporated the familiar into his animal fable as part of the "natural human" traits needed to gain plausibility for his drama of a revolution betrayed. But in so doing he inadvertently reveals something very important about this barnyard revolution: Like its human counterparts, it invariably re-creates the institution of patriarchy. (208)

Patai's perceptive work also provided the foundation for a recent critique by Stewart Cole of the speciesism evident in Orwell's oeuvre, particularly *Animal Farm*: "A cursory reading of these instances would place them firmly in line with the dominant current of Western thinking about the human/animal distinction, according to which animality is a state to which humans are reduced" (343). Acknowledging his debt to Patai, Cole explores the sociopolitical effect of Orwell's latent ambivalence toward animals: "In dialogue with these critical efforts, the substance of what I am undertaking here most basically amounts to replacing 'masculine' in Patai's formulation with 'the human': Orwell's adherence to traditional definitions of the human serves to undermine his commitment to social justice" (340).

It is strange that one as sensitive to hierarchical, regional, and racial biases as Orwell was essentially unaware of the sociopolitical consequences of other prejudices and of their presence in his own thought and output. This inattention, however, does not conclusively indicate that *Animal Farm* affords no hope or that Orwell's personal failings invalidate his work. Males and females fight alongside each other against oppression in *Animal Farm*, just as Orwell had known them to do in Spain. Consider his description of the expulsion of Fascist troops from the towns of eastern Spain: "Men and women armed only with sticks of dynamite rushed across the open squares and stormed stone buildings held by trained soldiers with machine guns" (*Homage* 53). The heroic determination of these women and men probably influenced Orwell's depiction of the animals' response to the obliteration of the windmill: "A mighty cry for vengeance went up, and without waiting for further orders they charged forth in a body and made straight for the enemy. This time they did not heed the cruel pellets that swept over them like hail. It was a savage, bitter battle" (118). As in Spain and as with the initial uprising against Jones by the animals over lack of food, it is once more the proletarians of both sexes who instinctively challenge evil without need of orders or encouragement from their so-called leaders. As Cole explains, "While women and the working classes are consistently animalized and therefore inferiorized within the novel's narrative frame, their animality is often also idealized as indicative of revolutionary potential" (337). Orwell did not see workers and women as clearly as he should have, but he did not count them out.

Moreover, the merging of the pigs and the humans at the end of the novel is also not nearly as discouraging and cynical as it initially seems. Orwell perceived fractious tensions within the governing classes:

> A number of readers may finish the book with the impression that it ends in the complete reconciliation of the pigs and the humans. That was not my intention; on the contrary I meant it to end on a loud note of discord, for I wrote it after the Tehran Conference which everybody thought had established the best possible relations between the USSR and the West. I personally did not believe that such good relations would last long; and, as events have shown, I wasn't far wrong. ("Preface" 180)

Written at the end of 1943 ("Proposed Preface" 161), *Animal Farm*'s denouement shrewdly forecasts the Cold War between the Soviets and their wartime Western allies. It also implies that such cracks in the establishment may provide fresh opportunities for renewal. For Dickstein, even the reversion to the farm's original name indicates prescience rather than pessimism: "At times Orwell seems to be looking ahead not only to 1943, when Russia and the West were meeting in Tehran as he was writing, but to 1991, when the Soviet Union was dissolved, predatory capitalism introduced, and cities like Leningrad reverted to their pre-Revolutionary names" (144).

This critique of predatory capitalism, which Reilly underscores in his analysis of *Animal Farm*'s conclusion, is an integral part of the satire:

> *Animal Farm* is manifestly an attack on Stalinism, but those on the right who gleefully embraced it somehow contrived to miss that it is just as palpably an attack on capitalism. Mr. Pilkington is no better than Napoleon—that's the point of the climactic confusion when the bewildered animals can no longer tell one from the other. Orwell did not expose the Soviets to make the world safe for General Motors. (86)

As Richard Voorhees makes clear, *Animal Farm* shows how the profit motive of the so-called free market undermines liberty by making bedfellows of capitalists and despots: "The early history of Animal Farm, then, is partly a satire of the Tory protesting against any form of social change because he fears and hates it; the latter history is partly a satire of the Tory wanting to get along well with dictatorships because it is good business to do so" (73). Smyer goes as far as to argue that Orwell attacks capitalism through a nuanced portrayal of Jones: "Sociologically, he seems representative of the small landholder described in a book reviewed by Orwell in May 1936, Alec Brown's *The Fate of the Middle Classes*, whom the expansionist imperatives of "monopoly capitalism" were allegedly pushing off the land in the 1930s" (Smyer 40). Though I read Jones more narrowly as an epitome of the dissipated gentry, Smyer's interpretation does indicate that a critique of capitalism runs through the novel.

Organized religion is another target of the satire. The blackness of Napoleon and Moses hints at the similarity between secular and religious totalitarian systems, anticipating the black overalls of Oceania's Inner Party—the high priesthood of *Nineteen Eighty-Four*'s omniscient, omnipotent Big Brother. In his role as spy and informant initially for the Tsarist Jones and then for the Bolshevik pigs, Moses embodies the tendency of organized religions to collaborate with socioeconomic and political authorities. John Rodden reminds us of the Marxian observation that faith assuages discontent, thereby subverting revolutionary tendencies:

> Orwell notes that the pigs tolerate Moses, that is, the Church, because they realize how effectively religious belief can suppress rebellion and even discontent, just as Stalin permitted the public return of the Russian Orthodox clergy because he realized that he could exploit the Church for his own purposes. (The name Moses is well-chosen, for it covers both the Russian Orthodox and the Catholic Church [and Judaism as well]). (322)

The appeal of Sugarcandy Mountain, with its material pleasures and abundant creature comforts, highlights how the credulity faith engenders makes people not only more easily swayed by political rhetoric but more susceptible to corporate advertising, allowing faith-based reasoning to determine their assessment of laissez-faire capitalism. Orwell understood that despite the austerity preached by Christ, in Western culture Adam Smith's invisible hand works interdependently with popular conceptions of divinity.

My brief survey of some influential interpretations of *Animal Farm* aims to showcase the richness and complexity of this topical satire. As David Dwan points out, the text invites a range of critical approaches: "The story can be read as a criticism of any number of political ideologies—communism, liberalism, democracy—partly because it is organized around a concept that is usually fundamental to each: namely, equality" (656). Even today in liberal democracies we struggle with what exactly equality means in political, economic, and cultural terms, and with how to address structural inequality, which is one reason why *Animal Farm* still resonates: "[Orwell] always remained convinced of the argument that significant inequalities of condition made genuine political equality impossible. But the removal of economic inequalities seemed to require a centralized administration that strained against democratic commitments to the equalization of power" (Dwan 663).Through the thorny complexity of the animal's social experiment, Orwell challenges us to move beyond "the egalitarian cant of the modern world" (Dwan 656) and take up our responsibility to each other.

Works Cited

Bowker, Gordon. *George Orwell*. Abacus, 2004.

Cole, Stewart. "The True Struggle": Orwell and the Specter of the Animal." *Lit: Literature Interpretation Theory*, vol. 28, no. 4, 2017, pp. 335-53.

Dickstein, Morris. "*Animal Farm:* History as Fable." *The Cambridge Companion to George Orwell*. Cambridge UP, 2007, pp. 133-45.

Dwan, David. "Orwell's Paradox: Equality in *Animal Farm*." *ELH*, vol. 79, no. 3, 2012, pp. 655-83.

Elbarbary, Samir. "Language as Theme in *Animal Farm*." *International Fiction Review*, vol. 19, no. 1, 1992, pp. 31-38.

Fergenson, Laraine. "George Orwell's *Animal Farm*: A Twentieth-Century Beast Fable." *Bestia*, vol. 2, 1990, pp. 109-18.

Kirschner, Paul. "The Dual Purpose of *Animal Farm*." *Review of English Studies*, vol. 55, no. 222, 2004, pp. 759-86.

Lee, Robert A. "The Uses of Form: A Rereading of *Animal Farm*." *Studies in Short Fiction*, vol. 6, no. 5, 1969, pp. 557-73.

Magráns, Ramón. "Anti-Totalitarianism in *Animal Farm* and *Time of the Hero*." *Maria Vargas Llosa: Opera Omnia*. Edited by Ana María Hernández de López, Pliegos, 1994, pp. 393-400.

Orwell, George. *Animal Farm*. Harcourt Brace, 1995.

_____. *Homage to Catalonia/Down and Out in Paris and London*. Houghton Mifflin Harcourt, 2010.

_____. "Proposed Preface to *Animal Farm*: The Freedom of the Press." *Animal Farm*. Harcourt Brace, 1995, pp. 161-71.

_____. "Preface to the Ukrainian Edition of *Animal Farm.*" *Animal Farm*. Harcourt Brace, 1995, pp. 175-80.

Patai, Daphne. *The Orwell Mystique*. U of Massachusetts P, 1984.

Reilly, Patrick. "The Utopian Shipwreck." *Modern Critical Interpretations: Animal Farm*. Edited by Harold Bloom. Chelsea House, 1999, pp. 61-90.

Rodden, John. "Big Rock (Sugar)candy Mountain? How George Orwell Tramped toward *Animal Farm.*" *Papers on Language and Literature*, vol. 46, no. 3, 2010, pp. 315-41.

Rorty, Richard. "The Last Intellectual in Europe." *George Orwell*. Edited by Graham Holderness et al., St. Martin's, 1998, pp. 139-60.

Smyer, Richard I. *Animal Farm: Pastoralism and Politics*. Twayne, 1988.

Voorhees, Richard. "Attack on Capitalism." *Readings on Animal Farm*. Edited by Terry O'Neill, Greenhaven, 1998, p. 73.

Biography of George Orwell

Thomas Horan

This brief overview of George Orwell's life emphasizes the circumstances and events that influenced the content of *Animal Farm*, though in making this claim I am admittedly on shaky ground. In a letter dated August 26, 1947, from Orwell to Richard Usborne, which Peter Davidson quotes in full in his introduction to Orwell's letters, Orwell cautions against reading his fiction autobiographically: "In general my books have been less autobiographical than people have assumed" (qtd. in *A Life* xi).

The writer who came to be known professionally—and ultimately even personally—as George Orwell was born Eric Arthur Blair in Motihari, India, on June 25, 1903. Orwell, the middle of three children, was of Anglo-French ancestry. His father, Richard Walmsley Blair, was an assistant subdeputy opium agent in British India. His mother, Ida Mabel Limouzin, though born in England, was a French national who grew up in Moulmein, Burma (present-day Myanmar). Ida was nearly twenty years younger than Richard, and their marriage was not a happy one (Bowker 9). In 1904, following an outbreak of plague, Richard settled his wife and children in Henley-on-Thames, Oxfordshire.

Gordon Bowker argues that Orwell's idyllic prewar childhood shaped his literary output: "In book after book, freedom is achieved at great risk and sacrifice, then lost again through deception or cheating, or under the crushing weight of convention or state despotism— Orwell's version of *Paradise Gained* and *Paradise Lost*. . . . This overarching metaphor of his life and work also reflects his sense of a lost 'Golden Age,' the pre-1914 years of his childhood" (xv). At the age of five, Orwell became a day student at a convent run by French Ursuline nuns. Here, apparently, were sown the seeds of his lifelong anti-Catholicism (Bowker 21).

Orwell received a partial scholarship to attend St. Cyprian's, a preparatory school for boys, located in Eastbourne, Sussex. He enrolled in September of 1911. In writing *Animal Farm*, Orwell drew upon his childhood experiences in the countryside, both at home and at St. Cyprian's: "The sights and smells of the farmyard were of course familiar to him since childhood around Henley and in Cornwall. Not far from St. Cyprian's School was a village called Willingdon with a Red Lion pub and a stone quarry nearby, which he could hardly have avoided on his schoolboy rambles across Sussex Downs" (Bowker 308). Orwell would remain at St. Cyprian's until 1917, ultimately winning a scholarship to Eton College, arguably the most prestigious independent secondary school in Britain. Orwell was unhappy at St. Cyprian's, recounting the grim experience of being a student there in his essay "Such, Such Were the Joys" (1947). Nevertheless, despite their mutual animosity, Cecily Vaughan Wilkes, the Headmaster's wife, who also served as St. Cyprian's English teacher, helped Orwell develop his clear writing style: "Her more admiring pupils recalled her great insistence on simplicity and clarity in prose, the very qualities that George Orwell later sought to emulate, and he had to admit that in certain ways she encouraged him" (Bowker 34). At St. Cyprian's Orwell also met his lifelong friend and fellow writer Cyril Connolly, through whom he would ultimately meet his second wife, Sonia Brownell.

In addition to his contempt for class hierarchy and class prejudice, Orwell developed his interest in and suspicion of the broad sociopolitical implications of nationalism during these school years while the First World War raged throughout Europe: "Jingoist propaganda during the Great War so horrified him that by 1916 he became repelled by the patriotic game, or so he said" (Bowker 432). These tendencies are evident in the rigidly hierarchical and rabidly patriotic climate of Animal Farm under Napoleon. Coincidentally, Orwell's French teacher at Eton was Aldous Huxley. Although he thrived intellectually at Eton, Orwell lacked the support of Andrew Gow, his tutor, and was thus unable to acquire a scholarship to attend university at either Oxford or Cambridge.

Graduating in 1921, Orwell left England in 1922 to work as a policeman in Burma, where many of his mother's relatives still lived. Orwell quickly came to loathe imperialism and the role his job compelled him to play in it; his time in Burma disabused him of the notion that he should be anything other than a professional writer. While home on leave in July of 1927, Orwell decided to remain in Europe, living initially in England and by 1928 in France. Witnessing mass unemployment, Orwell had by 1928 come to identify with the political left and was a published writer (under his given name) by October of that year.

In 1932, to placate his family and achieve some semblance of financial stability, Orwell began teaching English and French at The Hawthorns, a boys' school in Hayes, Middlesex. The following year, he left Hawthorns to become French Master at Frays College in Uxbridge and published his first book, *Down and Out in Paris and London*, a semiautobiographical account focusing largely on the circumstances of the desperately poor among whom he had lived. From this point forward Eric Blair would be known professionally—and increasingly personally—as George Orwell, a pseudonym that he selected with his first publisher, Victor Gollancz. Gollancz would go on to publish the novels *Burmese Days* (1934), *A Clergyman's Daughter* (1935), *Keep the Aspidistra Flying* (1936), and *Coming Up For Air* (1939).

While Orwell's early novels are somewhat uneven, his pioneering nonfiction established his literary reputation. According to Bowker, in 1936 Orwell "dedicated himself always to write in favour of democratic socialism and to turn political writing into an art" (178). *The Road to Wigan Pier* (1937) is what Orwell called a "political book," blending reportage, political criticism, and autobiography (Bowker 198); it begins with a vivid chronicle of his time living among the miners in Northern England and concludes with a revelatory assessment of middle- and working-class attitudes toward each other and socialism.

For a writer justifiably dogged by accusations of antifeminism and even misogyny, Orwell's output benefited greatly from the assistance of his first wife Eileen O'Shaughnessy, who had read (majored in) English at Oxford University and worked as a teacher and freelance journalist. They married in June of 1936 and resided in a small farmhouse in Wallington, which Orwell first occupied in

March of that year. "She could have pursued an independent career but chose to partner a man whose strange brilliance deeply attracted her. It is likely that the transformation in Orwell's work from *Wigan Pier* onwards owes a great deal to the intellectual stimulus his marriage brought him" (Bowker 190). Revealingly, the farm they occupied "had previously been an experimental farm named 'Manor Farm.'" (Weeks 103).

Orwell's relationship with Gollancz soured when Gollancz declined to publish *Homage to Catalonia* (1937), Orwell's account of his time fighting in the Spanish Civil War for the Republican cause in a quasi-Trotskyist militia in 1937. Denise Weeks notes that "Going to Spain gave Orwell a glimpse of a 'socialist utopia' that—like the ephemeral utopia in *Animal Farm*—is ultimately betrayed" (104). As the Spanish government increasingly relied on Stalin's support, non-Stalinist militias—such as Orwell's—were marginalized and ultimately outlawed. In Spain Orwell found an enormous gap between the news as reported by both government sources and the international press and what he knew to be true from firsthand experience. Bowker relates how Orwell complained in a letter to Connolly "that the war was being misreported in the English press which was repeating the Communist line uncritically" (218).

On May 20, 1937, Orwell was wounded through the neck by sniper fire. Following his convalescence, the party with which his militia was affiliated was outlawed. Orwell and wife were forced to flee Spain with the Spanish secret police in pursuit. Many of his militia confederates were incarcerated or murdered. Whereas on arriving in Spain he had been inspired by what he thought was a proletarian utopia, Orwell came to recognize that totalitarianism had ultimately arisen under the auspices of socialism, just as it does in both *Animal Farm* (1945) and *Nineteen Eighty-Four*:

> [H]e was left with persistent nightmares—the haunting fear of assassination (the later fate of some anti-Stalinists leftists in exile), of the concentration camp and the torture chamber.... [T]he cruel and tyrannical methods of medieval Catholicism had been revived— imprisonment without trial, confessions extracted under torture with summary executions to follow. . . . He had learned a hard lesson,

especially about the new political Europe. Totalitarianism, the new creed of "the streamlined men" of Fascism and Communism, was a new manifestation of his old Catholic enemy, the doctrine of Absolutism. (Bowker 226)

Since Gollancz continued to support Stalin and thus considered Orwell's political views unacceptable, Orwell published *Homage to Catalonia* with Secker and Warburg. Under the Secker and Warburg imprint, Orwell would take to their logical conclusion in both his fiction and nonfiction not just the consequences of totalitarianism but the susceptibility of liberals and progressives to totalitarian ideas and habits of mind, satirizing these tendencies and finally achieving critical and commercial success with *Animal Farm* and *Nineteen Eighty-Four*.

In July of 1937, Orwell and his wife returned to the farm in Wallington. Jack Branthwaite, with whom Orwell served in Spain, visited them there and may have inadvertently helped inspire Orwell to write *Animal Farm*: "Noting the number of animals around the place, Branthwaite remembered saying, 'I wonder if we handed over the reins of government to the animals, if they'd do any better?' He was thinking about the horrors of Spain, but Orwell, he felt, had been taken over by the idea, and after dinner disappeared upstairs" (Bowker 232). Although "the entire composition of *Animal Farm* took him only a few months [in late 1943] and was written at the same time he was working as editor and columnist" (Weeks 110-11), there were "six or seven years of gestation leading to its being written" (Bowker 223).

Unfortunately, Orwell's life was often hampered by itineracy, poverty, and overwork. All this, combined with his life-threatening war injury and subsequent hospitalization, led him to contract tuberculosis in 1938. This made him ineligible for military service when the Second World War broke out the following year. While continuing to publish essays and reviews, Orwell also "found occasional work for the Ministry of Information (Britain's answer to Goebbels's Ministry of Propaganda), which had its headquarters at the University of London's Senate House—one source for his

Ministry of Truth in *Nineteen Eighty-Four*" (Bowker 269). In June of 1941, he began working as an English language producer for the Indian Section of the BBC, producing programs and lectures for Indian students, the Section's target audience. Frustrated by not having time enough to write, Orwell left the BBC in November of 1943 and became literary editor of *Tribune*, a non-Stalinist left-wing paper founded in 1937. In addition to his editorial responsibilities, Orwell wrote a column called "As I Please." He would remain at *Tribune* until the beginning of 1945.

In June of 1944, Orwell and his wife adopted a three-week-old baby, naming him Richard Horatio Blair. However, unbeknownst to Orwell, Eileen had been seriously ill with uterine tumors for some time. She died under anesthesia administered in preparation for an operation on March 29, 1945. While still undergoing treatment intermittently in sanatoriums for tuberculosis, Orwell spent much of his remaining years living with his son and his younger sister, Avril, on the island of Jura. Believing that marriage would improve his chance of survival, Orwell persuaded Sonia Brownell, Cyril Connolly's assistant at the literary magazine *Horizon*, to marry him on October 13, 1949, while he was in London receiving medical treatment. Nevertheless, Orwell succumbed to pulmonary tuberculosis on January 21, 1950. He was forty-six.

Works Cited

Bowker, Gordon. *George Orwell*, Abacus, 2004.

Davidson, Peter. Introduction. *Orwell: A Life in Letters*, by George Orwell. Harvill Secker, 2010, pp. ix-xviii.

Weeks, Denise. "George Orwell and the Road to *Animal Farm*." *Understanding Animal Farm*. Edited by John Rodden, Greenhaven, 1999, pp. 93-116.

CRITICAL CONTEXTS

His Fable, Right or Left: Orwell, *Animal Farm*, and the Politics of Critical Reception

Erik Jaccard

In "My Country Right or Left," George Orwell attempts to synthesize two contradictory aspects of his political belief system. On the one hand, he was by this time fully committed to the international socialist cause, and more specifically to the development of English socialism in Britain. On the other, the beginning of the Second World War had led Orwell to question the value and function of his patriotism for an England he loved, but which he considered "the most class-ridden country under the sun" (*Essays* 303). Orwell ultimately fused this contradiction by deciding that it was only in supporting the British war effort—and thus British victory—that conditions for the emergence of socialism could ever emerge. This position allowed him, at least for a time, to fuse conventionally rightist and leftist frameworks into a unified whole: patriotically supporting the war enabled the survival of the nation and the possibility of a socialist future, while leftist critique of British capitalism hastened the breakdown of exploitative class relations, and thus worked toward that same future.

Unpacking this contradiction and the historical conditions that shaped it is central to understanding the history of critical debate about *Animal Farm*. Orwell wrote "My Country Right or Left" in 1940, as the German blitzkrieg was racing unchecked across Western Europe and the Battle of Britain raged above English cities. This situation directly informed Orwell's position: adopt a traditionally conservative patriotic stance so as to keep a traditionally leftist hope for socialism alive. However, by late 1943, the tide of the war had turned in favor of the Allies. With the Red Army keeping the Germans occupied on the Eastern Front, many Britons felt that they shared common cause with the Soviets. Anything critical of Stalin or communism was therefore considered anathema to the war effort. This was even truer among socialists, many of whom already supported Russian communism implicitly. Such naïveté in the face of Stalinist atrocities shocked Orwell, who had experienced the regime's brutality and obfuscation firsthand while fighting for the Republican cause in the Spanish Civil War. Orwell thus saw those who continued to defend Stalin after the horror of the 1930s as intellectually dishonest and, in the context of a developing English socialism, even dangerous. His experience in Spain had taught him that "the destruction of the Soviet myth was essential if we wanted a revival of the Socialist movement" in Britain (*Orwell* 319). With *Animal Farm*, Orwell attempted to shatter that myth by starkly presenting the betrayal of the Russian revolution in the form of a barnyard fable that could be widely understood. Yet, in doing so, he was once again forced to inhabit a political contradiction: criticize the left and the USSR so that a genuine socialism might flourish.

This paradox has dogged both popular and scholarly criticism of *Animal Farm* since its publication. For sure, many critical treatments background or marginalize the novel's political dimensions, and instead read the novel in terms of literary form, judging its merit on the successful execution of its satirical fable. However, the larger portion of criticism elevates the form's consequences above the form itself, focusing on the novel's send-up of Stalinism and, importantly, the ambiguous political positioning of its author. The latter point is significant because it is through readings of the author's politics that critics have often pursued their interpretations of *Animal Farm*. Indeed, what *Animal Farm* means has often depended on rhetorical context, on who was interpreting Orwell's political contradictions and why.

The Early Years: 1944-1946
The story of *Animal Farm*'s critical reception begins with the politics of finding a publisher. Had Orwell written the novel in the late 1930s, he would have had no problem locating a firm willing to publish an inventive fable critical of Stalinist Russia. By 1944, however, public support for the Soviets was high in Britain and, as Russell Baker notes, "even conservatives were pro-Soviet" (viii). Orwell's general publisher, Victor Gollancz, summed up the prevailing attitude: "We

couldn't have published it then. . . . Those people [the Soviets] were fighting for us and had just saved our necks at Stalingrad" (qtd. in Shelden 438). On the whole, four English publishers turned Orwell down, many out of fear of stirring up controversy (Shelden 438-40). Perhaps the most famous rejection came from T. S. Eliot at Faber and Faber, who noted in a rather cold letter that none among the firm's leaders had been sufficiently convinced that *Animal Farm*'s message was "the right point of view from which to criticise the political situation at the present time" (qtd. in Flood). Finally, in July of 1944, the small London publisher Secker and Warburg agreed to publish.

Due to wartime paper rationing, Secker and Warburg postponed British publication until the summer of 1945, while the American edition—published by Harcourt Brace—was delayed until 1946. This setback profoundly affected initial public reaction to the novel. As the Western world turned from the exigencies of World War II to the looming Cold War with the Soviet Union, public opinion predictably pivoted toward ideological opposition to communism. Morris Dickstein notes that *Animal Farm* was thus "quickly projected onto the front lines of the new East-West conflict" (134). Ironically, the novel's satire of the Russian revolution, the inauspicious reason for which it had been shunned by publishers in 1944, was by 1946 the cause of its massive popular success. In Britain the novel sold over 25,000 hardcover copies in only a few years. The American market proved even more surprising. Not long after its publication, it was included in the popular Book of the Month Club, and it remained on the *New York Times* Bestseller list for eight weeks in 1946. By 1950, it had sold close to 600,000 copies (Shelden 441). Despite this commercial success, immediate critical reaction to the novel was mixed, with opinion often split between those who deemphasized the novel's political implications and those who accentuated them.

Positive reviews during this period often backgrounded politics and emphasized the text's successful execution of literary form, highlighting in particular Orwell's skillful deployment of the satirical fable to communicate a powerful, albeit simple, message. For example, in a 1945 review, *The Guardian* described it as "a delightfully humorous and caustic satire on the rule of the many by the few" ("Books"). Following in this vein, the novelist Graham Greene lauded Orwell's successful use of the fable form to evoke genuine human pathos rather than "a mere echo of human failings at one remove" (196). Writing in *The New Yorker* (1946), Edmund Wilson praised the skillful economy of Orwell's style and form effusively: "Mr. Orwell has worked out his theme with a simplicity, a wit, and a dryness . . . and has written in a prose so plain and spare, so admirably proportioned to his purpose, that *Animal Farm* even seems very creditable if we compare it with Voltaire and Swift" (205). In what was perhaps the novel's most glowing early review, Arthur Schlesinger Jr., writing for the *New York Times Book Review*, gushed over Orwell's "superbly controlled and brilliantly sustained satire," which, he further noted, "[is written] with such gravity and charm that [it] becomes an independent creation, standing quite apart from the object of its comment" (qtd. in Garner). While none of these writers completely ignore the text's political implications, they also sideline or deemphasize explicit political positions. In one sense, we might see this as the granting of a respectful distance that allows the novel to speak for itself, as Orwell originally intended it to do (*Politics* 320). However, what might seem like respect from one angle is simply a willingness to accept oversimplified conclusions from another.

Predictably, it was also the text's formal execution and its supposedly simple message that provoked the majority of the novel's early negative reviews. Many held Orwell to harsh account for a failure to accurately or insightfully represent Russian history and politics, or for coloring that history with his own political despair. The essayist Cyril Connolly exemplified this approach when he wrote in a 1946 review for *Horizon* that Orwell allows "personal bitterness about the betrayed revolution to prejudice [his] attitude to the facts" (200). This charge of a "prejudiced attitude to the facts" was a common one. Writing for *The New Statesman and Nation*, for instance, Kingsley Martin accused Orwell of falling prey to disillusion and cynicism about the nature—and future—of humanity, and more importantly for sticking too close to history, thereby "[inviting] every kind of historical and factual objection" (198). As though on cue, George Soule's 1946 review for *The New Republic*—a publication that routinely defended Stalin through the 1930s and '40s (Rodden, *Understanding* 136)—blasted *Animal Farm* for its "dull," "creaking," and "mechanical" execution, its supposed historical inaccuracies, and its "stereotyped ideas about a country he [Orwell] probably does not know very well" (138). Some early reviewers looked past the focus on form to examine *Animal Farm*'s political implications in more depth. In a frequently anthologized 1946 review, Isaac Rosenfeld also condemned the novel for its historical reductionism, but further blamed Orwell for "a failure of imagination," where "failure to expand the parable, to incorporate into it something of the complexity of the real event . . . becomes identical with a failure in politics" (203). For Rosenfeld, the text's simple, plain style and straightforward plot leave one wondering after the novel's ultimate point or moral, making it both historically amateurish and politically inert.

As Rodden observes, these early reactions to *Animal Farm* were often characterized by a difficulty in understanding Orwell's purpose. While British reviewers were more familiar with Orwell, they still often misread the author's intentions (*Understanding* 125). This problem was only exacerbated in the American market, where most were comparatively unfamiliar with Orwell's early novels, his wartime journalism in the UK, or his political leanings. One common theme across critical reception in both countries, however, was that the hostility of a review tended to increase in correlation with the reviewer's support for Stalinism or global socialism, the former of which was viewed by some leftists as a standard-bearer for the latter. If this maxim held true throughout what Rodden calls "the crucial decade" of 1945-55, it shifted into a variety of complex permutations in the ensuing decades, as leftists were forced to reckon with the growing influence of Orwell and his fiction.

Orwell, *Animal Farm*, and the Left: 1955-1980
In the Britain of the fifties, along every road that you moved, the figure of Orwell seemed to be waiting (Williams, *Politics and*

Letters 384). Orwell's battles with the left have taken on something of the aura of myth in the nearly seventy years since his death. From the 1930s onward, Orwell frequently quarreled with members of the British left in particular, excoriating them in print for their hypocrisy, their inability to include the colonized world in theories of class struggle, their recalcitrance in the face of Soviet atrocities, and, perhaps most incisively, for their willingness to dispose of their intellectual independence, the one thing Orwell believed kept humans truly free. Orwell's premature death in 1949 instantly transformed a person with considerable cultural mystique into a full-blown myth, or what Lionel Trilling called "a figure" (Gale 499). As the British Marxist literary scholar Raymond Williams admitted many years later, leftist intellectuals in the decades after Orwell's death could not help but engage with this figure, a man who had expended a great deal of energy criticizing the left, but who was nonetheless often viewed as a leftist hero, in part because he sought to expose uncomfortable truths to which many orthodox leftists preferred not admit.

As is now generally acknowledged, Orwell's frequent attacks on his leftist contemporaries were not intended as expressions of disillusionment with socialism or as attempts to undermine revolutionary politics. Alex Zwerdling observes that "his criticism was always designed as internal; it was precisely Orwell's unquestioning fidelity to the ideals of the movement that, in his mind, justified his uncompromising critique of some of its theories, tactics, and leaders" (5). Nonetheless, since at least the publication of *The Road to Wigan Pier* (1937), orthodox leftists, including those associated with the British Communist Party, had frequently attempted to discredit or disclaim him as a turncoat or a petit bourgeois interloper (Rodden, *Politics* 185-87). When *Animal Farm* appeared, many on the orthodox left predictably received it as an insidious act of political betrayal, but one in keeping with an established image of the man as a disillusioned and pessimistic contrarian, contemptuous of ordinary people and bitter about possible socialist revolution. For instance, the American Marxist Milton Blau's scathing 1946 review for *New Masses* disparages the novel as the creation of "a mind which seethes with hatred for man and argues for nihilism, for the destruction of both man and art" (140). While overblown and inattentive to Orwell's purpose, Blau's characterization of *Animal Farm* as motivated by political despair and self-loathing foreshadows the more nuanced leftist arguments that would follow.

These arguments took a variety of forms, but most were motivated by a concern for the potential consequences Orwell's now-famous later novels might have on the socialist movement. In the context of the Cold War, both *Animal Farm* and *Nineteen Eighty-Four* came to represent the ultimate expression of principled opposition to totalitarianism. However, because Orwell's primary historical reference point in both cases is the Soviet Union, both were easily and popularly misinterpreted as direct attacks on any form of socialist politics. Orwell's rapid rise to posthumous fame in the 1950s popularized both his novels and such misinterpretations. Therefore, as public consciousness of both texts expanded, leftists were forced to excavate and attack the assumptions embedded in each. Some argued that *Animal Farm*'s depiction of the Russian revolution's betrayal extended far beyond its immediate historical context, ultimately promoting the idea that all revolutions are inevitably corrupted by power politics and totalitarianism (Hollis 150-52). If revolution was the engine of history, as many Marxists believed, then *Animal Farm*'s internal circularity seemed to demonstrate that real social progress was impossible. Others claimed, like Blau, that *Animal Farm* illustrates a bitter, ex-socialist's decaying faith in humanity (O'Neill 41, 86). For these critics, the crucial question was Why? Why does the Manor Farm revolution fail? Why do the pigs turn against the ideals of Animalism? Why don't the other animals rise up against Napoleon when he begins to consolidate privilege and power? In a brief discussion of Orwell near the end of *Culture & Society*, Williams concludes that in both *Animal Farm* and *Nineteen Eighty-Four*, the answer is that Orwell simply did not believe in the power of the working class to take the historical reins: "The hated politicians are in charge, while the dumb mass of 'proles' goes on in very much its own ways, protected by its very stupidity"

(293). It was precisely because Orwell had fashioned himself as a commonsense empirical thinker that these implications seemed so damaging. One of the most prevalent and powerful mythological constructions of Orwell was as the honest and plain-speaking man, unafraid to tell truth to power, no matter the political consequences. The worry was that people—and particularly future generations of political leftists—would believe in Orwell's critique of Stalinist socialism simply because of their more profound belief in the truth of the man himself (Norris 242-43).

This is why, in the 1960s and '70s, thinkers associated with the British New Left attempted to investigate the influence of Orwell and his work on the formation of a new era of socialist activists and scholars. In his 1971 monograph on Orwell, Williams turns on the 1950s reading of *Animal Farm* as pessimistic, admitting that the novel "carries a feeling that is more than disillusion and defeat," and that, at moments, it offers "a radical energy that goes far beyond its occasion and has its own kind of permanence" (*Orwell* 75). However, this reading is overpowered by Williams's subsequent criticism of *Nineteen Eighty-Four*, which he accuses of naturalizing a misrepresentation of socialist revolution as doomed to failure (78-82). At issue for Williams and his contemporaries was the notion that Orwell had effectively popularized political passivity by preemptively undermining the possibility of belief in progressive causes. For example, in "Outside the Whale" (1960), Williams's New Left contemporary E. P. Thompson asserted that Orwell's work "contributed a good deal to the form of a generalised pessimism which has outlasted the context in which it arose," and that it was by Orwell's hand that "not only was a political movement . . . buried, but so also was the notion of disinterested dedication to a political cause" (14, 17). While early cultural studies icons such as Williams and Richard Hoggart remained attentive to Orwell's writings on English popular culture, Thompson ultimately moved the political conversation further toward the radical left, shifting the context in which leftists received *Animal Farm* so that it came to be seen as an expression of political defeatism.

Orwell, *Animal Farm*, and the Right

Many of the qualities for which leftists chastised Orwell and *Animal Farm* were, conversely, the very same reasons the novel was championed by conservatives during the Cold War. As critics such as Williams and Thompson point out, Orwell's tendency to vacillate between precise observation and historical generalization sometimes made his political diagnoses tendentious and his historical renderings overly simple (Thompson 12-17; Williams, *Orwell* 71-75). From the perspective of the left, this made Orwell an imprecise thinker, but it also made his work vulnerable to incorporation by the right. Orwell's clearly dwindling faith in the efficacy of revolution, evinced in a number of his later essays, allowed the right to frame him much as the left had done—as a disillusioned and despairing former socialist. While this was patently untrue—Orwell remained committed to socialism until his death—it was nonetheless an argument many were capable of believing after reading *Animal Farm* and *Nineteen Eighty-Four*. Orwell's long history of conflict with the left made his supposed defection even easier to sell. Indeed, this led writers such as Norman Podhoretz to brand Orwell "the neoconservative 'guiding spirit'" and "the patron-saint of anti-Communism" (qtd. in Rodden, *Understanding* 142). This was particularly true in the United States, where Orwell's political history was relatively unknown. As Russell Kirk elaborates, "Orwell was, in the mid-fifties, a dramatic force for turning people away from socialism and progressivism. That was a period of painful reflection for Americans, who no longer believed left-wing ideas about the much-promised benefits of bigger government or the welfare state. Orwell's disillusion with socialism assisted such reflections" (144).

If misread properly, it is certainly possible to view *Animal Farm*'s attack on the Russian revolution as a general critique of socialism or revolutionary politics. In one such misreading, Stephen Sedley asserts that "Orwell's argument . . . is that socialism in whatever form offers the common people no more hope than capitalism, that it will be first betrayed and then held to ransom by those forces which human beings have in common with beasts" (158). William Empson, a poet and colleague of Orwell's during

World War II, is said to have told the latter that "[he] must expect [*Animal Farm*] to be misunderstood on a large scale," and even, much to Orwell's chagrin, that Empson's son, a conservative, had found the novel "very strong Tory propaganda" (qtd. in Rodden, "Ethics" 87). Indeed, the novel's value as propaganda went from figurative to literal soon after its publication.

This was in part due to Orwell's own involvement in its use. In the years leading up to his death, Orwell collaborated with British intelligence in the translation and distribution of *Animal Farm*, particularly to nations facing imminent threat from Soviet expansionism in Eastern Europe and Asia (Rodden, *Understanding* 145). Meanwhile, the American Central Intelligence Agency diligently promoted the distribution of the novel around the world as a means of ideological warfare against communism. According to Daniel J. Leab, the CIA played an integral role in the production of the first cinematic adaption of the novel in 1954 (11-20). By the mid-1950s *Animal Farm had* been canonized in the Anglo-American secondary school classroom for a variety of reasons, one of which was that it offered "an anti-Communist and anti-revolutionary 'lesson'" in easily taught and digested form (Rodden, *Politics* 385-86). The zealousness with which the right received and reused the novel was directly related to the degree to which it could manage the contradictions at the heart of the Orwell figure. By highlighting Orwell's historically situated critiques of the Soviet Union and then essentializing that criticism as universal truth, the right was able to revise and reconstruct a politically expedient conception of Orwell and *Animal Farm*.

Animal Farm in the 1980s

The 1980s saw a renewed critical and popular interest in Orwell and his work. The election of Ronald Reagan to the American presidency in 1980 ushered in a new era of militarism and Cold War anxiety, which in turn increased interest in Orwell, and in *Animal Farm* and *Nineteen Eighty-Four* in particular. As Rodden observes, it is from this moment that attention to *Animal Farm* often goes hand in hand with attention to its more contentious follow-up. This was especially true when the year 1984 occasioned a predictable explosion of scholarly and popular interest in Orwell's titular novel. Between 1980 and 1995 critics published more than twenty-five monograph-length studies on Orwell's work, life, and politics. A good portion of these scholars frame *Nineteen Eighty-Four/Animal Farm* through the lens of political commitment and character. For instance, Bonifas (1984), Patai (1984), and Rai (1988) echo earlier interpretations of *Animal Farm* and *Nineteen Eighty-Four* as statements of political and cultural pessimism and despair, while others elaborate on this thesis by exploring Orwell's evocation of the collapse of civilization and the arrival of a new (presumably Western) dark age. However, a handful of studies balance this focus on pessimism by reaffirming the power of Orwell's fiction—including *Animal Farm*—to generate hope for a future of individual autonomy, personal freedom, and political progress. As Erika Gottlieb contends, while this flurry of Orwell criticism during the 1980s produced a wealth of new studies and insightful approaches, it also in some ways left us back at the start, puzzling over the same contradictions between despair and hope, apathy and commitment, the right and the left (109, 119).

It was also during this decade that *Animal Farm* and *Nineteen Eighty-Four* saw their initial approved publications in portions of the socialist world, including the USSR. While Orwell's work had been available for decades in various underground formats, it was only in the 1980s that residents of the societies Orwell's novel could be said to target were officially able to acknowledge and respond to his treatments of the conditions under which they had been living. Rodden's *Understanding Animal Farm* presents a variety of Russian and East German reactions to the work, many of which, he observes, go to great pains to underscore that the novel "attacks the 'mockery' of socialist ideals, not socialism or its socialist ideas themselves" (173). Here we can see a new audience operating in full knowledge of how the novel had been deployed as a vehicle of American anti-Communist propaganda. As a result, they at times come much closer to capturing Orwell's original intentions for the book than, say, those in the United States who had uncritically accepted it as a useful ideological weapon during the Cold War (Rodden 175-82).

Animal Farm into the Twenty-First Century

Animal Farm is undoubtedly tied to the Cold War era in which it was published, promoted, and canonized; since the end of the Cold War in the late twentieth century, direct attention to the novel itself has waned considerably. However, it remains relevant into the twenty-first century in large part because the academic publishing industry and the global news media seem unable to let Orwell slip away. The centennial of Orwell's birth in 2003 occasioned a new round of critical reassessments of his work, many of which focused on the writer's relevance in a post-Cold War world. Among the most visible and popular of the centennial-era books was *Why Orwell Matters* (2002), by the English cultural critic and intellectual Christopher Hitchens. In his typically pugnacious style, Hitchens confronts Orwell's critics one by one, all the while expounding on the latter's humanism and his value as a lightning rod for discussions of English national identity, British imperialism, the importance of language and the natural environment, and issues of objective truth (10-14). Hitchens is surely correct in his assessment that both Orwell and *Animal Farm* still matter, as more than two dozen new monographs have been published on the man and his work since 2000.

While very few of these take *Animal Farm* as their primary object of inquiry, nearly all find a way to discuss it, often in the context of the issues Hitchens identifies. Robert Colls's *George Orwell: English Rebel* (2013), for example, moves away from the Cold War context and instead reads Orwell's barnyard archetypes relative to ongoing critical discussions of English national culture. This analysis dovetails with a vital current of academic inquiry into representations of English national culture in the context of British devolutionary politics and the post-Brexit construction of British identity. Michael Brennan (2017) discusses the novel relative to Orwell's long intellectual engagement with religion, particularly Orwell's fascination with similarities between Catholicism and communism. While new critical ground continues to be broken, more than a few recent studies use the novel as a lens through which to once again explore Orwell's relationship to the left, to Marxism, and to theories of revolution that have only grown more relevant in a twenty-first century geopolitical climate characterized by revolution, civil war, and political unrest.[1] If anything, what recent criticism reveals is that Orwell, *Animal Farm*, and the historical and political contradictions they entail continue to provoke critical thought across multiple intersecting spectrums of political belief, historical context, and cultural relevance.

Note

1. A sampling might include Bounds, *Orwell and Marxism* (2009), Rodden, *The Unexamined Orwell* (2011), Robbins, *George Orwell, Cosmopolitanism, and Global Justice* (2017), and Newsinger, *Hope Lies in the Proles* (2018).

Works Cited

Baker, Russell. Preface. *Animal Farm*, by George Orwell. Signet, 2015.

Blau, Milton. "Pig's Eye View." *Understanding* Animal Farm: *A Student Casebook to Issues, Sources, and Historical Documents*. Edited by John Rodden, Greenwood P, 1999, pp. 140-41.

"Books of the Day." *The Guardian*, The Guardian News and Media, 24 Aug. 1945, www.theguardian.com/books/1945/aug/24/georgeorwell. classics.

Connolly, Cyril. Review of *Animal Farm*, by George Orwell. *George Orwell: The Critical Heritage*. Edited by Jeffrey Meyers, Routledge, 1975, pp. 199-201.

Dickstein, Morris. "*Animal Farm*: History as Fable." *The Cambridge Companion to George Orwell*. Edited by John Rodden, Cambridge UP, 2007, pp. 133-45.

Flood, Alison. "It Needs More Public-Spirited Pigs': TS Eliot's Rejection of Orwell's *Animal Farm*." *The Guardian*, Guardian News and Media, 26 May 2016, www.theguardian.com/books/2016/may/26/ts-eliot-rejection-george-orwell-animal-farm-british-library-online.

Gale Research Company, et al. "Twentieth-Century Literary Criticism." *Twentieth-Century Literary Criticism*, vol. 2, 1978.

Garner, Dwight. "Inside the List." *New York Times*, 29 Aug. 2008. Accessed 17 March 2018.

Gottlieb, Erika. "Orwell in the 1980s." *Utopian Studies* 3.1 (1992), pp. 108-20.

Greene, Graham. Review of *Animal Farm*, by George Orwell. *George Orwell: The Critical Heritage*. Edited by Jeffrey Meyers, Routledge, 1975, pp. 195-96.

Hitchens, Christopher. *Why Orwell Matters*. Basic Books, 2002.

Hollis, Christopher. *A Study of George Orwell: The Man and His Works*. Hollis and Carter, 1956.

Kirk, Russell. Interview. *Understanding* Animal Farm: *A Student Casebook to Issues, Sources, and Historical Documents*. Edited by John Rodden, Greenwood P, 1999, pp. 144-45.

Leab, Daniel J. *Orwell Subverted: The CIA and the Filming of Animal Farm*. Pennsylvania State UP, 2007.

Martin, Kingsley. Review of *Animal Farm*, by George Orwell. *George Orwell: The Critical Heritage*. Edited by Jeffrey Meyers, Routledge & Kegan, 1975, pp. 197-99.

Norris, Christopher. "Language, Truth and Ideology: Orwell and the Post-War Left." *Inside the Myth: Orwell: Views from the Left*. Edited by Christopher Norris, Lawrence and Wishart, 1984.

O'Neill, Terry. *Readings on Animal Farm*. Greenhaven, 1998.

Orwell, George, and John Carey. *Essays*. Knopf, 2002.

_____. *Orwell and Politics:* Animal Farm *in the Context of Essays, Reviews, and Letters Selected from* The Complete Works of George Orwell. Edited by Peter Davison, Penguin, 2001.

Rodden, John. "On the Ethics of Admiration—and Detraction." Cushman, Thomas, and John Rodden, editors. *George Orwell: Into the Twenty-first Century*, Taylor & Francis, 2004, pp. 86-95.

_____. *George Orwell: The Politics of Literary Reputation*. Transaction, 2006.

_____. *Understanding* Animal Farm: *A Student Casebook to Issues, Sources, and Historical Documents*. Edited by John Rodden, Greenwood, 1999.

Rosenfeld, Isaac. Review of *Animal Farm*, by George Orwell. *George Orwell: The Critical Heritage*. Edited by Jeffrey Meyers, Routledge, 1975, pp. 201-04.

Sedley, Stephen. "An Immodest Proposal: 'Animal Farm.'" *Inside the Myth: Orwell: Views from the Left*. Edited by Christopher Norris, Lawrence and Wishart, 1984, pp. 155-62.

Shelden, Michael. *Orwell: the Authorized Biography*, Harper Perennial, 1992.

Soule, George. Review of *Animal Farm*, by George Orwell. *Understanding Animal Farm: A Student Casebook to Issues, Sources, and Historical Documents*. Edited by John Rodden, Greenwood, 1999, p. 138.

Thompson, E. P. *The Poverty of Theory and Other Essays*. Merlin, 1978.

Williams, Raymond. *Culture & Society: 1780-1950*. Columbia UP, 1983.

_____. *George Orwell*. Viking, 1971.

_____. *Politics and Letters Interviews with New Left Review*. Lowe and Brydon, 1979.

Wilson, Edmund. Review of *Animal Farm*, by George Orwell. *George Orwell: The Critical Heritage*. Edited by Jeffrey Meyers, Routledge, 1975, pp. 204-05.

Zwerdling, Alex. *Orwell and the Left*. Yale UP, 1974.

Animal Farm and the American Left, 1945-1947____
Bradley Hart

In March 2003, journalist and commentator Christopher Hitchens delivered the keynote address at the George Orwell Centenary Conference at Wellesley College. At the time, Hitchens was in the midst of controversy over his support for the recent invasion of Iraq, and much of his paper was devoted to polemically defending himself against criticism from former left-wing friends who disagreed with his newfound views. "A thing that I am no longer interested in is the question of whether or not George Orwell would take my view or anyone else's if he was still with us. . . . All I can say for sure is that it would be a pleasure to disagree with him," Hitchens wrote. "And that is not a compliment I find one can very often bestow these days" (85).

Amidst this fundamentally self-serving argumentation, Hitchens made an intriguing observation about two of Orwell's final and most famous works: "Though I believe I might have to stand a challenge on this—I don't think that anyone has pointed out that in neither *Animal Farm* nor *Nineteen Eighty-Four* is there any Lenin figure," Hitchens wrote. He continued:

> There is only a Trotsky and a Stalin. There's only Snowball and Napoleon [in *Animal Farm*]. There's only Goldstein and Big Brother [in *Nineteen Eighty-Four*]. The Lenin phase of the argument on the left about what went wrong with Marxism and with the revolution is by Orwell amazingly and interestingly and reprehensibly skipped. But he did see the point that remains with us, which is that any attempt to trade freedom for security contains a death trap within it (84).

With this, Hitchens had stumbled—perhaps inadvertently—into one of the longest-standing controversies surrounding *Animal Farm*: What is the book actually about? At first glance, this seems simple to answer—it is an allegory for a revolution turned exceedingly violent and corrupted into tyranny. But beyond this, interpretations

Critical Insights

have varied to a surprising degree. Orwell scholars have long poked fun at a 1944 letter from Dial Press rejecting *Animal Farm* on the grounds that "it was impossible to sell animal stories in the USA," as if the story had no deeper significance (realizing the error of their ways, the editors recanted two years later but the rights had already been sold to Harcourt Brace) ("Letter" 109-10). Orwell himself expressed uncertainty prior to publication in the United States about "whether one can count on the American public grasping what it is about" ("Letter" 109-10). He needed not worry: as will be seen, nearly all the American critics *did* recognize the book's satirical intent. What they could not agree on, however, was what exactly Orwell was satirizing.

There were—and remain—two general sides to this debate. Given Orwell's well-established skepticism by this point toward orthodox communism and the Soviet Union, commentators on the left generally argued he was writing specifically about the Russian Revolution and its bloody aftermath.This view generally aligned with those of leftist but anti-Soviet groups in Europe and North America at the time, as criticism of the USSR and Josef Stalin began to mount. Critiquing the Russian Revolution was therefore politically expedient for American liberals who now wanted to distance themselves from Moscow, and *Animal Farm* offered a way to do just this.

Other critics, primarily those on the political right of the time, made a different argument. In their reading, Orwell's satire was intended to include *all* revolutions, not just the Russian case. In this view, *Animal Farm* provides not only a biting satire of Soviet brutality and ideological corruption but also a stark warning about the risks of overthrowing the established order. Along these lines, Craig L. Carr has recently argued that Orwell fundamentally saw himself as "a liberal still fighting the revolutions of the seventeenth and eighteenth centuries in the after-revolution," in this case by warning that revolutionary action can easily descend into totalitarianism (82). In this interpretation, the Soviet Union was merely one historical example of a revolution descending into illiberal dictatorship and tyranny. The same trend could, and likely would, happen in other revolutions too.

This essay examines the initial reaction of American critics to the release of *Animal Farm* to explore how the issue that opened this section has historically been addressed: Is *Animal Farm* a work satirizing specific historical circumstance and a set of actors, or is it a wider commentary on the vagaries of revolutions in general? Further, the contemporary political implications of these views will be examined to shed light on how *Animal Farm* was received and interpreted by the American left, ranging from mainstream liberal critiques to socialist-leaning analyses of the time. Together, these sections provide a sense of the wider political climate in which *Animal Farm* was released and understood by its first readers in the United States.

Before doing so, however, we must first return to Hitchens's statement and deliver him the challenge he invites. Hitchens was assuredly correct when he stated that *Animal Farm* contains no allegorical version of Vladimir Lenin. However, he was wrong when he claimed to be the first to arrive at this conclusion; as it turns out, Orwell scholar Alex Zwerdling discussed the same insight at some length as far back as 1974 (91). This is more than a pedantic correction because it relates closely to how *Animal Farm* has been interpreted since its initial publication. Undoubtedly, the nearest potential analogue to Lenin in the text is the character of Old Major, an elderly boar whose philosophy inspires the revolution after his death. However, since Lenin actually *led* the Russian Revolution, most scholars have associated Old Major with the philosopher Karl Marx who died in 1883, well before the revolution. (One prominent dissenter was British writer and Conservative politician Christopher Hollis, who asserted in 1956 that Old Major was intended to represent Lenin without explaining how he came to this unorthodox view) (145).

For Zwerdling, the omission of Lenin from *Animal Farm* is significant and suggests Orwell:

wants to emphasize the enormous disparity between the ideals of the revolution and the reality of the society it actually achieves. Lenin was the missing link in this process, both visionary and architect of his new state, but from Orwell's longer historical perspective, his brief period of power must have seemed like an irrelevant interlude in the stark drama that was unfolding. . . . In order to demystify the Russian Revolution and present the Bolshevik leaders as they really were, Orwell must have felt compelled to eliminate the mythical hero altogether. (91)

In addition, Zwerdling argues that Orwell may have intended *Animal Farm* to represent the Russian Revolution specifically, but the text can also be read as an allegory of revolutions generically. "As the Stalinist period recedes into the distant past, Orwell's book . . . will more and more be appreciated as generic rather than topical satire, just as *Gulliver's Travels* has come to be," Zwerdling contends (92). In other words, Orwell's meaning lies as much in the eye of the reader as in the pen of the author—a common postmodernist argument.

This may well be true, but there is still merit in analyzing how a text was read and interpreted by its contemporaries. Indeed, as already noted, *Animal Farm*'s meaning has always been the source of controversy. Some readers, including the misguided editors at Dial Press, took the superficial interpretation that Orwell was trying to tell a children's story about talking animals. This was not merely an American phenomenon, as a number of London bookshops initially stocked the book in the children's section until chastised by the author himself. Orwell scholar John Rodden has reported that some twenty-first-century university students have been known to make the same error by overlooking the wider meaning of the novel (47). Most of the better-read critics of Orwell's time seem to have grasped his satirical intentions, however, and a debate over the book's meaning swiftly ensued.

The American edition of *Animal Farm* was first published in August 1946 under the Harcourt Brace Book of the Month club imprint. Remarkably, the book had already been the subject of discussion in the American press. One of the first American commentaries was published on the editorial page of the *Green Bay Press Gazette* on January 4, 1946. This was surprisingly early for the book to be receiving publicity in the United States since it had only been published in the UK the previous August. No hint is given as to why a Wisconsin-based newspaper saw fit to editorialize about a British novel a few days after the holiday season had passed. That said, the *Press Gazette*'s commentary largely predicted the discussions that would take place in US literary circles over *Animal Farm*.

Beginning with the acknowledgement that Orwell "is an Englishman to whom an introduction is due," suggesting that the average reader was not familiar with his work, the columnist identified him as "a rather radical Englishman" who turned to writing after fighting in "other people's wars," presumably referring to the Spanish Civil War. The column went on to summarize the plot of *Animal Farm* before concluding:

> Fortunately Orwell is an Englishman. A Finn wouldn't dare to publish that book. If a Turk, so close to Russia, printed it, Istanbul would shake in insecurity. Although Orwell has been rated a fellow traveler of the Reds the disillusionment of Communism he breathes through his printed pages will never be accepted by the Kremlin lying down. The next thing we will learn about Orwell [from the Soviets] is that he is a wolf in sheep's clothing, a Trotskyite, a Fascist and a hard-bitten traitor of the masses, that is the sheep [in *Animal Farm*]. ("Blithering Trotskyite")

This was a telling statement. For this critic, *Animal Farm* was an effective denunciation of the USSR and so dangerous that authors in other countries might face physical peril for publishing it. Yet there was no mention here of any wider significance of this story in terms of other revolutionary movements or American politics. For the *Gazette*'s editorialist, *Animal Farm* was little more than a biting satire of Soviet Communism.

Over the coming months, *Animal Farm* received little attention in the American press until the floodgates opened with its publication in August. The book did make one notable and humorous appearance, however. In March, the *New York Times* published a short article describing the deteriorating relationship between the Soviet Union and its former wartime allies. The Soviet government's official line at the time was that the USSR had no objection to the principle that all states were equal and entitled to determine their own political destinies (despite Stalin's increasing attempts to overturn this in Eastern Europe). An anonymous British diplomatic source interviewed by the *Times*'s London correspondent sardonically likened Stalin's conception of equality to the notion espoused by the pigs of *Animal Farm*:

> With a straight face the spokesman referred to George Orwell's political satire, "The Animal Farm" [sic]. Pigs take over government of a farmyard in this book under the slogan that all animals are equal. Later the pigs substitute another slogan, "All animals are equal except some more so than others." This spokesman evidently sees a parallel between the barnyard government's idea of equality and Mr. Stalin's plea for "maintaining the principle of equality." ("British Voice")

Here again we see the direct relation of *Animal Farm* to the Soviet Union specifically, though admittedly from a British source. It is telling as well that the *Times* writer not only saw fit to explain the analogy to readers, but also gave an incorrect name for the book. *Animal Farm* was clearly still not widely known, at least by Americans.

This would soon change when the book's American release opened the floodgates of controversy. In some senses, the book provides an interesting Rorschach test for the ideological predilections of its reviewers. Some focused on the book's humorous and satirical aspects and all but ignored its ideological undertones. A *Los Angeles Times* book reviewer, for instance, never mentioned communism (though the headline used the term "Comrades") and instead concluded that the novel was "a gay little masterpiece" and "A tonic book of laughter" (P.J.S.). For those who focused more on the book's political undertones, however, two main trends emerged in this early period. As a general rule, conservative-minded readers appear to have interpreted the book broadly while more left-leaning reviewers read its satirical intent more narrowly. An intriguing example of the latter impulse can be found in the *Detroit Free Press* review of the book, written by renowned journalist and arts critic Helen Bower. Describing Orwell as both "anti-communist and anti-fascist," Bower initially took a broad interpretation of the book, with a particular twist:

> His fantasy of an English farm taken over and run by animals is a two-way blast. Its tragedy is in portrayal of the lengths of self-delusion to which men are capable of going, the conditions they will ensure for the illusion of freedom. Its rage is directed against the hypocritical greed and selfishness of the world's pigs and sheep. The over-all [sic] story satirizes the disintegration and degradation of an ideal. Human history, unfortunately, is not lacking in comparable examples of Utopias come to grief. Always, as on the animal farm, it is the little people or animals of good intent and devotion who suffer and sacrifice, like Boxer, the faithful horse, in the story. (6)

Thus far, one might be tempted to lump Bower's review among the critics who believe Orwell intended to condemn all revolutions for their totalitarian impulses. Yet Bower later turned this on its head in a summary of the book remarkable for its contrarian interpretation of the text: "Leaders emerge. Snowball and Napoleon, the only young boars, come into conflict. Napoleon becomes the Hitler of the animal farm, with a pig called Squealer as his Goebbels. In the light of German history after 1933, it is downright chilling to see the dream move step by step toward tyranny and despotism" (6). For Bower, *Animal Farm* was therefore about the threat of *fascist* tyranny, not communism. In fact, neither the term "communism" nor "socialism" even appeared in her review. Her conclusion was thus that Orwell's "purpose is as obvious as his fable. But since men's memories are short, it would be a good idea if leaders and citizens of the world's democracies were to re-read 'Animal Farm' every year or so, as a refresher course in recognition of danger signals" (6). Here we see a broad interpretation of Orwell's intentions, but one intended to recast his story to suit left-wing sensibilities by evoking the specter of fascism rather than Stalin.

Bower's attempt to interpret *Animal Farm* along these ideological lines clashed markedly with the approaches of most other reviewers. To take just one example, the markedly more conservative *Waco News-Tribune* reviewed the book just a week after Bower. Its unnamed reviewer concluded that Orwell's intention in the book was not only to mock the Soviets but to draw larger conclusions about human nature and politics. "I thought for some pages that Orwell's satire was intended principally to make a couple of pigs out of Stalin and Trotzky [sic], but I concluded that he meant to make pigs out of you and me, too," the review read. "He may be anti-communist, but he's also a pessimist. There'll always be a whip and a hand to wield it, he says" ("Book Review").According to this reviewer, *Animal Farm* was thus a statement on wider human politics and the human condition, not just communism.

Nowhere was this dichotomy of responses more pronounced than in the pages of the *New York Times*, which had the perhaps unique distinction of reviewing *Animal Farm* twice in two days. The first review, published on August 25, 1946, was penned by famed liberal commentator and future Kennedy administration official Arthur M. Schlesinger Jr. and headlined "Mr. Orwell and the Communists." In a lengthy essay that filled the entire front page of the *New York Times Book Review* and jumped to another, Schlesinger argued that the book should be used to illustrate the dangers of supporting communism to his fellow liberals:

It now appears that the question of the ownership of the means of production—though interesting and important—does not necessarily contain all the ambiguities and complexities of human motivation. In the phrase of one of the most influential of the leftist critics of communism, we tend to recoil from the Commissar into the arms of the Yogi. Most of us do not really much care for the Yogi either. But nearly all of us will now concede that the lesson of the Russian Revolution is that the historical process does not suspend the dark interior passions of man, whether you want to talk about them in the vocabulary of Freud or of Augustine. (1)

Animal Farm, he continued, should be viewed as Orwell's "most compact and witty expression of the left-wing British reaction to Soviet communism." In the final reckoning, he continued, Orwell had produced perhaps the most effective argument for why the left should refuse to support the Soviet Union. "The story should be read in particular by liberals who still cannot understand how Soviet performance has fallen so far behind Communist professions," Schlesinger concluded. "'Animal Farm' is a wise, compassionate and illuminating fable for our times" (28).

Schlesinger's essay was perhaps the most clearheaded liberal review of *Animal Farm* in this early period. By arguing that Orwell was directly condemning Stalin's USSR, liberals could appropriate the novel for their own purposes. The author's reference to the "means of production"—and the troubling results that had come from their seizure in the Soviet Union—indicates that changing views on this doctrine of Marxist theory were consuming the international left in this period. For Schlesinger, Orwell's satire was thus a powerful tool for convincing his fellow left-wingers that supporting socialist ideas did not have to lead to sympathies for Moscow. This point would become increasingly important in the coming era of McCarthyism, when many who had supported communism both quietly and loudly in earlier years would find themselves in serious peril. *Animal Farm* was therefore, Schlesinger wrote, a "simple story . . . but a story of deadly simplicity" (1).

A sharply contrasting view could be found in the pages of the *Times* the following morning as the paper's chief literary critic, Orville Prescott, weighed in. Prescott was well known for taking contrarian positions. His obituary later characterized him as "challenging sacred cows and often crossing swords with artistic experimentalists while pursuing his own predilection for novels with strong narratives and characterization" (Gussow). On this occasion, Prescott labeled *Animal Farm* "an odd little book" with "nothing so startlingly brilliant about this quite elementary fable... to justify a tempest in anything larger than a teacup" (33). Orwell himself, Prescott continued:

is on record as a determined foe of totalitarians, including the Russian variety. But he still believes in socialism of an abstract sort and does not seem aware of any connection between it at totalitarianism. He seems to believe that totalitarianism is caused either by wicked men, oppressing stupid men, or by the very nature of revolution by force instead of by peaceable revolution. But in which of these theories he believes is not clear. It is not clear in "Animal Farm," although this book is a satire on totalitarianism in general and the Russian variety in particular. As a satire it is neat, moderately clever and so simple and explicit that "Animal Farm" could be read in grade schools with salutary results for democratic education. But it is not particularly witty or amusing. (33)

Prescott's general distaste for the novel aside, this analysis betrays his own views of *Animal Farm*'s intent. Rather than a specific satire of the Russian Revolution, as Schlesinger had argued the previous day, Prescott now claimed Orwell was an opponent of revolutions in a broad sense. His purported confusion as to which view Orwell was advocating was in fact mere cover for Prescott's own view on the matter. Just a few paragraphs later, Prescott more or less admitted this explicitly: "'Animal Farm' in a few pages demonstrates once again the ancient cycle of revolution—first brotherhood, then organization and then tyranny. The sequence should be a warning well known to all, but, since it isn't, another warning is always in order" (33).

Just as Schlesinger's review had argued for a liberal, anti-Soviet interpretation of *Animal Farm*, Prescott's review the following day presented more or less the conservative reading that Orwell was intending to condemn revolutions generally as threats to human freedom. This would become the prevailing view of the novel among conservatives in coming years. Christopher Hollis would argue in 1956 that *Animal Farm* was more than "an attack simply on Communism." Instead, he wrote, "Orwell's whole record from the Spanish days onwards shows his impartial hatred of all tyrannies and of all totalitarian claims. . . . The lesson of *Animal Farm* is clearly not merely the corrupting effect of power when exercised by anyone." In other words, *Animal Farm* was not merely about

Soviet Communism but about the dangers posed by any regime that overthrows the old order. Hollis then went further and concluded that Orwell's main objection to British Conservatism was thus that it had actually gone too soft for its own good. "While the case for Conservatism was that it stood for traditional ways and ancient liberties against the menace of new philosophies, the Conservatives had in practice, he [Orwell] complained, had shown themselves always only too ready to do a deal with the new philosophies. . . . Orwell despaired of the Conservatives because the Conservatives despaired of Conservatism," Hollis wrote. "They were without principle" (153). It seems very unlikely that the lifelong socialist Orwell would have agreed with this analysis, but it is telling that a conservative like Hollis could use *Animal Farm* to argue that its author was really a disaffected Tory.

The debate over *Animal Farm* continued on both the left and the right well after Orwell's death in January 1950. The author's obituary in the *New York Times* acknowledged the controversy, describing *Animal Farm* as "a brief, trenchant allegory in which most reviewers saw an indictment of Soviet communism, traced the rise of a dictator by using animals as its characters and a barnyard as the locale. The novel was also praised for its wit and charm, independent of any political implications" ("George Orwell, Author, 46, Dead"). Clearly this interpretation was by no means universal. Later adaptations of the novel did little to clarify the controversy. A 1955 film adaption ended with the animals embarking on a second revolution to overthrow Napoleon and the pigs (Hollis described this as "a happy ending. . . . But of course this ending makes nonsense of the whole thesis. It was the Orwellian thesis, right or wrong, that power inevitably corrupts and that revolutions inevitably fail of their purpose") (147). A 1999 television adaptation controversially changed the novel's ending to have a new human family arriving on Manor Farm to take over and return matters to normalcy, symbolizing the (relatively) peaceful end of the Soviet Union a few years early. To justify the new ending, the series director stated that *Animal Farm* is "more about repression than Stalinism" and was "an anti-dictatorship book. It applies to Kosovo today as much as it applied to Hungary then" (Rodden 45). Clearly, the debate over what *Animal Farm* is actually about—and the lessons it may hold for the post-Soviet world—are far from resolved.

This leaves one significant remaining question, however: what did Orwell himself intend the book to be about? Thanks to the recent publication of Orwell's selected letters there is direct evidence on this question. Shortly after the publication of *Animal Farm*, American author and left-wing social critic Dwight Macdonald wrote to Orwell to ask about the book's intent (Macdonald himself held the view that the book should be applied narrowly to the Soviet case only and had no wider implications for revolutions in general). Orwell told Macdonald he actually had both intentions in mind:

> Of course I intended it primarily as a satire on the Russian revolution. But I did mean it to have a wider application in so much that I meant that *that kind* of revolution (violent conspiratorial revolution, led by unconsciously power-hungry people) can only lead to a change of masters. I meant the moral to be that revolutions only effect a radical improvement when the masses are alert and know how to chuck out their leaders as soon as the latter have done their job. . . . What I was trying to say was, "You can't have a revolution unless you make it for yourself; there is no such thing as a benevolent dictat[or]ship. ("What Orwell Really Meant")

Orwell thus seems to have seen both sides of the controversy. The Russian Revolution was clearly the event he was most closely evoking in *Animal Farm*, yet he himself saw the wider implications of the work. One need not share Hollis's view that Orwell was really a frustrated Tory to see that his message was wider than a mere commentary on the Soviet Union, however convenient that interpretation may have been for left-wing American critics of the time. As was typical throughout his career, Orwell's views were simply too contrarian and unusual to fit into neat and tidy ideological boxes.

The continuing debate over Orwell's legacy and *Animal Farm* in the twenty-first century demonstrates the remarkable resonance of the novel. Just as Hitchens deemed it necessary to weigh into a decades-old controversy in the midst of his own battles over the Iraq War, scholars and the general public alike remain fascinated by Orwell. This is in many ways a reflection not only of his personal genius but of the way he defied the standard political categories of his own time and after. For both the American left and the right, *Animal Farm* could be appropriated to support their political positions. On the left these could range from Bower's conviction that the book was a belated condemnation of Nazi Germany and a warning against fascism, to Schlesinger's view that the book was a warning for liberals about the dangers of supporting Stalin. For conservatives, *Animal Farm* was a warning against the accumulation of government power and the revolutionary overthrow of traditional governments. Regardless of one's political views, Orwell's writing could be construed to support them. As Rodden has written, "*Animal Farm* is simple on the surface—and quite subtle beneath it" (47). As with so much of his writing, Orwell's combination of accessibility and subtlety will undoubtedly make *Animal Farm* the subject of controversy for decades yet to come as new generations find themselves exploring and interpreting the events on Manor Farm.

Works Cited

"A Blithering Trotskyite Down On the Farm." *Green Bay Press Gazette,* Jan. 4, 1946, p. 4.

"Book Review: Animal Farm, by George Orwell (Harcourt, Brace; $1)." *Waco News-Tribune,* Aug. 31, 1946, p. 4.

"British Voice Skepticism." *New York Times,* March 23, 1946, p. 2.

"George Orwell, Author, 46, Dead." *New York Times,* Jan. 22, 1950, p. 77.

Bower, Helen. "Pigs Rule the World in Animal Satire." *Detroit Free Press,* Aug. 25, 1946, part 2, p. 6.

Carr, Craig L. *Orwell, Politics, and Power.* Bloomsbury, 2010.

Gussow, Mel. "Orville Prescott, Times Book Critic for 24 Years, Dies at 89." *New York Times,* Apr. 30, 1996. www.nytimes.com/1996/04/30/ books/orville-prescott-times-book-critic-for-24-years-dies-at-89. html. Accessed May 9, 2018.

Hitchens, Christopher. "George Orwell and the Liberal Experience of Totalitarianism." *George Orwell: Into the Twenty-first Century.* Edited by Thomas Cushman and John Rodden, Taylor and Francis, 2004, pp. 77-85.

Hollis, Christopher. *A Study of George Orwell.* Hollis and Carter, 1956.

Orwell, George. "29. Letter to Leonard Moore." *The Collected Essays, Journalism and Letters of George Orwell: In Front of your Nose 1945-1950.* Edited by Sonia Orwell and Ian Angus, Secker and Warburg, 1968, pp. 109-11.

Orwell, George. "'Animal Farm': What Orwell Really Meant." *New York Review of Books*, vol. 60, no. 12, July 11, 2013. www.nybooks. com/articles/2013/07/11/animal-farm-what-orwell-really-meant/. Accessed May 9, 2018.

P. J. S. "Animals Take Over Farm and Oust Man." *Los Angeles Times,* Aug. 25, 1946, p. C4.

Prescott, Orville. "Books of the Times." *New York Times*, Aug. 26, 1946, p. 33.

Rodden, John. *Scenes from an Afterlife.* ISI, 2003.

Schlesinger, Arthur M., Jr. "Mr. Orwell and the Communists: His 'Animal Farm' is a Compassionate and Illuminating Fable for our Times." *New York Times Book Review,* Aug. 25, 1946, pp. 1, 28.

Zwerdling, Alex *Orwell and the Left.* Yale UP, 1974.

Rendering Animals: Thought for Food, Meat for Metaphor

Gregory Brophy

> On my return from Spain I thought of exposing the Soviet myth in a story that could be easily understood by anyone and which could be easily translated into other languages . . .
>
> (Orwell, "Author's Preface" 403)

> If a lion could talk, we could not understand him.
>
> (Wittgenstein, *Philosophical* 225)

Institutional Renderings: Agricultural and Educational Contexts of Reading

What is it about *Animal Farm* that makes it not only "easily understood" but "easily translated"? Certainly, the compact novella's direct and simple prose, its stark and expressive conflicts—hallmarks of much of Orwell's fiction—help in this regard. But the singular feature that sets this text apart from the rest of his body of work is its committed use of "fairy tale" (as the novella's subtitle would have it), a choice that allows the author to draw upon a deep imaginative wellspring of all languages. Orwell's stated aim is "exposing the Soviet myth," though his strategy—rather than a historical or journalistic exposé—is, paradoxically, to clothe that myth in allegory, a fictional mode in which characters and actions represent historical persons and events, or more abstractly emblematize values, concepts, and aspects of consciousness. Critics Carolyn Burke and Joby Copenhaver grasp at this raiment of allegory when they characterize Orwell's tale as "a *costumed* version of the promise and betrayal of the Russian Revolution set in a barnyard" (207; emphasis added). In like manner, Peter Edgerly Firchow reads the fable as the story of socialism's perversion "disguise[d] . . . in animal *dress*" (129; emphasis added). To unravel the fable's core concern, then, discerning readers coax the actors out of their fur coats and animal hides, disrobing the metaphor.

But why enlist animals in the first place? Is there a significant relation between the animals on the surface and the theme at the core, or are they merely the text's disposable wrapper, flesh to be torn from the book's bones? Though particular associations and connotations vary wildly from culture to culture, the allegorical use of animals is a universal practice. Orwell intuits the fundamental mythological fact that Claude Lévi-Strauss would articulate seventeen years later in his *Totemism*: that "[n]atural species are chosen" to serve as metaphors for social distinctions and conflicts "not because they are 'good to eat' [*bonnes à manger*] but because they are 'good to think' [*bonnes à penser*]" (89).

What makes animals so easy to understand, and so easy to translate—to *render* into something else? The aim of writing in the allegorical mode is to solicit translation on the part of the reader. Orwell, the story goes, works within one system of signs (animal), and expects his reader to transpose these signs into another register (twentieth-century political figures, to use the most readily familiar interpretation of our text). To understand *is* to translate. Fail to perform the latter action, choose to take things at face value, and you have missed Orwell's point entirely.

Pet Theories: Critical Animal Studies

Parrying this interpretive thrust, critical animal studies is responsible for a surprisingly recent development in the novella's critical reception. It seeks—stubbornly resisting the best advice of schoolteachers round the globe—to interpret Orwell's animals *as animals*. The dominant reading of *Animal Farm* as historical parable understands the animals as decoys; fashioned from words not wood, they are nonetheless human devices that serve human ends. Literate readers will quickly recognize the barnyard drama as a stand-in for (human) historical and political conflict. At first blush, the modest refusal of such interpretative overtures is likely to read as nothing more than a dogged literalism. But in fact, animal studies provide a meta-analysis of the ideological work performed by these animal metaphors. Individual acts of allegorical reading feature audacious flights of critical ingenuity that enable breathtaking interpretive leaps. (Most students are shocked to find Josef Stalin crouched within the pigskin of Napoleon.) But these local interpretations provide textual illumination while leaving undisturbed the underlying thinking that prompts authors and readers always to translate creatures of the imagination out of existence, systematically sacrificing animal experience to allegories of human concern.

Orwell dramatizes the process of reading and the development of critical literacy, and, like a surprising number of the dystopian novels that end up on secondary school curricula, *Animal Farm* features a classroom (with the significant difference being that this educational institution has been built on the rubble of an agricultural institution). Paying special attention to the widespread institutional use of *Animal Farm* as an instructional text commonly directed to adolescent students, we must connect the agricultural context of Orwell's plot with the educational context of its reception, asking why we train young readers to conflate literary interpretation with this "rendering" of animals.

Animal studies finds its ethical underpinnings in 1975's groundbreaking work of moral philosophy, Peter Singer's *Animal Liberation: A New Ethics for Our Treatment of Animals*. Following Jeremy Bentham, Singer insists it is the animal's capacity for suffering that must serve as the basis for our ethical responsibility to them. His wide-ranging study of human-animal interactions takes particular notice of the exploitative *uses* to which we put animals— as clothing, as food, as experimental research subjects, and as domesticated companions. The mentality that encourages callous and systematic disregard for the suffering these acts produce Singer calls "speciesism." Analogous to racism or sexism, speciesism is an exclusionary principle through which humans "allow the interests of their own species to override the greater interests of members of other species" (6). Reading literature in light of this pervasive mentality of speciesism impels critics to interrogate the insidious strategies through which literature instills readers with systematic disregard for animals, even—or perhaps especially—when we are reading stories that seem to be about animals.

Orwell's plot represents the neglect and abuse of animals (Jones lets his animals go hungry and whips them when they seek the feed on their own), but it is hardly necessary to preface *Animal Farm* with a disclaimer (as one finds in the cinema) that "no animals were harmed in the making of this book." Animals possess a special metaphorical allure that sees them endlessly absorbed into comparison with the human. Critics have found in this ritual immolation of animals to human "meaning" something predatory. To examine this rendering process is to take a hard look at the ingenious ways in which readers refuse to look at animals.

Educational institutions have put to the test Lévi-Strauss's theory on animals as aids for thinking, introducing *Animal Farm* as a key text in the education of adolescents. For more than half a century now, *Animal Farm* has been taught worldwide, and in varied educational contexts and levels (Scherff). We train young readers to become discriminating consumers of fiction, but in the process, we are also teaching them lessons about consuming animals. Just as the parent of an infant will introduce solid food to her diet as her development permits, so educators introduce this complex food for thought. Meaty with meaning, the story will need to be broken down in order to offer up its full value, digested through interpretation and allegory. The child's instinctive, imaginative affinities with animals will be recalibrated by the educator, who introduces allegory as a transformative model of reading. Adolescent readers, many in the midst of their own pubescent metamorphoses, begin to discern a human shape emerging from within the animal figure.

Anthropomorphism and Allegory

Anthropomorphism is the term we give to this misrecognition. It names the attribution of human characteristics to objects, gods, and—our present concern—animals. The figure describes not animals that are shaped *like* humans, but shaped *by* humans. It was Victorian literary critic and amateur physiologist George Herbert Lewes who first used the term "anthropomorphism" to describe how humans misrepresent animals. Writing in 1858, the same year that Darwin and Wallace would present their revolutionary work on natural selection, Lewes criticized habits of reasoning that made sense of animal behaviors by appealing to human metaphors and models. Scientific discourse, he averred, was "incessantly at fault" in its reliance on this trope, a failure of scientific objectivity that projected onto its animal subjects human language, cognition, emotion, and values (385).

Lewes draws our attention to the literary tropes that, often unconsciously, frame our understanding of the world around us. This insight has proven crucial to animal studies, as a field of critical inquiry that interrogates the framing of nature within culture and explores the symbolic uses to which animals are put. While some critical animal studies thinkers have been trained as biologists, many more approach the animal from the fields of history, philosophy, and literary and cultural studies. As such, they are ideally positioned to examine and contest cultural representations that depict the animal in human terms, providing ideological support for exploitation.

Anthropomorphic reading, whether in a biology textbook or in a children's bedtime story, peddles the vain conceit that every animal story is at heart a story about us. For Nicholas Howe, that writers "burden animals by asking them to teach us how to behave like human beings seems no more than yet another way of exploiting them. We force animals to do physical labor, we raise them under cruel conditions, we mistreat them in all sorts of ways, and then we domesticate them most fully by moralizing them" (231). As Steve Baker argues, this pervasive stance, "that talking-animal narratives are not really about animals—that the worthwhile ones, at least, must surely be about something more than mere animals—is quite consistent with the far wider cultural trivialization and marginalization of the animal" (138). Not simply a literary figure or scientific fallacy, anthropomorphism is a formative technique in our most intimate relations with animals. The malformations it breeds, read critically, betray the unseemly and inhumane relationship between domestication and domination.

While *Animal Farm* employs this common figural strategy, Orwell's handling of anthropomorphism is unprecedented, even revolutionary. First, the revolution upends not only the presumed "natural order" of the farm, but also the conventions of animal narrative. When the abused creatures "[fling] themselves upon their tormentors," readers familiar with the unspoken laws of fable are likely to be just as shocked as Jones and his men. This "sudden uprising of creatures whom they were used to thrashing and maltreating just as they chose, frightened them almost out of their wits," because they "had never seen animals behave like this before" (12). Nor in all likelihood have we. Orwell's animals cast off with violence what Steve Baker identifies as "the myth of willing submission almost universally imposed on all manner of animals in children's stories," along with the conventional "eagerness to please humans, to be acknowledged, observed and valued by them" (xiv).

This species revolt, entirely unpremeditated by the animals, sprouts from a revolution in consciousness. The remarkable fact in this regard is that Orwell grants his animals a critical awareness of anthropomorphic comparisons. Rather than serving as the unwitting instruments of this trope, they are self-conscious of the ways in which certain traits and acts make them more or less human. We can examine Orwell's innovation through two textual examples that chart the animals' quickly mounting consciousness of their own figuration. Consider Clover the mare, the butt of Orwell's first modest attempt at humor. Our narrator notes two facts connected with Clover's maternity. She is "motherly," and she has "never quite got her figure back after her fourth foal" (2). Now, to be told that Clover is a mother and that she is "motherly" may sound redundant, but in fact the second term shifts the reader from the ground of biological facts to the field of cultural values. As an adjective, motherly describes not all mothers, but a select group who not only *are* mothers but also perform that identity in a manner that confirms social conceptions and values of motherhood. Thus, to describe Clover as maternal is to view her through the lens of a classic anthropomorphism that ascribes human values to the animal, domesticating our encounter by enclosing Clover within reassuringly familiar structures of the familial and the feminine.

This classic anthropomorphic lens fractures somewhat under the weight of the narrator's curious next comment, that Clover has "never quite got her figure back" after the fourth foal. Orwell here makes subtle comic use of our uncertainty as to where this observation comes from. Is this our narrator's voice, chiming in to assess the shapeliness of horses, or is it Clover who is self-conscious about her "figure"? Do these animals know they *have* figures or that they *are* figures? Orwell's indirect discourse equivocates. Clover's self-consciousness is superficial, not yet rising above a vague sense of vanity, all the while satirizing human insecurities by sketching an animal caricature of feminine pride. Accordingly, Orwell withholds the radical gesture of plainly granting her ownership of this internal voice.

Old Major's speech conveys a reflexive understanding of anthropomorphism that is more broadly conscious. He politicizes this trope of resemblance when he warns his comrades that "in fighting against Man, we must not come to resemble him" (6). Old Major will not live to see it, but the metamorphosis of animal into human animal marks the ignominious end of their revolution. Staring through the farmhouse window at their leadership, the animals gaze "from pig to man, and from man to pig, and from pig to man again; but already it was impossible to say which was which" (95). This is a grotesque piece of satire, every bit as unsettling as the political caricatures of Jean-Jacques Grandville. Orwell's humanizing metamorphosis of the animal serves as a principle of dramatic conflict. It gives farcical but tragic expression to the animals' capitulation to anthropocentric values, and it embodies the threat that revolutionary action might ultimately lead to the reification of the same power relations. Teetering absurdly on his hind legs, whip grasped in his front hoof, Napoleon's human resemblance is a parodic performance and a shocking catachresis. This troubling categorical confusion is felt more deeply for the conceptual paradoxes it incarnates: bestial and brutal behaviour is the mark of humanity; Napoleon's evolution into this form is a degenerate mark of devolution.

Reading Animals Reading

The most fantastic point of resemblance between human and nonhuman animals is not physical, of course, but linguistic. However, while Orwell's humans and animals share a common language, this commonality only highlights the divergent uses to which each group puts that language. They share a tongue, but not their words. Old Major's address, the novella's first significant speech act, mounts a plea to rebuff human intercourse. "Never listen," he insists, "when they tell you that Man and the animals have a common interest" (5). The animals are miraculously capable of communication with humankind, but aware that this is merely the channel of their subjection through ideological manipulation. To know the language of humanity is to recognize that "[i]t is all lies" (5).

This common language provides the battlefield for competing interpretations and world views. Consider what happens, for instance, when these two distinct groups fasten their gaze on a contested object. The given name of Farmer Jones's homestead is Manor Farm. After the Rebellion, however, a mutiny in language takes place. Led by Napoleon, Snowball "painted out MANOR FARM from the top bar of the gate and in its place painted ANIMAL FARM. This was to be the name of the farm from now onwards" (15). Neighboring farmers recognize the rejection of the human name for this territory as an act that expresses political allegiances. Confirming their human solidarity with Jones, they pointedly refuse to acknowledge this new name.

This animal speech-act of renaming reveals to the animals that words are not attached to things by any immutable law. Names are arbitrary: the selfsame object can be given two different and even contradictory names, and the animals needn't passively accept as reality the names that humans have given to the things of this world. This is a dicey lesson in double coding, the full significance of which is intuited only by the pigs, who have the firmest grasp on the subtleties of language. It opens up the horizon of hypocrisy, manipulation, and the ideological use of language to obscure the material circumstances of the animals' existence. Indeed, before long, Napoleon has begun to apply this principle to manipulate physical as well as verbal signs. A set of footprints leading to a hole in the hedge is fastened upon as evidence that Snowball has destroyed the windmill (48). For the majority of the animals on the farm, every sign inscribed by Napoleon and Squealer is received as constative and evidential, read as if it were unalterable evidence of material reality. All that Squealer has to do to silence the animals' complaints of hunger and exhaustion is to "[read] out the figures in a shrill, rapid voice," which "proved to them in detail that they had more oats, more hay, more turnips than they had had in Jones's day, that they worked shorter hours, that their drinking water was of better quality, that they lived longer, that a larger proportion of their young ones survived infancy, and that they had more straw in their stalls and suffered less from fleas" (75). Utterly false, but extremely detailed, these "figures" exploit writing's surprising power to overrule the animals' personal experience.

Animal Farm is a satire that depends for its effects on a peculiar species of dramatic irony: human readers bear the burden (and the pleasure) of knowing what the animal cannot. In a rudimentary fashion, and with varying degrees of success across species lines, the animals have become literate. Speaking appears to have come "naturally," though they must be taught to read and write, and most retain a dangerously credulous relation to these signs. The tragedy of misreading that follows from such naïveté is employed to pedagogical ends with adolescent students. Satire is always teaching and testing its readers. Rather than express its truth in a direct manner, the text offers oblique access through coded prisms of discourse. Satire critiques hypocrisy by mimicking its structure, saying one thing while meaning and doing another. The text invites readers to infer significance by discerning the distance between rhetoric and truth, the difference between appearance and reality. A reader who can parse satire in fiction will be well armed to puncture hypocrisy in the real world.

Consider, for instance, the hands-off approach that our narrator takes with Napoleon's news concerning management's modified expectations for laborers: "Throughout the spring and summer they worked a sixty-hour week, and in August Napoleon announced that there would be work on Sunday afternoons as well. This work was strictly voluntary, but any animal who absented himself from it would have his rations reduced by half" (40). The announcement is transmitted without authorial commentary, and no murmur of dissent is heard from the barnyard. The practical contradiction, we assume, along with the ambiguity of this "strict" voluntarism, goes unnoticed by the animals. In like manner, we later find that Napoleon has "commanded that once a week there should be held something called a Spontaneous Demonstration, the object of which was to celebrate the struggles and triumphs of Animal Farm. At the appointed time the animals would leave their work and march round the precincts of the farm" (77). Again, Orwell telegraphs the conspicuous contradiction of a "commanded" and choreographed "spontaneous" act. The irony may be obvious, but it is still unanswered, and this unresolved paradox gives the scene resonant power. When neither narrator nor animal intervenes to disentangle these ironies, the contradiction is left to vex the silent reader.

Animals serve Orwell's satire well because they express the incomprehension and susceptibility of an illiterate or uncritical public. Their credulity and obedience incite revolt within readers, who may be inclined to identify against not only the oppressor, but also his unappealingly pliant subjects. Orwell's bleating sheep, Napoleon's "greatest devotees" (77), still serve as an expressive figure for the susceptibility of "the masses" to deceptive political rhetoric.

Napoleon and Squealer's campaign of coercive manipulation builds to the novella's signal moment of horror, when Boxer is carted off in Alfred Simmonds's van. In this critical scene of reading, Benjamin, the highly literate and skeptical donkey, discerns the "writing on the wall," revealing to his naïve companions their friend's true fate: "Fools!" he shouts, impatient with the agonizing slowness of his fellow readers. "Do you not see what is written on the side of that van?" (81). As Muriel the goat stumbles over the text, Benjamin breaks through to recite to the silent crowd: "'Alfred Simmonds, Horse Slaughterer and Glue Boiler, Willingdon. Dealer in Hides and Bone-Meal. Kennels Supplied.' Do you not understand what that means? They are taking Boxer to the knacker's!" (82).

The animals make their fraternal appeal to the horses driving the cart, but the "stupid brutes, too ignorant to realize what was happening, merely set back their ears and quickened their pace" (82). If these horses cannot hear the truth of things, however, the farm animals have seen the lie exposed. In the face of this bitter realization, readers might reasonably expect the animals will experience the kind of epiphany that would lead to mutiny and revolution. If they have just been witness to the novella's Soylent Green moment, why are the animals not moved by this revelation? Boxer's comrades are delivered from their own desperate grief by Squealer, who explains that "the van had previously been the property of the knacker, and had been bought by the veterinary surgeon, who had not yet painted the old name out" (83). We learn that the animals "were tremendously relieved to hear this" (83). Orwell's description of this turn mirrors a similar formulation earlier in the same chapter: when Squealer insists to his comrades that the miserable conditions on the farm are still far better than they were in Jones's day, we are told that the creatures "were glad to believe so" (75). The preposition that prefaces these acts of hearing and believing suggest it is desire that drives the animals to belief, a state where "relief and gladness" might be seized. Squealer's lie relieves the animals of the burden of a truth they do not want to believe. They happily accept the palliative of Squealer's propaganda, the words that numb and inoculate against the reality of Boxer's fate.

Squealer's spurious explication *does* teach the animals a truth of writing that it seems many had yet to intuit: writing grants expression to situated perspectives that are historically contingent. The words may be permanent, but the referent to which they gesture is not. Recall that, as the original commandments are amended one by one, each alteration is received as an original and timeless truth (73). When *"to excess"* is hastily appended to the decree that "No animal shall drink alcohol" after the pigs discover a taste for it, Muriel corrects the record of her memory, before imagining that the authoritative commandments might have been altered (73). Squealer is a cynical teacher, we know, seeking only to teach the animals a sophistication that will enable their complicity as readers. He trains his pupils how to unread what they have just read. Benjamin, playing to type as a stubborn donkey reader, insists on a manifest and simple truth of the text. Snowball introduces the more seductive possibility that an unwritten truth overwrites what they see plainly on the surface.

Few readers will be taken in by Squealer's fiction, but we are nonetheless just as likely to reassure ourselves that a horse has not "really" died. We quickly translate the thought of "Boxer" into whatever it is we have decided this horse stands for. The first time we read this book, many of us were told, plausibly enough, that Boxer's betrayal at the hands of the pigs allegorized Stalin's betrayal of the proletariat (who, like Boxer, provided the muscle for the Tsar's overthrow and the drive to industrialization in the new era). We can choose to call this a critical insight or a critical oversight. Either way, we eclipse the object presently in front of us with an absent concept.

For Helen Tiffin, this substitutive procedure, which marginalizes the animal in order to center upon the human lesson, enacts a "disappearance of animals as characters in their own right" (252). To Kimberly Benston, this enterprise of writing and reading is a process of "making and enlarging 'humanity' by effacing (writing over) animality" (551). We hardly need bother with altering the text on Simmonds's cart. We are still rendering the animal, stripping back the hide of the fable and breaking down the figure for its thematic value. Boxer provides the glue that holds together our allegory.

Boxer is denied a burial. His comrades blithely accept the explanation that: "It had not been possible . . . to bring back their lamented comrade's remains for interment on the farm" (84). Napoleon delivers a self-serving eulogy and arranges a raucous night of drinking for the pigs at Boxer's expense but not exactly in his honor. The abrupt shift forward in time marked by the subsequent chapter's opening line—"Years passed" (85)—marks the enormity of the loss, but eradicates any period or process of mourning. To catch a glimpse of such animal sorrow, we must travel all the way back to the very first morning following the revolution, as the animals venture warily toward the farmhouse. Momentarily frozen at the threshold of this taboo human space, they "halted in silence outside the door … frightened to go inside" (14). What will it mean to cross that boundary? These animals are surely not the first, but on what drastically different terms have their forebears entered! Having already proven their bravery in the previous day's Rebellion, the audacity of this act still somehow gives them pause. They are breaking and entering—what is sometimes called "housebreaking," a term that risks confusion with the name's more familiar use. Typically, it is the house that breaks the animal: owners tame and train their pets, replacing animal instincts with human behaviors. To *break*, especially where animals are concerned, is to *crush resistance*. To be sure, domesticated animals are treated with special care, sheltered, fed, and often coddled. However, pet keeping typically involves confinement, facilitated through a host of tools, from leash and collar to kennel and cage. Yi-Fu Tuan's term for the curious treatment reserved for these privileged animals is *petrification*, the ritualistic acts of ownership and mastery that combine cruelty and affection.Whether in house or field, to be domesticated is to be dominated. Tuan reminds us that the two acts share "the same root sense of mastery over another being—of bringing it into one's house or domain" (143).

The Jones's domicile is a space of domination, and the signs of that subjection fill the animals with "awe." The animals decide unanimously "on the spot that the farmhouse should be preserved as a museum. All were agreed that no animal must ever live there" (14). Mausoleum would perhaps be closer to the point, as many have died there. If it is to be a museum, the farmhouse's animal artefacts will bear mute witness to a history of animal bondage. There are touches of the slaughterhouse here, but the ascendant note is, rather than explicit violence, foremost a sense of the house's "unbelievable luxury" (14). Human comfort inspires in these creatures reverent dread because these are comforts snatched from their own bodies. As they "tipto[e] from room to room," the narrator pauses to note "feather mattresses" and a "horsehair sofa" (14), among other human luxuries of animal origin.

Moving through this haunted house, the animals arrive at the kitchen to find "some hams hanging" (14). The scene is a grisly one (and likely gristly as well . . .), though our narrator grants it mention in suitably terse and mundane terms. No doubt these hams have been hanged for practical purposes, so that the meat can be dry-aged with the goal of a more tender and flavorful meal. And yet, try to picture the scene through Snowball's eyes, to see the dismembered and unidentifiable bodies of his peers strung up and swaying from the ceiling. If we consume this passage without choking on its bones, it is only because the word we digest as readers has been prepared for us by Orwell and his human narrator. The term *ham* shields the human gaze from direct exposure to such an image; to see it for what it is, one must reverse the successive acts of euphemistic translation that transform in language a pig to *pork*.

The animals restore these victims to their identity and integrity through a symbolic act, taking the hams "out for burial" (14). Later in the plot, we will hear tell of chicken interments as well (51), though we aren't privy to the ritual details of these ceremonies. The spectacle of burial for these "hams" is absurd on the face of it, a ceremony that struggles to reverse the disfiguration of human butchery by ritualistically reconnecting this hunk of meat to a whole pig. Synecdoche is a figure of speech in which a part of something is used to refer to the whole of that thing, or vice versa. Most often read as a benign poetic device, it is also a figure of understanding that guides human action. What allows a part to stand in for the whole? In human relations, this tendency is often tangled up with objectification and alienation. When it comes to animals, which human society encourages us to perceive as objects at our disposal, the means by which a part is separated from the whole is often a violent and even fetishistic process.

To imagine the details of such mourning, as I have just done here, no doubt involves a fair bit of projection. It is to Orwell's credit that his fable retains his tautness of tone in moments like these, never descending into such somber or sentimental mawkishness.

But doing critical justice to the power of this ceremony, of which we are permitted only the barest of glimpses, means coming to terms with the spectrum of exploitative uses to which we put animals, all the way from the knacker's trade in "Hides and Bone-Meal" to the racket through which readers of allegory harvest fictional plots, tilled by animals, for their own anthropocentric ends.

Analysis of culture through the lens of critical animal studies prompts us to examine how the imaginative dismantling of literary animal figures mirrors, and arguably provides the ideological support for, the literal exploitation of animals. As Gillian Beer contends, the true interest of animal narratives "is certainly not in the whole animal but in the animal as pointer to or satire on human behavior" (311). Her distinction between whole and part is an evocative one; when applied to the use of animals, it suggests that interpretation is a kind of poaching or trophy hunting. The dissection of animal figures confirms our sophistication as readers of signs, but masks our basic incapacity to encounter the animal on its own terms. When we use animal decoys, whether deployed as lure or deterrent, our gesture prompts misreading and misinterpretation from a range of animal species with a demonstrated incapacity to read these signs *as signs*. Human consciousness reverses this problem of recognition: unable and unwilling to recognize animal sovereignty, we are always converting them into signs within our own systems. The animal is always and only grasped as a metaphor of something beyond itself. Fur, furniture, fable; meat or metaphor: could it be possible for us to gaze upon an animal and avoid some such act of translation?

Works Cited

Baker, Steve. *Picturing the Beast: Animals, Identity, and Representation.* U of Illinois P, 2001.

Beer, Gillian. "Animal Presences: Tussles with Anthropomorphism." *Comparative Critical Studies*, vol. 2, no. 3, Oct. 2005, pp. 311-22.

Benston, Kimberly W. "Experimenting at the Threshold: Sacrifice, Anthropomorphism, and the Aims of (Critical) Animal Studies." *PMLA,* vol. 124, no. 2, March 2009, pp. 548-55.

Bentham, Jeremy. *An Introduction to the Principles of Morals and Legislation*. Clarendon, 1789.

Burke, Carolyn L., and Joby G. Copenhaver. "Animals as People in Children's Literature." *Language Arts*, vol. 81, 2004, pp. 205-13.

Firchow, Peter Edgerly. "George Orwell's Dystopias: From *Animal Farm* to *Nineteen Eighty-Four*." *George Orwell's Animal Farm*. Edited by Harold Bloom, Bloom's Literary Criticism, 2009, pp. 125-50.

Howe, Nicolas. "Fabling Beasts: Traces in Memory." *Humans and Other Animals*. Edited by Arien Mack, Ohio State, 1999, pp. 229-47.

Lévi-Strauss, Claude. *Totemism*. Translated by Rodney Needham, Merlin, 1964.

Lewes, George Herbert. *Sea-side Studies at Ilfracombe, Tenby, the Scilly Isles, and Jersey*. Blackwood, 1958.

Orwell, George. *Animal Farm*. Penguin, 2008.

_____. "Author's Preface to the Ukrainian Edition of *Animal Farm*." *George Orwell: As I Please, vol. 3: 1943-1946*. Edited by Sonia Orwell and Ian Angus, Nonpareil, 2000, pp. 402-06.

Scherff, Lisa. "Rethinking Literature 'Instruction.'" *International Perspectives on the Teaching of Literature in Schools: Global Principles and Practices*. Edited by Andrew Goodwyn et al., Routledge, 2017.

Tiffin, Helen. "Pigs, People, and Pigoons." *Knowing Animals*. Edited by Laurence Simons and Philip Armstrong Brill, 2007, pp. 244-65.

Wittgenstein, Ludwig. *Philosophical Investigations*. Translated by G. E. M. Anscombe, Basil Blackwell, 1958.

From "A Fairy Story" to "Darning a Worn-Out Sock, Cadging a Saccharine Tablet, Saving a Cigarette End": Narrative Strategies in George Orwell's *Animal Farm* and *Nineteen Eighty-Four*_____

Rafeeq O. McGiveron

Although the British writer Eric Blair (1903-1950), far better known by his pseudonym of George Orwell, authored six novels, three books of nonfiction, and hundreds of pieces of journalism, literary criticism, and other essays, it is of course *Animal Farm* and *Nineteen Eighty-Four* for which he is most remembered. The intellectual echoes of these two grim yet artfully rendered dystopias have shaped public discourse for generations now, with Orwellian coinages such as the wry notion of some members of a group being *more equal than others*, the mysterious *Big Brother* and his sinister *thought police*, and various ironic euphemisms and obfuscations of *Newspeak* helping us identify, make sense of, and combat a multitude of encroachments against individual freedom for well over half a century.

Animal Farm and *Nineteen Eighty-Four* were written just years apart, with both investigating the totalitarianism that can spring from even the highest-seeming ideals, yet Orwell in each of his two most well-known and culturally significant novels uses very different strategies of narration to further their ever-timely warnings. One book purports to be, as its subtitle wryly suggests, "a fairy story," and hence uses a deceptively simple presentation, while the other, which deals not with a revolution but with the time of a generation afterward, tells its story both with a subtler point of view and with a richer depiction of the individual's life of the mind. Each approach allows for a different kind of storytelling, thus producing significantly different reading experiences aptly suited for the subjects of their respective plots.

The "fairy story" of Orwell's *Animal Farm* employs a third-person omniscient narrative that covers many characters, though delving only a little bit beneath the surface, while *Nineteen Eighty-Four* employs a third-person limited narrative that focuses on protagonist Winston Smith, delving deep into his conscious and subconscious, and wallowing there. But why? What makes these different approaches so appropriate and so effective?

Animal Farm: The "Fairy Story" Beginning

Animal Farm covers what in the real world would be an extraordinarily complex situation: the overthrow of a longstanding form of sociopolitical organization for a revolutionary one that changes almost every aspect of governance, economy, and even personal and familial relations. To tell such a story in the form of a standard novel—that is, a sizeable work with one or more well-developed characters whose outward actions and inner emotions and conflicts are revealed, and with a plot that both chronicles the ideological and political upheavals of the time and also shows how they affect individual characters and the shape of the new society as a whole—would require a sizable and complex book. Orwell could have produced such a text had he wanted, but he did not. He chose a very compact format of only about 30,000 words, and he kept the narrative closer to the surface rather than moving into a great deal of interiority, for this made a novel whose ironies are crisp and cutting.

A "fairy story," as *Animal Farm* is subtitled—or fairy tale, as we more commonly call the genre in the United States—generally begins in some unspecified period "once upon a time," often "in a land far away," and is told by a narrator who somehow knows everything there is to know about every important character, the populace in general, and the history of the land, but who often will not spare more than a sentence or two here and there about their feelings and motivations. On the one hand, *Animal Farm* begins in a land not so far away at all: a cozy agrarian England of the mid-twentieth century, where quaintly "old-fashioned" (54) small farms still are plowed by draft horses, protected from foxes by the occasional "charge of number 6 shot" (24), and accessed by a mere "cart-track" on the way to the road proper (29). Of course, the animals of Manor Farm can reason and philosophize and organize just as humans do, and they can speak intelligibly across their different species and with people, too, so . . . well, this is a land very far away indeed.

This fairy tale kingdom is reported to us with a calm, patient, sometimes- droll narrative voice not too far removed from those that for centuries have relayed the details—although often only the rather superficial details—of the trials of the likes of Little Red Riding Hood or, perhaps more apropos, the Three Little Pigs. Orwell here is particularly fond of a broad-brush approach that a neophyte writer still unskilled in the craft might use without thought, but which a master can deliberately employ to great effect. Eschewing the "Show—don't tell" advice now a cliché in creative writing classes, Orwell instead *tells* with gusto, and often tells so broadly as to treat whole groups as, essentially, a single unit.

In the very beginning of the book, for example, when the Lenin of the plot, the wise old boar called Old Major, first wishes to speak to the animals of Mr. Jones's farm, "*everyone* [is] quite ready to lose an hour's sleep in order to hear what he had to say" (15; italics added)—every single one of the animals, without exception, and without reservation. Some of the main characters receive quick descriptions as they come into the barn and settle down to hear Old Major's speech, but none of these is shown responding individually to the stirring call for the overthrow of "Man . . . the only real enemy" (19). Indeed, no reactions are shown at all until the singing of Old Major's revolutionary anthem, "Beasts of England," and then they are those of the entire group as the act "thr[ows] the animals into the wildest excitement" (23). Orwell distinguishes only very broadly among the "low[ing]," "whin[ing]," "bleat[ing]," "whinn[ying]," and "quack[ing]" of the different species, but he comes immediately back to a monolithic presentation: "They were so delighted with the song that they sang it right through five times in succession, and might have continued singing it all night if they had not been interrupted" (24). After the interruption of Jones's shotgun blast intended to scare away a supposed fox, "[e]veryone fle[es] to his own sleeping-place," and then somehow, without any animals venturing to talk further in little groups or even having to lie awake in the wonder of their own private thoughts, "the whole farm [is] asleep in a moment" (24).

Orwell does not neglect individual characters, naturally, and soon we will see the actions and hear the words of, say, horses Boxer and Clover, donkey Benjamin, or pigs Snowball, Napoleon, and Squealer. Descriptions of "the animals," "all the animals," or "they" as an undifferentiated and unified group, however, abound throughout the book. Waking up after the unexpected but successful Rebellion that drives out Mr. and Mrs. Jones and their four farmhands, the inhabitants of the farm, which now is to be renamed Animal Farm, act as one:

> [S]uddenly remembering the glorious thing that had happened, *they all* raced down out into the pasture together. A little way down the pasture there was a knoll that commanded a view of most of the farm. *The animals* rushed to the top of it and gazed round them in the clear morning light. Yes, it was theirs—everything that *they* could see was theirs! In the ecstasy of that thought *they* gambolled round and round, *they* hurled themselves into the air in great leaps of excitement. *They* rolled in the dew, *they* cropped mouthfuls of the sweet summer grass, *they* kicked up clods of the black earth and snuffed its rich scent. Then *they* made a tour of inspection of the whole farm and surveyed with speechless admiration the ploughland, the hayfield, the orchard, the pool, the spinney. It was as though *they* had never seen these things before, and even now *they* could hardly believe that it was all their own. (30-31; italics added)

Yet who first suggests going to the pasture? Does any animal *not* feel like rolling in the dew, or jumping in their air, or kicking up chunks of earth? Who first begins the tour of the entire farm? Are all truly speechless, or might any animals murmur comments here and there? Such questions are moot, though, in the land of fairy tale, where the populace is so conveniently unified that the complexities and subtleties of real life do not detract from the broad thrust of the tale.

The level of interiority in fairy tale is similarly, and purposefully, shallow. How exactly do Hansel and Gretel feel, for instance, about being abandoned in the woods, presumably to starve to death? How shamed and crushed is the trusting Jack upon being scolded that he has traded a valuable cow for a mere bean that appears to have no worth at all? We do not know, and neither does Orwell's novel give more than the briefest summaries of his characters' states of mind, even during events that should shock and perplex them. Life under a real-world dictatorship, when propaganda turns facts upside down and suspected dissidents are executed at will, presumably could spur much angst and second-guessing, but the "fairy story" of *Animal Farm* does not show these. Instead, through occasional use of bland passive voice and through a steadfast refusal to reveal more, the narrative carefully keeps to the shallows of its characters' inner lives.

On the day the animals first expel the humans from the Manor Farm, the inhabitants of the newly renamed Animal Farm are about to head to the field to begin the harvest when the cows, with their udders "almost bursting," protest that they need to be milked first. The pigs do so, producing

> five buckets of frothing creamy milk at which many of the animals looked with considerable interest.
>
> "What is going to happen to all that milk?" said someone.
>
> "Jones used sometimes to mix some of it in our mash," said one of the hens.
>
> "Never mind the milk, comrades!" cried Napoleon, placing himself in front of the buckets. "That will be attended to. The harvest is more important. Comrade Snowball will lead the way. I shall follow in a few minutes. Forward, comrades! The hay is waiting."
>
> So the animals trooped down to the hayfield to begin the harvest, and when they came back in the evening it was noticed that the milk had disappeared. (33-34)

The scene begins with an active rather than passive voice—meaning that a subject clearly performs an action, such that *animals look* or *someone says*—and in one instance it even narrows down one of the speakers as being "one of the hens." This really is not much of a narrowing, however, for that hen is not named and hence is no more a specifically identifiable character than the "someone," be it duck, dog, horse, sheep, or what have we, who first asks hungrily about the fate of the milk. Only Napoleon, the Stalin of tale, is identified by name, his high-sounding shiftiness thus better remembered by the reader. And by the final one-sentence paragraph Orwell switches to the ironically bland passive-voice construction of "it was noticed," refusing to trouble us with specifics about exactly who noticed the missing milk, let alone what discussion might have followed. He ends the chapter without showing or even suggesting that any animal wondered inwardly about the matter.

This lack of questioning or inward second-guessing can be seen throughout the book. "The animals had assumed as a matter of course," for example, that any apples ripening and falling by themselves in the orchards "would be shared equally" (42). We are told that when the order is given that these should go solely to the rulings pigs, "some of the other animals murmured" (42), but Orwell does not name any of these grumblers, even by species, and instead, after a little noble-sounding flimflam, "it [i]s agreed without further argument that the milk and the windfall apples (and also the main crop of apples when they ripened) should be reserved for the pigs alone" (43).

Once Napoleon's reign of terror begins in earnest, Orwell finally gives us a little more interiority regarding other characters, but only a very little more, and again he retreats with deft swiftness to the surface. When the Stalin figure, flanked by guard dogs "as fierce-looking as wolves" (58), for the first time prohibits any debate of policy, "the animals [a]re dismayed," and "[s]everal of them would have protested if they could have found the right arguments" (59). These animals, though—who are not named, categorized by species, or narrowed down in any way—cannot find the arguments, nor are lingering private doubts revealed later. Regarding the farm's model uncomplaining worker, the narrative finally notes that "[e]ven Boxer was vaguely troubled." Yet we are told that while the earnest draft horse "set his ears back, shook his forelock several times, and tried hard to marshal his thoughts . . . in the end he could not think of anything to say" (59). No deeper life of the mind is shown for the earnest Boxer, and instead "[h]is two slogans, 'I will work harder' and 'Napoleon is always right,' [seem] to him a sufficient answer to all problems" (65).

As the first show trials and executions begin, and Napoleon's cult of personality grows, Boxer's mate, Clover, realizes perplexedly that

> they had come to a time when no one dared speak his mind, when fierce, growling dogs roamed everywhere, and when you had to watch your comrades torn to pieces after confessing to shocking crimes. There was no thought of rebellion or disobedience in her mind. She knew that, even as things were, they were far better off than they had been in the days of Jones, and that before all else it was needful to prevent the return of the human beings. Whatever happened, she would remain faithful, work hard, carry out the orders that were given to her, and accept the leadership of Napoleon. But still, it was not for this that she and all the other animals had hoped and toiled. It was not for this that they had built the windmill and faced the bullets of Jones's gun. Such were her thoughts, though she lacked the words to express them. (85-86)

This may be the deepest and most prolonged dive into interiority in *Animal Farm*, but even here, Orwell closes off all inner argument, and the simplicity of Clover's trust in the path of the Rebellion provides all the better irony for later events: the selling off of her exhausted companion to a rendering plant, with the profits buying more whiskey for the pigs (116); the animals' acceptance of the explanation that the van "marked 'Horse Slaughterer'" recently had been purchased by a veterinarian "who had not yet painted the old name out" (115); and the fact that "it [does] not seem strange" at all that finally the pigs learn to walk upright, carry whips just as Jones's hated men formerly did, subscribe to conservative publications such as *John Bull* and the *Daily Mirror*, and wear Jones's old clothing (123). As Orwell concludes when Napoleon and his dandified cronies host a group of neighboring human farmers, "[s]ome of

---

them ha[ve] five chins, some ha[ve] four, some ha[ve] three," and "already it [is] impossible to say which [is] which" (128).

Nineteen Eighty-Four: The Deeply Personal Ever-After

Whereas *Animal Farm*, grimly pessimistic as it may be, is told with scathing irony as a "fairy story," a broad-brush tale in which talking animals are presented with only the briefest glimpses of interiority, *Nineteen Eighty-Four* is the personally focused and deeply psychological end-game counterpart. The time of a book such as *Animal Farm*—that of a revolution whose ideals seem intended to free the masses from oppression and misery—actually is almost a fairy tale to the people of only a generation later, who live in the reality that replaces the supposed "happily ever after." A children's textbook describes the period prior to the rise of Ingsoc, or English Socialism, as being "[i]n the old days," a term as cozily vague as "once upon a time," and then continues with an exposition worthy of fairy tale. According to the propaganda of the ruthless Party that rules Oceania, "[c]hildren . . . had to work twelve hours a day for cruel masters, who flogged them with whips if they worked too slowly and fed them with nothing but stale breadcrusts and water"; the capitalists "were fat, ugly men with wicked faces," each of whom wore

> a long black coat which was called a frock coat, and a queer, shiny hat shaped like a stovepipe, which was called a top hat. This was the uniform of the capitalists, and no one else was allowed to wear it. The capitalists owned everything in the world, and everyone else was their slave. They owned all the land, all the houses, all the factories, and all the money. (62-63)

The language is as superficial and sweeping as any describing the plight of Cinderella, and yet, as protagonist Winston Smith asks himself, "How could you tell how much of it was lies?" (63).

The answer, of course, is that, after a generation of police state tactics that include relentless propaganda and the rewriting of history, pervasive surveillance and warrantless arrest, and the brainwashing or execution—or, just as commonly, the brainwashing and *then* execution—of suspected or even potential dissidents, one cannot. What the deeply intimate third-person limited narration of *Nineteen Eighty-Four* does so well, however, is explode "the ideal set up by the Party," that of "a nation of warriors and fanatics, marching forward in perfect unity, all thinking the same thoughts and shouting the same slogans, perpetually working, fighting, triumphing, persecuting" (63-64). The reality is that the so-called "glorious Revolution" (62) has not delivered on what it had promised, and life in the oppressed and impoverished Oceania instead consists more commonly merely of "darning a worn-out sock, cadging a saccharine tablet, saving a cigarette end" (63) . . . and not running afoul of the Thought Police.

Whereas the narrative of *Animal Farm* speaks only broadly of the texture of physical existence and without much real feeling, Orwell throughout *Nineteen Eighty-Four* instead focuses with great effectiveness on portraying the niggling, nagging annoyance of everyday life, a life of elevators "seldom working" (5), "coarse soap and blunt razor blades" (6), and constant shortages of random "necessary article[s]" (43) in a London of "rotting nineteenth-century houses, their sides shored up with balks of timber, their windows patched with cardboard and their roofs with corrugated iron . . ." (7). We hear of the "itching" of Winston's inflamed varicose vein, his fits of "violent coughing" upon waking up (29), and the eye-watering jolt of a slug of the "oily-tasting" Victory Gin (45), but even physical details that are not specifically part of Winston's own bodily experience nevertheless are filtered, via the third-person limited narrative, through his observation and interpretive evaluation.

Orwell describes the lunchroom at Winston's workplace, for example, as

> a low-ceilinged, crowded room, its walls grimy from the contact of innumerable bodies; battered metal tables and chairs, placed so close together that you sat with elbows touching; bent spoons, dented trays, coarse white mugs; all surfaces greasy, grime in every crack; and a sourish, composite smell of bad gin and bad coffee and metallic stew and dirty clothes. (52)

Through such passages we know that it is Winston's perspective that informs the narrative. Although Winston is not the narrator, his private point of view provides verisimilitude, explaining how "you" are always compelled to sit too close to other patrons. Political awareness and protest arise from his personal discomfort: "[a]lways in your stomach and in your skin there [is] a sort of protest, a feeling that you ha[ve] been cheated out of something you ha[ve] a right to" (52).

This third-person limited narration not only allows Orwell to filter descriptions through Winston's perspective but also, more importantly, lets him dive into Winston's inner consciousness to show the crushing effects of the Party's self-righteous but cynically self-serving totalitarianism upon the mind of the individual. Winston, of course, knows what facial expression is "considered proper" for any even semipolitical occasion (30), just as he knows, "Never show dismay! Never show resentment! A single flicker of the eyes could give you away" (34). This is *knowing*, combined though it is with the "sudden hot sweat" (34) of a panicked reaction, but even more profound, and far more hidden, is truly *feeling*.

One of the most poignant revelations of Winston's felt experience is when he dreams of his mother, who, along with his father, "must evidently have been swallowed up in the purges of the Fifties" (28). In the surreal staging of dream—the kind that is so beautifully significant, for it occurs in literature rather than in the randomness of real life—Winston's mother, and the sister whom he remembers only "as a tiny, feeble baby, always silent, with large, watchful eyes," gaze up at him from "some subterranean place" such as "the bottom of a well, for instance, or a very deep grave":

[I]t was a place which, already far below him, was itself moving downwards. They were in the saloon of a sinking ship, looking up at him through the darkening water. There was still air in the saloon, they could still see him and he them, but all the while they were sinking down, down into the green waters which in another moment must hide them from sight forever. He was out in the light and air while they were being sucked down to death, and they were down there *because* he was up here. He knew it and they knew it, and he could see the knowledge in their faces. There was no reproach either in their faces or in their hearts, only the knowledge that they must die in order that he might remain alive, and that this was part of the unavoidable order of things. (28)

This finely grained, deeply intimate depiction of Winston's inner life helps reveal the contrast between "the ancient time . . . when there were still privacy, love, and friendship, and when members of a family stood by one another without needing to know the reason" (28) and the time of his own society, when instead "there [are] fear, hatred, and pain, but no dignity of emotion, or deep or complex sorrows" (28-29).

Winston for a brief period does experience some of the emotions of "the ancient time" during his strictly forbidden love affair with his coworker Julia. In addition to his physical desire, he comes to feel "a deep tenderness" for her (116), and in the illicit couple's too-good-to-be-true hideaway—literally too-good-to-be-true, for it actually has been provided as a trap by the Thought Police—he wonders in a sort of disbelief "whether in the abolished past it had been a normal experience to lie in bed like this, a man and a woman with no clothes on, in the cool of a summer evening, making love when they chose, talking of what they chose, not feeling any compulsion to get up, simply lying there and listening to peaceful sounds outside" (119). After the trap has been sprung and the torture and brainwashing go on and on, however, natural human emotion is eradicated, until the thought of their lovemaking makes "[h]is flesh fr[ee]ze with horror" (239) . . . and in the end, any semblance of feeling has been transferred instead to the figurehead of the State that so thoroughly has destroyed him: "He loved Big Brother" (245).

Conclusion

Fairy tales sometimes end "happily ever after." Subjugating the individual to some supposedly noble ideal that in actuality requires the abandonment of thought, conscience, and personal and familial relationships, however, does not. When George Orwell wrote his classic dystopias, the lessons of the then-contemporary Nazi and

Soviet regimes already were apparent to any who truly chose to look. *Animal Farm* and *Nineteen Eighty-Four*, using different narrative strategies of ironically superficial "fairy story" and compellingly nuanced and introspective third-person limited point of view, respectively, have given generations the emotional and intellectual tools to help ward off tyranny. And surely these two volumes, one deceptively thin and the other appropriately thick and weighty, will continue to be read and will continue to warn us for generations to come.

Works Cited

Orwell, George. *Animal Farm*. 1945. Signet, n.d.

_____. *Nineteen Eighty-Four*. 1949. Signet, 1984.

CRITICAL
READINGS

Are Rats Comrades? Metaphor and Allegory in George Orwell's *Animal Farm*_____

Brian Ireland

The subtitle of George Orwell's *Animal Farm* is "a fairy story." However, a more apposite subtitle would be "a fable," which, it can be argued, is a kind of subgenre within the fairy tale tradition, albeit rigid definitions are difficult to discern, and often tales can fit into both genres (Calder 6). While fairy tales tend to feature a range of fantastic creatures as well as animals and may or may not contain a moral lesson, fables usually present a moral lesson and regularly feature animals as protagonists. The audience for fairy tales is normally children, whereas the audience for fables can be broader. A useful, concise definition of fables is "instructive tales that teach morals about human social behavior" (Doniger 772).

Orwell's intention in *Animal Farm* was to provide one of these "instructive tales" not only about one of the most significant events of the twentieth century, the 1917 Russian Revolution and its aftermath, but also about the effects of human social behavior on the application of political power (Orwell, *Life* 334). In presenting his thoughts as a fable with farmyard animals standing in for historical figures, Orwell was following in a long tradition of anthropomorphism in which human traits are assigned to nonhuman objects. Most relevant here is Claude Lévi-Strauss's assertion that animals "are good to think with" (128); due to the associations we apply to them, they can serve as metaphors for the human condition. This was particularly important when *Animal Farm* was written: in Nazi propaganda, Jews were compared with rats, and Allied propaganda against the Japanese compared them to insects, vermin, and apes (Dower 9). In addition, countries typically use animal totems to denote national power: for example, the American eagle, the British bulldog, and the Russian bear.

Orwell called himself a democratic Socialist, and he despised how the Russian Revolution had spawned a totalitarian political system whose practices he equated with Nazism (Kirschner 151). For him, totalitarian communism was as big a threat to genuine socialism as totalitarian fascism. When the Soviet-Nazi pact ended and the Russians entered the war against Germany, Russia, and Stalin in particular, became popular allies in a common cause against the Axis powers and Nazi ideology. The image of affable "Uncle Joe" Stalin was particularly grating: Orwell wrote in his wartime diary, "One could not have a better example of the moral and emotional shallowness of our time, than the fact that we are now all more or less pro Stalin. This disgusting murderer is temporarily on our side, and so the purges, etc., are suddenly forgotten" (*Patriot* 522).

His opinion of Russian-backed communism was shaped by his experiences during the Spanish Civil War. He traveled to Catalonia to join anarchist and Trotskyist forces in their struggle against Franco's fascists. In Spain he witnessed how communist groups undermined other leftist, anti-Franco groups, and put Russian national interests first (Dickstein 133). There were purges, arrests, show trials, imprisonments, and disappearances. He also witnessed how, in the West, pro-Russian communist propaganda became the accepted version of the events of the Spanish Civil War (Rodden and Rossi 21). He wrote *Homage to Catalonia* (1938) as an indictment of Stalinist tactics. However, his experiences planted the seeds for a more ambitious work to undermine Soviet communism: "On my return from Spain I thought of exposing the Soviet myth in a story that could be easily understood by almost anyone and which could be easily translated into other languages" (qtd. in Weeks 112). This idea for a story became *Animal Farm*.

There is almost total critical consensus that the characters and events in *Animal Farm* parallel characters, countries, and events related to Russian history, including the 1917 Revolution and events up to World War II. Orwell stated, "Of course I intended it primarily as a satire on the Russian revolution" (*Life* 334). For instance, Old Major represents Karl Marx; Napoleon is Joseph Stalin; Snowball is Leon Trotsky; and the dogs are the communist secret police. There is some division among critics as to whether Vladimir Lenin is represented in *Animal Farm*: there may be some elements of Lenin in the character Snowball; in addition, Old Major's role as a leader of the revolution, together with the preservation and public display of his skull, suggests some parallels with Lenin, whose body has been on display in a mausoleum in Moscow since his death in 1924; but mainly Lenin is notable by his absence from the novel (Pearce 51).

In a similar vein, Pilkington represents England (or perhaps more broadly, he represents capitalist, Western countries, which would include the United States) and Frederick signifies Germany. The attempt by the farm's previous owner to retake power with the aid of local farmers, bankers, and businessmen is representative of the Allied invasion of Russia in 1918; the "battle of the windmill" is suggestive of the Nazi invasion of Russia in 1941; the meal shared between the pigs and the humans at the end of the story is suggestive of the 1943 Tehran Conference in which the leaders of the United Kingdom and the United States met with Stalin and agreed, among other strategic plans, to the postwar boundaries of Poland, which included giving Russia Polish land in the East. This decision was a betrayal of the many free Poles who were, at that time, fighting in and alongside British armed forces. Individual events related to the Russian Revolution and civil war are also represented in *Animal Farm*: a few indicative examples are the pigs' harsh response to the hens' protest, which is analogous to Trotsky's ruthless response to the 1921 *Kronstadt rebellion; the socialist anthem* "The Internationale" is represented in the novel when the animals adopt the song "Beasts of England" as their patriotic anthem; building and rebuilding of the windmill evokes memories of Stalin's five-year economic plans; and when Napoleon brings back Moses the raven—who is a symbol of religion in the novella—it recalls Stalin's rapprochement with the Russian Orthodox Church during World War II.

Regarding *Animal Farm*'s literary origins, Pearce points to a broad range of popular authors including Jonathan Swift, Thomas Hobbes, Joseph Conrad, T. S. Elliot, and H. G. Wells. More specifically, however, Pearce points to Beatrice Potter's *Pigling Bland* (1913), which Orwell read twice to a childhood friend. Pearce observes that the frontispiece of this book was an illustration of two pigs walking on their hind legs (50). Pearce also points to Malcolm Muggeridge's *Winter in Moscow* (1934) in which Stalin is compared to Napoleon, and Tolstoy's *Confession* (1882), in which the Biblical Ten Commandments are amended in similar fashion to the Seven Commandments in *Animal Farm* (50).

Orwell also had American cinematic examples to choose from, for example, the Mickey Mouse, Donald Duck, and Porky Pig cartoons of the 1930s. Disney's anti-Nazi cartoons also showed how powerful political points could be made using anthropomorphic animals. For example, in *Donald Duck in Nutzi Land* (1943) Donald has a nightmare in which he works in a German munitions factory and is forced to read Nazi propaganda. Other Disney propaganda films featuring anthropomorphic animals include *Donald's Decision* (1941), *Donald Gets Drafted* (1942), *The Spirit Of '43* (1943), *Herr Meets Hare* (1943), *The Old Army Game* (1943), and *Commando Duck* (1944) (Betts 30). They are successful not because of qualities necessarily associated with the species of animal (duck and hare) but instead because the characters are fast-talking, quick-thinking, hot-tempered, mischievous, and antiauthority. As such, they are ideally placed to satirize the pretentions of Hitler and his coterie of flunkies.

Critics seem to have missed one particular context of Orwell's anthropomorphic story—the use of animal imagery by World War II propagandists to boost their own country and its allies and to demean and dehumanize the enemy. Depictions of animals in comics and newspapers as representations of countries became fashionable in the late eighteenth and nineteenth centuries. The Russian bear, the American eagle, and the British bulldog were particularly popular (Lamarre 76). While these representations were often based on supposed national characteristics or depicted animals indigenous to and therefore evocative of individual countries, the nature of the representation was subject to change based on the context of the depiction. When countries were depicted to make a political or satirical point, the emphasis might change from national characteristics to traits associated with individual animals. For example, Fred W. Rose's *Serio-Comic War Map for the Year 1877*, shows Russia as an octopus spreading its tentacles threateningly into neighboring countries. Similarly, in his map entitled *L'Europe animale, physiologie comique*, André Belloguet identifies the countries of Europe and their near neighbors with animals, with each portraying supposed national characteristics: France is a cockerel; Germany is a fox; Austria is an owl; and Russia is a bear. A different dynamic is at work in Belloguet's portrayal of non-European countries. Drawing on a long tradition of depicting non-European, non-Caucasian countries as animals to identify them as wild, primitive, and dangerous, Belloguet portrays North Africa as a lion, Turkey as a camel, and areas further east as an ape.

Like the bulldog, the lion has come to represent Britain. Indeed, both the lion and the unicorn are ancient heraldic symbols, appearing on the royal coat of arms of the United Kingdom since the early 1600s and also on current United Kingdom passports. The lion and the bulldog are often deployed during times of war for their fearsome qualities (the unicorn less so, for obvious reasons). For example, numerous World War I British propaganda images depicted Britain as a lion, including Arthur Wardle's 1915 design "The Empire Needs Men!" which illustrates the point by depicting Britain as a lion with a full mane and countries of the empire such as Australia, Canada, India, and New Zealand as young lions without manes.

In 1782, the Continental Congress adopted the eagle design for the new official seal of the United States. Since then, the eagle has become the most obvious and routinely used symbol of the country. Prior to this, during the Revolutionary Era, the only other competition for an animal national symbol was the rattlesnake, because it is indigenous to the American colonies and because of the political slogan "Don't tread on me," which served as a powerful warning to Great Britain not to mistreat the American colonies since they might bite back. The snake also represents treachery, and it is a lower animal when compared to humans and mammals. It is, therefore, not an ideal national symbol, especially when compared to the eagle, which represents both power and freedom.

Just as the Germans referred to Jews as vermin and the Russians as *untermenschen* (sub-human), both Britain and the United States regularly referred to and depicted the Japanese as beasts or vermin.

For instance, in magazines, speeches, documentaries, and other anti-Japanese propaganda, Americans compared the Japanese to animals, insects, vermin, and snakes. In each case, the comparison intended to dehumanize, but each category of beast meant different things. Comparisons to baboons, gorillas, and monkeys implied that the Japanese were not as evolutionally advanced as Americans; it also suggested a reason why the Japanese enjoyed some initial military success—supposedly they were at home in the jungle. Comparisons of the Japanese to herds of cattle and sheep suggested that they were similarly herdlike—easily manipulated and with little capacity for individual thinking. Referring to Japanese as mice, rats, and cockroaches reinforces the spurious notion that they are verminous. Comparing them to spiders and beetles suggests they are pests that can easily be disposed of. References to Japanese cities as beehives and anthills combines two unsavory metaphors, that the Japanese act without individual thought and are also pests. And comparing Japan to an octopus suggests that its tentacles will reach into other countries in a predatory fashion (Dower 80-85). In turn, the Japanese also had their own racial views of Westerners, depicted the Allies in numerous animal forms such as birds, reptiles, alligators, and serpents (Dower 240). The intent in all of this was, of course, to dehumanize the enemy, which makes it easier to hurt and kill them, or even to exterminate them. John Dower points out, for example, that the Allies' anti-Japanese lexicon increasingly utilized the language of cleansing and extermination, often with fire (81-83, 90-92), an effort to justify Allied firebombing and nuclear destruction of Japanese cities. In contrast, the Allies rarely used such language to describe Germany and Germans, nor, with the exception of Dresden, did they firebomb Germany to the same extent and with the same zeal as the Americans firebombed Japanese cities.

Eschewing the propagandistic use of animal imagery to dehumanize other people, Orwell uses farm animals firstly to illustrate how power corrupts decent people and noble ideas and secondly to allegorize the Russian Revolution, its aftermath, and Russian history up to the Second World War. More novel interpretations of *Animal Farm* are also possible: Dickstein suggests, for example, that it can even be read as a polemic about animal rights (135). Orwell's allegory is tested, however, when Old Major challenges the farm animals with the question "Are rats comrades?" (11). This takes place as Old Major reveals his plans for revolution. In the farmyard, rats may be animals, but they remain vermin, so are they to be accepted as equal in the eyes of the revolutionaries? Initially the answer is no: when four rats appear, they are chased into hiding by farmyard dogs who would otherwise have killed them as, we assume, they had been trained to do. But when Old Major asks the question, the animals agree that rats are indeed comrades, meaning they will be part of the egalitarian future without humans.

It is at this point that Old Major sets out the rules or commandments by which the animals will now be required to live:

> remember always your duty of enmity towards Man and all his ways. Whatever goes upon two legs is an enemy. Whatever goes upon four legs, or has wings, is a friend. And remember also that in fighting against Man, we must not come to resemble him. Even when you have conquered him, do not adopt his vices. No animal must ever live in a house, or sleep in a bed, or wear clothes, or drink alcohol, or smoke tobacco, or touch money, or engage in trade. All the habits of Man are evil. And, above all, no animal must ever tyrannise over his own kind. Weak or strong, clever or simple, we are all brothers. No animal must ever kill any other animal. All animals are equal. (11-12)

It is unclear whether Old Major planned for this sequence of events to unify all animals. It seems unlikely, as the rats were not originally at the meeting. From this point on, however, rats are to be considered "comrades," as are wild nonfarmyard animals such as rabbits. But there is a caveat: after the revolution is successful and humans have been chased off the farm, Snowball establishes a Wild Comrades' Re-education Committee, as Orwell tells us, to "tame the rats and rabbits" (29), who are then no longer mentioned in the novel. A number of points arise from this part of the story. The rules/commandments of this new social order are visionary, egalitarian, and utopian: nothing like it had existed before. However, while it is left to Old Major to articulate these rules, they exist as a response to the question Old Major posed to the crowd: are rats comrades? His improvised response, done "on the hoof" so to speak, reflects the wisdom of the crowd and their willingness to adopt a new social order. It is not the intelligentsia (represented by Old Major) who makes this great social leap, it is the crowd—the proletariat. Orwell thought it important to make this distinction. He did not believe that Russia was a socialist country; he saw it as a totalitarian state. He saw how intellectuals in England were duped by communist myths about Russia and also how they accepted misleading communist propaganda about the Spanish Civil War. His views about this are best illustrated by an observation he made to writer Humphry House: "I have never had the slightest fear of a dictatorship of the proletariat. . . . But I have to admit to having a perfect horror of a dictatorship of theorists, as in Russia" (qtd. in Dickstein 139).

It was important to Orwell to make the point in *Animal Farm* that the proletariat was capable of visionary thinking and making correct moral choices. They did not need Old Major to make those choices for them. In fact, if left to his own devices, and following Orwell's logic, Old Major would perhaps conclude that rats are not comrades. And if that was the case, some of the rules of the new society could not be enacted: "Whatever goes upon four legs, or has wings, is a friend" (except rats, rabbits, and other wild animals); "no animal must ever tyrannise over his own kind" (except rats, rabbits, and other wild animals); "we are all brothers" (except rats, rabbits, and other wild animals); "No animal must ever kill any other animal" (except rats, rabbits, and other wild animals); and especially "All animals are equal" (except rats, rabbits, and other wild animals). Unless rats are considered comrades, the new social order is undermined at the roots.

But what or whom do rats represent? They conjure up ideas of filth, poverty, and disease. For humans, being compared to a rat suggests that one cannot be trusted. There are, therefore, a number of possible parallels with real life. Old Major claims that "Man is the only creature that consumes without producing" (9). He says this before the rats make an appearance, so it is possible he had not, at that point, considered vermin or wild animals as part of the antihuman revolution. Within the framework of the story, it is possible that the rats are also considered "consumers without producing" anything of benefit to society. Old Major also complains that "nearly the whole of the produce of our labour is stolen from us" (8) and that "Man serves the interests of no creature except himself" (11)—charges that could also be leveled against vermin. It is possible then that this is an entirely diegetic point that needed to be resolved by the author. However, it is also possible that the wild nonfarmyard animals such as rats and rabbits are representative of nondiegetic groups. For example, Robert Savage notes that rats appear so frequently in Orwell's oeuvre that he speculates Orwell suffered from some deep-seated loathing perhaps grounded in a childhood experience (87). Savage also points out that Orwell encountered rats during his time as a soldier in Spain. They infested trenches and dined on corpses. Orwell opened fire on them more than once. Savage believes that rats symbolize both fascists and the pro-Soviet communists who Orwell believed helped sabotage the Spanish leftist cause during the civil war (88). Savage's eloquent conclusion, therefore, is that "rats are indeed comrades because the Comrades, alas, are rats" (89). Orwell was not antirevolutionary; he simply despised totalitarianism. He supported the Russian Revolution but not the system that it spawned because he did not believe that Soviet Russia was a genuinely socialist country. It is possible then that the rats represent those people or parties who opposed the Revolution, but Orwell believes, nevertheless, that they should be considered equals. As a believer in democratic socialism, Orwell considered dissent an essential ingredient of the political process.

Perhaps, however, Old Major's question about the status of rats also reflects Orwell's concern about the validity of his allegory. A useful comparison can be made here with Art Spiegelman's *Maus* (1980), a two-volume illustrated biography of his father, Vladek Spiegelman, who was a former Auschwitz inmate and a Holocaust survivor. Art Spiegelman portrays the characters in *Maus* as anthropomorphic animals, with Jews drawn as mice and the Germans as cats. This works as a metaphor for the relationship between the Nazis and the Jews in the 1930s and 1940s, drawing particularly on

Nazi propaganda comparing the Jews with rats. In this allegorical tale, Poles are depicted as pigs, Americans as mongrel dogs (rather than pedigreed, which perhaps suggests an American "melting pot"), the French as frogs, the British as fish, and the Swedish as reindeer. Spiegelman bases the metaphor on nationalities, aside from Jews, whom he depicts as mice no matter what their nationality. The author frequently breaks the fourth wall by inserting himself into the story to make asides and observations about the writing process. At one stage, for example, he illustrates himself as a middle-aged man in a mouse mask; in another scene, he converses with his psychiatrist about the guilt he feels at profiting from writing a successful Holocaust memoir. The question of representation is always on his mind: at one point he debates how he should depict his French girlfriend: she is Jewish, so should she be a mouse? But she is also French, so should he depict her as a frog? This serves to illustrate the author's decision-making processes with regard to the cat/mouse metaphor. The further he gets from that central idea, the more difficult it becomes to maintain the metaphor.

Orwell's introduction of troublesome animals such as vermin threatens the integrity of the story. This is reflected in part in some of the critical reactions to his use of a fable to make a serious point about real historical events. For example, Dickstein argues that the "weakness of Orwell's tale was . . . that it was written in the form of allegory, which was a form that, if effectively done, was prone to quite different interpretations and could take on meanings of its own" (144). Pearce argues that a fable is always a simplification and, as such, suffers from misinterpretations. He explains that Orwell's "simple farmyard story" led many readers to believe that *Animal Farm* was critical of all revolutions rather than just the Russian experience (Pearce 53). George Soule raised a similar criticism in an early review of *Animal Farm* in the magazine *New Republic*. Soule referred to Orwell's allegory as, "a creaky machine for saying in a clumsy way things that have been better said directly" (qtd. in Rodden and Rossi 23). Yet Orwell knew both the value of simplicity and the power of anthropomorphism. He saw how simple communist propaganda and brazen but unsophisticated lies influenced how the

West viewed the events of the Spanish Civil War. He also noticed how readily the West consumed pro-Russian propaganda during World War II. In "The Lion and the Unicorn: Socialism and the English Genius" (1941) Orwell advocates for an English version of socialism based on a moral code, in stark contrast to the Soviet model. Tellingly, Orwell refers to the "the lion and the unicorn on the soldiers' cap-buttons" as "an anachronism" which, nevertheless, remained a powerful symbol of essential Britishness: "in England traditional loyalties are stronger than new ones," he suggested (qtd. in Miller 599). Orwell indicates that these outdated symbols might be retained along with other feudal reminders of Britain's unequal past, even as land and industries are nationalized. It is that generosity and magnanimity that marks Orwell's version of moral socialism, which contrasts so widely with the version that developed in Stalinist Russia. It is also that simple message about immoral abuse of power that Orwell wanted to convey in *Animal Farm*. The allegory worked because it was simple and uncomplicated; "if it does not speak for itself it is a failure" (qtd. in Orwell and Angus 372), he asserted, and he trusted his readers to understand this. In the end, his faith in ordinary people was proved correct.

Works Cited

Belloguet, André. *L'Europe animale: Physiologie comique*. Vincent, 1882.

Betts, Raymond F. *A History of Popular Culture: More of Everything, Faster and Brighter*. Routledge, 2004.

Calder, Jenni. *Animal Farm and Nineteen Eighty-Four*. Open University, 1987.

Lévi-Strauss, Claude. *Le totémisme aujourd'hui*. Presses Universitaires de Paris, 1962.

Dickstein, Morris. "Animal Farm: History as Fable." *The Cambridge Companion to George Orwell*. Edited by John Rodden, Cambridge UP, 2007, pp. 133-45.

Doniger, Wendy, editor. *Merriam-Webster's Encyclopedia of World Religions*. Merriam-Webster, 1999.

Dower, John W. *War Without Mercy: Race and Power in the Pacific War*. Pantheon, 1986.

Kirschner, Paul. "The Dual Purpose of Animal Farm." *Bloom's Modern Critical Views: George Orwell.* Edited by Harold Bloom, Chelsea House, 2007, pp. 145-80.

Lamarre, Thomas. "The Biopolitics of Companion Species: Wartime Animation and Multi-ethnic Nationalism." *The Politics of Culture: Around the Work of Naoki Sakai.* Edited by Richard Calichman and John Namjun Kim, Routledge, 2010, pp. 72-90.

Miller, Stephen. "Orwell Once More." *Sewanee Review,* vol. 112, no. 4, 2004, pp. 595-618.

Orwell, George. *A Life in Letters.* Edited by Peter Davidson, Norton, 2013.

_____. *Animal Farm.* 1945. Penguin, 1985.

_____. *A Patriot After All 1940-1941.* Secker and Warburg, 1998.

Orwell, Sonia, and Ian Angus, editors. *The Collected Essays, Journalism and Letters of George Orwell,* vol. 1. Penguin, 1971.

Pearce, Robert. "Animal Farm: Sixty Years On." *History Today,* vol. 55, no. 8, 2005, pp. 47-53.

Rodden, John, and John P. Rossi. "*Animal Farm* at 70." *Modern Age,* vol. 58, no. 4, 2016, pp. 19-27.

Rose, Fred W. *Serio-Comic War Map for the Year 1877.* G. W. Bacon, 1877.

Savage, Robert. "Are Rats Comrades? Some Readings of a Question in Orwell." *Colloquy: Text Theory Critique,* vol. 12, 2006, pp. 83-90.

Wardle, Arthur. "The Empire Needs Men!" Parliamentary Recruiting Committee, 1915.

Weeks, Denise. "George Orwell and the Road to Animal Farm." *Understanding Animal Farm: A Student Casebook to Issues, Sources, and Historical Documents.* Edited by John Rodden, Greenwood, 1999, pp. 93-116.

Writing Revolution: Orwell's Not-So-Plain Style in *Animal Farm*_____

Paige Busby

Animal Farm is often described as a child's *Nineteen Eighty-Four*—a simple experiment in fairy tales and allegory and an insubstantial foray into Orwellian dystopia. Yet *Animal Farm* has legitimacy as a serious commentary on language as both a revolutionary and an authoritarian tool. Language is the key power structure in *Animal Farm,* a power superior to violence and fear. Orwell's presentation of language in *Animal Farm* is unique in that, unlike in *Nineteen Eighty-Four*, there is complete efficacy in totalitarian control. *Animal Farm* is not a story of a revolutionary underground but rather a postrevolution return to the status quo. There are no dissidents left at its conclusion, and those who were part of the revolution do not recognize how language has been used against them. Literacy becomes a political and social advantage, but one that is powerless when compared to the spoken word. *Animal Farm* presents the fluidity of the spoken word and its manipulative effects as a productive force—creating actuality from nothingness—while also emphasizing the ease of altering the concreteness of written record.

While scholars such as Roger Fowler have argued that *Animal Farm* is a successful product of Orwell's plain style, Orwell's desire for plain language is itself a "fairy story." Though Orwell's best attempt at producing a text in plain style, *Animal Farm* instead reinforces the highly complex and performative nature of language. Language is indeed oppressive and obfuscating when placed in a totalitarian context as Orwell claims, but Orwell shows this oppression by using his own creative and performative power over language. Despite his best efforts to keep language transparent, Orwell's prose is like a smudged windowpane, but those smudges tell an even more compelling story.

Literary Aesthetics, Political Engagement, and Plain Writing

To understand Orwell's plain style, it is essential to contextualize it alongside his literary aesthetics and political engagement. There is a lasting tradition of viewing Orwell's writing through these lenses. Most recently, Alex Woloch's *Or Orwell: Writing and Democratic Socialism* has reasserted this traditional analysis. As Woloch claims, Orwell's "motive for such plain style is . . . the sheer desire (both palpable and unfulfilled) to express his political orientation, directly and without distortion, in writing" (9).

Orwell's expresses his features of writing in his summary of "four great motives for writing [prose]" (*Why I Write* 5). The first motive, egoism, relates both to his commitment to aesthetics and political engagement: for Orwell, it is important to have *his* ideals presented, including his political beliefs, his ideology about language, and his personal interiority. While this first motive for writing reinforces Orwell's desires for clarity of expression, in as far as the egotistical writer desires to express himself or herself, one must also acknowledge that the writer can obfuscate, persuade, lie, exaggerate, and that the egotistical writer is also a potential propogandist and a biased voice. When approaching Orwell's writing, one should bring to bear a healthy skepticism even of Orwell's own words.

The second motive for writing, Orwell says, is "aesthetic enthusiasm" (*Why I Write* 5). Orwell explains aesthetic enthusiasm as the "perception of beauty in the external world, or, on the other hand, in words and their right arrangement. Pleasure in the impact of one sound on another, in the firmness of good prose or the rhythm of a good story. Desire to share an experience which one feels is valuable and ought not to be missed" (*Why I Write* 5). However, even the word *perception* allows for subjectivity, and while it is clear that Orwell sees the clarity of plain language as being the mark of "good prose," aesthetics is itself just as complex as language. Even in Orwell's definition of aesthetic enthusiasm and his attempt to clearly outline its parameters, the language that has to be used in describing "beauty" and "valuable experiences" allows for a slippage not conducive to Orwell's ideal plain style. Regardless, from this definition, one can clearly see how Orwell connects politics and plain style with aesthetics. Orwell's aesthetics are defined by the plain style coupled with experiences deemed "valuable," which to Orwell include historical and political attentions.

Orwell's third motive—the "historical impulse"—is a "desire to see things as they are, to find out true facts and store them up for the use of posterity" (*Why I Write* 5). For Orwell, this historical impulse is intimately reflected in his concerns about how obscure language leads to authoritarian power structures. As an allegory of a Stalinist Soviet Union, *Animal Farm* not only fictionalizes historical figures and events, but also reflects Orwell's concern with the rewriting of history through the pigs' control over the animals' very memories through language and deception. In *Nineteen Eighty-Four*, this same process of revisionist history is represented through the Ministry of Truth. Orwell's fiction permits insight into what happens if history is not recorded "for the use of posterity."

Finally, in Orwell's fourth motive, "political purpose," he explains how aesthetics and politics are inseparable: "no book is genuinely free from political bias. The opinion that art should have nothing to do with politics is itself a political attitude" (*Why I Write* 5). Integrating the motives of "historical impulse" and "political purpose," Orwell says he writes, "because there is some lie that I want to expose, some fact to which I want to draw attention . . . but I could not do the work of writing a book . . . if it were not also an aesthetic experience" (*Why I Write* 8). This aesthetic experience is not only tied into *what* Orwell creates (his characters, setting, plot, etc.) but *how* Orwell writes, thus leading to the third element of Orwell's writing: the plain style.

Plain Language and Demotic Speech

Fowler's *Language of George Orwell* traces the evolution of Orwell's linguistic style over the course of his essays and novels and connects these changes to Orwell's ideals about language. In *Why I Write*, Orwell argues for simple, concrete language; he sees that the "ultimate evil effect of the 'corruption' of language is totalitarianism," an effect that readers see unfold in both *Animal*

Farm and *Nineteen Eighty-Four* (Fowler 20). In both *Why I Write* and *Politics and the English Language* (1946), Orwell makes an intellectual and moral argument concerning "plain language," that is, language that embraces demotic speech. Demotic speech is "'simple, concrete language,' 'clear, popular, everyday language,' 'spoken English,' 'ordinary language,' 'ordinary slipshod, colloquial English'; not the 'bloodless dialect,' the 'stilted bookish language' of broadcast speeches and news bulletins" (Fowler 24). Despite Orwell's illogical causality in this context ("corrupted language" causing totalitarianism), he holds this belief very deeply; this is clear in Orwell's writing, especially in *Animal Farm*, where he attempts to embrace consistently plain language. In *Why I Write*, Orwell expresses his greatest hope: "to make political writing into an art," and *Animal Farm* became "the first book in which [he] tried, with full consciousness of what [he] was doing, to fuse political purpose and aesthetic purpose into one whole" (*Why I Write* 5, 10). According to Fowler, "The quest for simplicity of expression is part of the triumph of the Orwellian voice," and it is because of the consistent application of this linguistic simplicity that Fowler argues "*Animal Farm* is so central to his craftsmanship" (36).

Orwell's shift from a more stylistic writing in earlier novels to the simplicity readers see in *Animal Farm* is a clear result of "his thinking about politics and morality of language use" (Fowler 164). As Fowler explains, "this simplification, one might even say purification, of his own language in *Animal Farm* no doubt reflects his desire for linguistic honesty in political writing, and is the foil against which the degradation of language by the pigs is presented" (165). *Animal Farm*'s narrator illustrates how Orwell struggles to reconcile his new ideas about simplicity with the complexity that is political discourse, the aesthetic complexity in literature, and the very complexity of language itself. This struggle is best represented through *Animal Farm*'s narrative voice, which not only reflects, as Fowler argues, a shifting in Orwell's focus on morality of language, but also ironically adopts the language of the characters, employing narrative intrusions, reported speech, and free indirect discourse. Narrative intrusions are instances in *Animal Farm* where the action or dialogue is interrupted by narrative commentary and description. Reported speech is, instead of direct dialogue, the narrator taking over to explain what the characters are saying. Finally, with free indirect discourse, at different points of the story the narrator's voice adopts the tone of the pigs or the other animals in addition to the narrator's own separate tone.

While Fowler argues that the narrator in *Animal Farm* empathizes with the nonpig animals while also maintaining distance, the narrator is not wholly empathetic, nor does the narrator necessarily maintain distance. On several occasions, the narrator adopts the voices of the pigs, a type of focalization or free indirect discourse that Fowler discusses but upon which he does not completely elaborate. While we assume Orwell's narrator is on the side of the animals and against the obscuring of "truth," these allegiances are not clear since the narrator adopts free indirect discourse on multiple occasions. This shifting narrative voice indicates that the narrator is unreliable, subverting our own expectations of a clear dichotomy between truth and propaganda. Orwell's lack of clarity on this point is inherently un-plain.

From the beginning of *Animal Farm*, Orwell's narrator establishes that the animals adhere to the stereotypical characteristics of their species. The narrator also clearly establishes a hierarchy of intelligence, labeling the pigs as "clever" and the other animals as "stupid" on multiple occasions throughout the text (Fowler 174). While there are differences in the animals' capacities for literacy, there are also differences concerning with whom the animals can communicate, as well as whether or not they are comprehensible. The different species are described as having their own languages on multiple occasions, one such instance being when they sing "The Beasts of England" for the first time: "The cows lowed it, the dogs whined it, the sheep bleated it, the horses whinnied it, the ducks quacked it" (13). However, while Orwell references the animals as having their own species-specific languages, there is still a common interspecies language that they all understand and speak even before their literacy lessons.

Communication with humans is similarly complex. At certain junctures, animals and humans seem incapable of communication, such as when "the uproar" of the animals singing "The Beasts of England" awakens Mr. Jones who, thinking the animals have been disturbed by a fox, fires a gun toward the barn (14). However, after the animals have successfully taken over Manor Farm, the animal languages are not incomprehensible to humans: "the words of 'Beasts of England' were known everywhere. . . . The human beings could not contain their rage when they heard this song, though they pretended to think it merely ridiculous. They could not understand, they said, how even animals could bring themselves to sing such contemptible rubbish (39)." The animals are therefore incomprehensible to humans until they inherit a new level of power through their successful seizure of Manor Farm. With power, the animals gain the privilege of empowered language, and since the pigs are at the top of this linguistic hierarchy, they are the ones who have the privilege of engaging in animal-human communication directly. This animal-human communication is most evident via the pigs' continued business dealings with other farmers (primarily Frederick and Pilkington). There is no indication that these animal-human business dealings entail either party learning a new language or needing a translator. Although all animals are shown to understand human speech, not all animals are shown in *Animal Farm* as capable of communicating with humans. Just as there is a hierarchy of literacy, wherein some animals can read more effectively than others, there is also a hierarchy of spoken power, wherein nonpigs are shown as constantly listening instead of speaking, even though it is clear from these other examples that all of the animals have the capacity to speak at least to one another. As the power dynamic shifts to favor the pigs, they inherit a new level of spoken agency, one so clear that even humans can understand them. The humans initially hear only empty noise, but as the animals gain power through their revolution and the pigs become "more human," their language simultaneously becomes comprehensible.

While the narration often reflects the perspective of either the pigs or other animals, incidents such as casting judgment on the "stupidity" or "cleverness" of the animals shows that the narrator *can* maintain distance to provide context for the reader. This also shows that the pigs are only "playing" human, which becomes more apparent through the increasingly grotesque descriptions of their human behavior. As Fowler argues, "Their physical traits are at the onset individuating, but the grotesquerie of the bodies is more and more emphasized until, finally, standing on their hind legs and wearing clothes, they have become men-monsters" (171). Where the qualities of literacy and oral prowess at first set them apart as superior to the other animals, the end of the book presents a transformative Kafkaesque depiction of the pigs: "Some of [the pigs] had five chins, some had four, some had three. But what was it that seemed to be melting and changing?. . . No question, now, what had happened to the faces of the pigs. The creatures outside looked from pig to man, from man to pig, and from pig to man again; but already it was impossible to say which was which" (141). In this moment of transformation, the narrator takes complete control of the narrative, although readers see the transformation through the animals' sight (specifically, Clover's).

Unlike the beginning of *Animal Farm*, where Old Major's speech dominates the text, the end of the book sees narrative intrusions and reported speech rather than dialogue as the main methods of narration. By the novel's conclusion, there is little direct dialogue, but the narrator's reporting of this dialogue is presented as an accurate representation of the speakers' interiority. This same narrative structure works throughout *Nineteen Eighty-Four*. Orwell proposes that all language is corruptible by inappropriate use, and this corruption leads to totalitarianism, the result of which is explicitly expressed through *Nineteen Eighty-Four*'s Newspeak, mass censorship, and rewriting of history.

However, what has not been addressed in analyzing Orwell's ideal for language is how performativity factors into this paradigm. Even though Orwell does not directly mention performativity, a contemporary theory in his time, it is significant in understanding not only his ideals of language (and its limitations), but also how language functions in *Animal Farm*. Through Orwell's narrator, we see how his "plain language" is a flawed approach and not the most effective interpretative medium to understand language in *Animal Farm*. If instead one applies theories about performative language, one sees that where Orwell's views of plain language fail, his principles of the power of language in authoritarian contexts remain.

Performativity in *Animal Farm*

All language is performative. While the initial theoretical backing for performative language came from J. L. Austin's performative utterances, scholars have since established that language "performs," regardless of intention or syntactical structure. John Searle and Jacques Derrida elaborated upon (and debated) Austin's original theories; Judith Butler expanded Austin's utterances to gender and sexuality studies; and Eve Sedgwick argued that performativity is an inseparable part of language. As James Loxley summarizes, "words do something in the world, something that is not just a matter of generating consequences. . . . The promises, assertions, bets, threats, and thanks . . . are actions *in themselves*" (2). Searle expands Austin's ideas, saying "it is essential to any specimen of linguistic communication that it involve a linguistic act," meaning, "linguistic communication essentially involves acts" (253-54). If one sees performativity in standard usages of language as Searle and later theorists postulate, Orwell's idea of language as being a direct path to totalitarianism does not seem such an illogical stretch. However, as later examples will show, just because language is performative and is part of a power structure within Orwell's imagined authoritarian regimes, it does not necessarily follow that misuse of language will lead to these political shifts.

One of the defining characteristics of authoritarianism is the manipulation of persuasive language—being able to shift language and understanding to one's advantage. Many scholars use George Orwell's *Nineteen Eighty-Four* to begin the conversation about dystopian societies that exhibit this mastery over language. However, Orwell was clearly thinking about the performativity of language before *Nineteen Eighty-Four*: in *Animal Farm*, he experiments with language as being not just performative, but also as generative and sometimes incontestable.

To understand how language in *Animal Farm* operates, how power influences that language, and how language can create from nothing, Austin's performative utterances is the most appropriate entry into this discussion. While there must be some variation to Austin's performative utterances to make them fit *Animal Farm's* narrative, his concepts are most closely tied to the ideas of orality being both speech and act. Austin's definition of performative utterances is an "utterance which looks like a statement and grammatically . . . would be classed as a statement, which is notnonsensical, and yet is not true or false . . . [and] if a person makes an utterance of this sort we should say that he is doing something rather than merely saying something" (235). With this definition of utterances, it is appropriate to first ask how truth and falsity are treated in *Animal Farm*.

Traditionally, the pigs' power of language has been compared to *Nineteen Eighty-Four*'s doublespeak or other dystopian rhetorical methods. As Andreea Popescu argues in "Four Legs Good, Two Legs Bad: The Dystopia of Power," the methods the pigs use to control the animals include, "discourse power. . . . The rhetoric of power implies that the moment the speaker chooses to talk he has to be able to convince the others of the truth . . .to manipulate" (194). She attributes this power to the "subtle process of brainwashing," which she then connects to *Nineteen Eighty-Four*'s well-known motto, "Truth is lie and lie is truth" (194). Orwellian scholarship clearly connects *Animal Farm* and *Nineteen Eighty-Four* through the theme of language as a tool of totalitarian control. However, Popescu takes this line of thought a bit further, emphasizing "the mechanism by which the brainwashing succeeds in the one of psychological conditioning . . . the modification of voluntary behavior through reinforcement, controlling, and extinction" (199). While this direct manipulation of the animals' minds presents the pigs as having complete agency of power and its effects, Popescu and other scholars attribute the overall success of this brainwashing effort to the other animals' intellectual capacities. When Squealer engages in his linguistic gymnastics, he and Napoleon "exploit their listeners' lack of facility for recall, and their textual-comparison ineptitude" (Elbarbary 35-36). Even with her theory of psychological conditioning playing a factor, Popescu also agrees that the animals, "though starved, tired, and overworked, remain convinced of the truth of the words. Squealer even abuses the animals' poor memory and invents numbers to show their improvement" (199). However, while brainwashing and the animals' malleable memory are useful explanations for how linguistic power is so influential in *Animal Farm*, language has a more direct and immediate effect, one that relies on Austin's idea of performative language and language-as-act.

Austin's analysis of language is not the first to unite "act" with utterance. The examples Austin provides of speech-as-act from "Performative Utterances" include the groom or bride saying "I do" during a marriage ceremony, or during a ship's launching if the person with the champagne says "I name this ship the *Queen Elizabeth*" (235). He says that these performative utterances need appropriate context as well as an appropriate script, in as far as an audience member at the wedding saying "I do" is not performing the act of being married, nor is the groom who responds to "Do you take this bride/groom" with an incomprehensible or unfitting response. *Animal Farm* shows the pigs as not only always having the appropriate context, but also always having the appropriate script because of the fantasy world in which they possess an all-powerful authority over language. In some cases, the pigs possess a monopoly over language (for instance, their ability to communicate with humans and their control over education and literacy) and in other cases they are at the top of the linguistic hierarchy through their superior abilities of reading, writing, and manipulation of language. While an indirect analogy, the best comparison between the power of language in *Animal Farm* and Austin's performative utterances would be the similarity in activity between Squealer and God in *Genesis*: the structure "God said. . . . And God made" creates the direct relationship between "speaking" into being (or speaking into truth) that readers see in *Animal Farm*. Although the pigs' statements do not always have the marked structure Austin outlines as required of performative utterances, the same idea is present because it is the power of language and specific characters who have this power that provide the necessary context.

The narrator of *Animal Farm* provides an (assumedly) true description of events as they unfold. Even if the narrator's shifting focalization and narrative intrusions make his voice appear occasionally unreliable, the narrator, in contrast to the other voices in *Animal Farm*, "is characterized by syntactic tidiness and verbal pithiness" (Elbarbary 31). Therefore, readers know what the omniscient narrator knows: what happened, how the characters responded, and how, subsequently, those events or words were rhetorically modified to suit the pigs' purposes. However, for the animals within *Animal Farm*, the truth of direct experience is always subject to change by the pigs' linguistic gymnastics. These linguistic gymnastics extend to the written word as well. The main executor of this power over the truth is Squealer, Napoleon's mouthpiece, who "can project his own mental linguistic images onto the minds of the underprivileged or onto the fabric of reality itself" (Elbarbary 32). Once Squealer performs a speech act, the utterance revises the truth of experience. Therefore, while Austin's limitation on performative utterances as not being aligned with a value of truth or falsity is legitimate for his purposes, for a fantasy world wherein language can change the very memories of experience, truth value is a necessity.

In "Language as Theme in *Animal Farm*," Samir Elbarbary argues that *Animal Farm* has a "distinct language: the crassly elitist, manipulative, unintelligible, and circumlocutory discourse of the pigs, through which the fictitious passes off as factitious and the animals' world is created for them" (31). There are instances where the truth is reformulated through a simple utterance, which immediately transforms (or at the very least, brings into doubt) the truth. One example occurs when Boxer is injured and the pigs tell the other farm animals that Boxer will be taken to a veterinary hospital. However, when the ostensibly veterinarian van arrives, the animals realize that the van's siding reads, "Alfred Simmonds, Horse Slaughterer and Glue Boiler, Willingdon. Dealer in Hides and Bone-Meal. Kennels Supplied" (122). Even though the animals witness this event—personally reading or having the van's words read to them—they nonetheless believe Squealer's "correction" that the van was not bound to the knacker's, but that the confusion was merely a case of mislabeling:

> Some of the animals had noticed that the van which took Boxer away was marked "Horse Slaughterer," and had actually jumped to the conclusion that Boxer was being sent to the knacker's. It was almost unbelievable . . . that any animal could be so stupid . . . surely they knew their beloved Leader, Comrade Napoleon, better than that? But the explanation was really very simple. The van had previously been the property of the knacker, and had been bought by the veterinary surgeon, who had not yet painted the old name out. . . . The animals were enormously relieved to hear this. (124-25)

Thus, the fabric of reality is altered as this new truth becomes actuality. The animals illustrate an overall inability to reconcile a contradiction in logic when faced with the pigs' rhetoric, even if there is significant proof against what the pigs are saying. What readers also see in this selection is an example of the narrative reporting explained earlier: the narrator adopts the presumptuous tone of the pigs (particularly, Squealer) with the phrases, "[they] had actually jumped to the conclusion," "it was unbelievable . . . that any animal could be so stupid," "surely they knew," and "the explanation was really very simple." Additionally, the van scene undermines the expectation of the performative dimension of language—the expectation being that a van labeled as "Horse Slaughterer" would be a van devoted to the act of horse slaughtering. The label of "Horse Slaughterer," in this case, does represent the object it labels until the pigs redefine the circumstances under which the label is performing. Therefore, the pigs use the performativity of language to make "Horse Slaughterer" instead represent "Veterinary Surgeon."

Another example of performative language transpires when the animals are first faced with Napoleon's assertions that Snowball is a traitor, and the animals' recollections about Snowball's commendations in battle contradict what they are being told. Morris

Dickstein clearly articulates a pattern of "corrective" steps once Napoleon takes over the farm:

> The first is personified by the mouthpiece of the system, Squealer, who "could turn black into white," the second by the bloodthirsty dogs—the secret police—whom Napoleon has secretly trained as instruments of a new reign of terror. Bolstering this oppression is the habit of obedience represented by the sheep, who drown out dissenters as they bleat in unison whatever the current official slogans happen to be. (5-6)

With Snowball's expulsion, the narrator describes the animals as "dismayed," "even Boxer was vaguely troubled," and there is a desire to protest "if they could have found the right arguments" (54). But, with any disapproval, "the dogs sitting round Napoleon let out deep menacing growls" (54). Guaranteeing that no other objections could be voiced, "the sheep broke out into a tremendous bleating of 'Four legs good, two legs bad'" (55). Squealer then addresses the animals' concerns by pivoting away from their objections and rhetorically redirecting them. After an animal argues against Squealer's labeling of Snowball as a criminal by saying "he fought bravely at the Battle of the Cowshed," Squealer retorts, "Bravery is not enough. . . . Loyalty and obedience are more important. . . . I believe the time will come when we shall find that Snowball's part in [the battle] was much exaggerated" (55). Despite these clear incongruences between the lived experiences of the animals (Snowball's commendation and participation in battle juxtaposed against the pigs' recounting), at the end of this exchange, all of the animals are not only convinced that Snowball is their enemy, but Boxer's motto, "Napoleon is always right," resounds. In addition, Squealer's assertion that "loyalty and obedience are more important" resituates the conversation rhetorically—away from the "bravery" of the revolution to the "loyalty" needed from followers, a sentiment encapsulated by Boxer's "Napoleon is always right." Later, Snowball becomes not only an enemy, a bogeyman and object of fear, but also Jones's secret agent, despite the contradictions the animals experience between their memories and what Squealer tells them.

Napoleon (with Squealer as his propagandist) transforms Snowball into an ever present (and yet, invisible/amorphous) entity who seeks to destroy Animal Farm: "Every night, it was said, [Snowball] came creeping in under cover of darkness and performed all kinds of mischief. . . . Whenever anything went wrong it became usual to attribute it to Snowball. . . . It seemed to them as though Snowball were some kind of invisible influence, pervading the air about them and menacing them with all kinds of dangers" (77-78). By the mere utterance of Snowball's name do the animals see the physical manifestations of his presence, even when Snowball is never actually seen. Although the rumor begins with Squealer and Napoleon, who attribute the failures of Animal Farm to Snowball, as the attribution continues, the other animals begin to believe and make those assertions as well. The power of language in *Animal Farm* does not stop with the oral and written revisions of history but also has spontaneous, generative powers. For example, in the creation of Snowball as a bogeyman, language's creative power allows for the mere utterance of Snowball's name to give form to the acts attributed to him. Even though the animals are all present at the commendation of Snowball as "Animal Hero, First Class" after the Battle of the Cowshed, it only takes Squealer's "correction" to alter the very shape of history. The "commendation" itself is an act of performance—a physical performance tied to a linguistic label. This performance, linked to the Rebellion, is mirrored later by Napoleon's various performances (for example, the Spontaneous Demonstration that is at an "appointed time" (115) or Napoleon's growing number of formal titles (93)).

Language in *Animal Farm* works on various levels ranging from totalitarian rhetoric to a force *creatio ex nihilo*. Despite Orwell's attempt to achieve a plain-language novel, one that warns of the dangers of obscured language leading to totalitarian control, *Animal Farm* instead illustrates the performativity of language. Even if Orwell's theories of plain language are inapplicable, his claims about the inextricability of power and language allow *Animal*

Farm to hold its own against *Nineteen Eighty-Four*. When Napoleon rechristens the farm "Manor Farm," readers understand that not only has nothing changed compared to Mr. Jones's managing of the farm, but that the pigs are even more reprehensible because they betray the revolution itself by continuing to sell, kill, and manipulate their own. Not only does spoken language create something out of nothingness, but through Napoleon's utterance, the farm returns to its original state and the pigs are themselves transformed into Joneses. When Napoleon says the Rebellion is complete, he is right. The animals are no longer in revolution; they have lost their will to revolt, even when faced with hypocritical injustices. They have witnessed their revolution succeed and falter, yet they have subsequently been unable to understand the consequences of that failure or the treachery of their leaders. Their memories of revolution have been lost. This mass amnesia is not conditioning over multiple generations or an effect of doublespeak as in *Nineteen Eighty-Four* but is instead a condensed, rapid, and wholly penetrating cleansing of facts. While Orwell's *Animal Farm* is not a "simple" fairy story or a product of perfected plain style, it can be reclaimed through performative language as a serious discourse about the complexity of language, politics, and aesthetics.

Works Cited

Austin, J. L. "Performative Utterances." *Philosophical Papers*. 1961. Clarendon, 1979.

Dickstein, Morris. "Animal Farm: History as Fable." *The Cambridge Companion to George Orwell*. Edited by John Rodden, Cambridge UP, 2007.

Elbarbary, Samir. "Language as Theme in *Animal Farm*." *International Fiction Review,* vol.19, no.1, 1992, pp. 31-38. *JSTOR*.

Fowler, Roger. *The Language of George Orwell*. St. Martin's, 1995.

Loxley, James. *Performativity*. Routledge, 2007.

Orwell, George. *Animal Farm*. Signet, 1996.

_____. *Why I Write*. Penguin, 1984.

Searle, John R. "What Is a Speech Act?" *Perspectives in the Philosophy of Language*. Edited by Robert Stainton, Broadview, 2000.

Popescu, Andreea. "Four Legs Good, Two Legs Bad: The Dystopia of Power in George Orwell's *Animal Farm*." In *From Francis Bacon to William Golding: Utopias and Dystopias of Today and of Yore*. Cambridge Scholars, 2012.

Speech Acts, Mind, and Social Reality. Edited by Gunther Grewendorf and Georg Meggle, Kluwer Academic, 2002.

The Philosophy of Language. Edited by A. P. Martinich, Oxford UP, 2008.

Urmson, J. O. "Performative Utterances." *Midwest Studies in Philosophy*, vol.2, no.1, 1977, pp. 120-27.*Wiley Online Library*.

Woloch, Alex. *Or Orwell: Writing and Democratic Socialism*. Harvard UP, 2016.

"This World and the Next": Religious Text and Subtext in *Animal Farm*

Camilo Peralta

Of the many important themes explored by George Orwell in *Animal Farm*, few seem to have received as little attention from critics and readers as that of religion, despite the author's lifelong interest in the subject and the extensive analysis to which his treatment of it in other works has been subjected. Most criticism of religion in *Animal Farm* begins and ends with Moses, a raven who spins fantastic stories about an otherworldly paradise called Sugarcandy Mountain and is often regarded as a symbol of the Orthodox Church. But Orwell's choice of name here is far more significant than is commonly recognized. Moses is not just one of many biblical figures, after all, but a legendary prince and lawgiver who freed the Jews and led them out of bondage in Egypt. In naming the raven after him, Orwell invites us to consider other ways in which the influence of religion might be felt in the novel, from the characterization of the animals as lost, wandering, and easily influenced, to the authoritarian manner in which the Seven Commandments are created and subverted. Far from being a minor theme in *Animal Farm*, a critique of religion can be found on almost every page.

Orwell and Religion

As a recent biographer notes, Orwell consistently expressed a "hostile and dismissive" attitude toward organized religion (Brennan 2). In "Such, Such Were the Joys," published shortly after his death, he recalls his childhood years at a boarding school in Eastbourne, Sussex, with unmistakable bitterness: "Broadly, you were bidden to be at once a Christian and a social success, which is impossible. At the time I did not perceive that the various ideals which were set before us cancelled out" (31-32). In "Lear, Tolstoy, and the Fool," Orwell points to an existential "quarrel between the religion and the humanist attitudes towards life," arguing that the two cannot be reconciled: "one must choose between this world and the next. And the enormous majority of human beings, if they understood the issue, would choose this world" (526). His antagonism toward Christianity—and Catholicism especially—figures to some extent in all of his major works, as John Rodden and John Rossi remind us:

> Orwell mocked the idea of heaven and the Catholic (and Anglican) priesthood in *Down and Out in Paris and London* and *A Clergyman's Daughter*, denounced "Romanism" as the ecclesiastical equivalent of Stalinism in *The Road to Wigan Pier*, compared "orthodox" Catholic intellectuals to Communist Party writers throughout his journalism, and linked religious with political orthodoxy in O'Brien's power-crazed speech in *Nineteen Eighty-Four*. (18)

For all his criticism of Christianity, Orwell had an impressive knowledge of its central tenets and practices. Furthermore, his experiences as a colonial officer overseas introduced him to some of the religious traditions of the East, including Buddhism and Hinduism (Brennan 101).

But it is the Russian Orthodox Church that bears the brunt of his satirical fury in *Animal Farm*. With his black coat and somber appearance, Moses the raven is surely meant to call to mind images of an Orthodox priest. The other animals dislike and mistrust him because he performs no work on the farm and is closely associated with their tyrannical owner. Orwell describes him as the "spy" and "especial pet" of Mr. Jones, who feeds the raven "crusts of bread soaked in beer" (37-38). After the revolution, Moses disappears for a while, before returning with new claims that he has seen Sugarcandy Mountain for himself. Though the pigs were initially glad to see him go, they soon realize that his stories provide the animals with a bit of distraction from the daily grind of their miserable lives, and offer him a ration that is comparable to his previous one. In linking the raven with both the animals' original and their subsequent oppressors, Orwell points to the opportunistic complicity of the Orthodox Church in preserving the status quo of the lower classes in Russia. The portrayal of Moses "has been taken to symbolize Stalin's wartime entente with the Orthodox Church,"

Paul Kirschner observes, adding that "more generally it reflects the potential convenience of religion to dictators" (780). This is how most critics of *Animal Farm* have interpreted the character and where much of the discussion of religion in the novel comes to an end.

A Wandering and "Stiff-Necked" People

But Orwell's choice of name here has radical implications for how the novel might be read and interpreted by succeeding generations of readers, who have never even heard the names Stalin and Trotsky, and cannot recall a time when socialism was ever regarded as a serious threat to their way of life. After all, Orwell could have picked any number of characters from the Bible to represent the Church or organized religion—why go with Moses, one of the key prophets in the Abrahamic religions, a teacher, mediator, and "mouthpiece of God," who is traditionally credited with writing the first five books of the Bible (Gravett 164)? At first glance, he would seem to be a poor match for the sly-tongued raven. Though the biblical Moses is heroic and wise, willing to defy the most powerful ruler in the world and risk his life to lead his people to freedom, his animal namesake can hardly be bothered to lift a finger to relieve his comrades' suffering. They "hated" him, Orwell tells us, "because he told tales and did no work" (37). When the animals finally succeed in overthrowing Jones and other humans, he takes off after them, confirming the reader's suspicions about whose side he is really on.

But if the character of Moses does not accord well with that of his fictional representative, certain aspects of his story, at least, appear to be accurately depicted in *Animal Farm*. There are striking similarities between the characterizations of the Jewish people in Exodus and the animals in Orwell's book, for instance, which validates the idea that Orwell picked the name carefully. After the Israelites have escaped from Egypt, they soon reveal themselves to be "a model of undesirable behavior," complaining constantly and questioning their leadership and faith (Langston 171). When, at Marah, they discover that the water is bitter, they "grumble against Moses," who appeals to God for help in making it drinkable (Exod.

15:24-25). Soon after setting off from there, in an astonishing display of ingratitude, they complain about being hungry: "Would that we had died by the hand of the Lord in the land of Egypt, when we sat by the meat pots and ate bread to the full, for you have brought us out into this wilderness to kill this whole assembly with hunger" (Exod. 15:3). God obligingly sends down manna from heaven, though it is not enough to prevent them from complaining again at Rephidim about a lack of water to drink (Exod. 17:1-7). The bad behavior continues in Leviticus and Numbers.

The overall impression of the ancient Israelites that emerges in the Hebrew Bible is of a flawed and fickle people, unworthy of the salvation that has been offered to them. Repeatedly, God denounces them as "stiff-necked," a term that carries certain agricultural implications (Exod. 32:9, 33:3). The same term might be applied to the mutineers in *Animal Farm*, who, after their initial triumph, allow themselves to be led astray by a priestly class intent on its own glorification. The end result in both cases is bloodshed, though Napoleon's reign of terror only seems to be nearing its peak in the closing pages of the novel. The revolution certainly begins with noble enough intentions: after overthrowing Jones and establishing the ground rules that will govern their new society, the animals put extraordinary effort into ensuring that their first harvest will be a success. And it is, at first: "In the end," Orwell writes, "they finished the harvest in two days' less time than it had usually taken Jones and his men. Moreover, it was the biggest harvest that the farm had ever seen" (46). But even at this point, when the promise of the revolution seems closer to being fulfilled than it will ever be, there are warning signs that no one pays attention to. From the first day, the pigs seem disinclined to join their comrades in performing the hard daily labor that awaits them: "With their superior knowledge," Orwell claims, "it was natural that they should assume the leadership" (45). But there is really nothing "natural" about it.

The animals are not stupid. Most are able to learn how to read and write at least a little, and they all demonstrate the capacity to understand their role in the running of the farm. But as a collective, they often demonstrate a willingness to ignore the obvious and turn a blind eye to danger. No one tries to prevent Napoleon from taking away the litter of puppies born to Jessie and Bluebell or even thinks to ask him what he is doing with them over the long months until their sudden and dramatic reappearance (51). Few think to challenge the pigs' relentless but gradual accumulation of power or question the legitimacy of the privileges they claim for themselves. Even if one accepts that the pigs may need a break from hard labor due to their responsibilities managing the farm, it does not follow that they also deserve all of the choicest milk and apples. Simple logic dictates that Boxer and the other workhorses would benefit more from the extra nutrition. But in response to Squealer's claims to the contrary, all that is offered in dumb obeisance. In Exodus, after Moses goes up the mountain to receive the Ten Commandments, he seems to take with him all of the courage and sensibility that was in his people. So it is with the animals in Orwell's story, whose revolution begins to sour almost as soon as it has started.

Perhaps no one better represents how gullible and "stiff-necked" they can be than Boxer. Even as conditions continue to deteriorate on the farm, he clings to his stubborn and unfounded belief that "Napoleon is always right" (Orwell 70). After catching Squealer in a bald-faced lie about Snowball's actions at the Battle of the Cowshed, he abruptly drops the matter once the expected appeal to Napoleon's authority has been made. Shortly after, Boxer almost kills a dog that attacked him without provocation. At a gesture from Napoleon, he agrees to let it go, then watches impassively as it joins its brothers in executing several animals who have been accused of a variety of improbable crimes. Of the dozens present, only Boxer is physically capable of resisting the pigs' slaughter, yet declines to do so. "And so the tale of confessions and executions went on, until there was a pile of corpses lying before Napoleon's feet and the air was heavy with the smell of blood, which had been unknown there since the expulsion of Jones" (93).

There is a striking parallel here to a scene at the end of Exodus when Moses is summoned to receive the Ten Commandments. The people grow restless in his absence, and implore Aaron, Moses' brother and helper, to make new gods for them to worship (Exod.

32:1). He agrees and directs them in the construction of an enormous golden calf, which they offer sacrifices to and even credit for helping them escape from Egypt. God, understandably annoyed, warns Moses that the Israelites have fatally "corrupted themselves," and that he intends to destroy this "stiff-necked people" once and for all (Exod. 32:7-10). Moses begs the Lord for mercy and receives it. But on his way down the mountain, he catches sight of the golden calf for himself and is so enraged that he throws down the stone tablets on which the Ten Commandments had been inscribed, shattering them to pieces. He stands before his people and draws a line in the sand: "Who is on the Lord's side? Come to me" (Exod. 32:26). He orders the loyal Levites to pick up their swords and slaughter everyone in the camp, resulting in thousands of deaths (Exod. 32:28). Boxer is like those doomed men and women, unable to recognize his error in abetting Napoleon's rise to power and blindly standing by when decisive action is required. He refuses to come to his senses until he is riding in the van that will take him to his death—and by then, it is far too late to do anything about it.

Perhaps the most significant factor in the animals' downfall, however, is their poor collective memory. They seem to suffer from the same mass amnesia that the ancient Israelites often demonstrate toward their own history and the many instances in which God came to their rescue (Smith 645). No sooner have events transpired on the farm than they are already being forgotten, or misremembered. The pigs are only able to get away with flouting the Seven Commandments so conspicuously because no one can quite remember their original form. As each is broken, Squealer simply rewrites it to excuse what they have done. When, for instance, Napoleon takes to living in the farmhouse and even sleeping in Jones's old bed, Muriel knows this to be in violation of one of the rules. She goes to check the wall on which they were written, but Squealer has gotten there first: "as it was there on the wall, it must have been so" (79). The scene repeats itself over and over again, as the pigs grow more confident in their ability to manipulate the others' memories.

Given the portrayal of the animals as gullible and forgetful, it is tempting to see the pigs as a parody of the priestly class. Orwell was surely familiar with the incident involving the golden calf and the controversy surrounding Aaron's culpability in creating it. Rather than "violently suppressing" the people's misguided desires, as a priest ought to do, he can and has been faulted for enthusiastically embracing them, leading everyone to ruin (Watts 428). Likewise, despite its questionable utility, Napoleon insists that the animals devote considerable time and resources to building a windmill. Even after it has been partially destroyed, he urges the others to set about immediately to rebuild it. Snowball's extravagant notion of the lifestyle they will enjoy after it has been completed might be compared to the promises of a mystic who thinks he knows the way to heaven: "The animals had never heard of anything of this kind before," Orwell writes, "and they listened in astonishment while Snowball conjured up pictures" of the wonderful lives they would enjoy after it was built (64). Though it is often taken to symbolize the debate between Stalin and Trotsky over whether to consolidate the revolution or immediately try to export it to the other countries, the windmill also works as a powerful symbol of the arrogance of the priestly class.

The ending pages of the novel provide additional support for such a reading. As has been noted, Orwell had an especial dislike for the Catholic Church, dating back to his early experiences at St. Cyprian's. By the 1940s, when he wrote *Animal Farm*, he had come to regard Catholicism as "a reactionary force working against left-wing movements in the world" (Dugan 227). Undoubtedly, he would have identified with the long tradition of criticism centered on the power and wealth of the Church, which dates back at least to the start of the Protestant Reformation. Like the medieval clergy, who sold indulgences for money and fathered children with their mistresses, the pigs shamelessly indulge themselves at the expense of those whose care they have been entrusted with. They take to drinking whiskey, eating human food, and even walking around on their hind legs, while the other animals starve and drop dead from exhaustion. Finally, long after the early promise of the revolution has all but been forgotten, the pigs invite a party of humans over for a riotous meal. The other animals, looking back and forth between the faces, are surprised to discover that it has become impossible to distinguish between man and pig: "Some of them had five chins, some had four, some had three ... they were all alike" (138-39). So the majority of priests must have seemed to Orwell, professing their faith outwardly but living the same sinful and corrupt lives as the ruling classes they represented.

The Making and Breaking of Laws

Shortly after overthrowing their human rulers, the animals devise a set of principles to govern their new society. Orwell refers to them as "Commandments," and one cannot help but wonder why he would choose to employ that particular word to describe them. Orwell, being familiar with the importance of precise language, would likely have considered the alternatives very carefully. Why did he not go with "laws," "rules," "policies," or "decrees," then? There is no suggestion of compulsion or force in the rules the animals devise, either when they are being written up or after they have been adopted. Even when Napoleon begins terrorizing the others, it is not so much for their breaking of specific commandments but for their perceived failures to submit to his will without question or complaint. Only the pigs can be accused of breaking any of the Seven Commandments, and they are obviously not punished for doing so.

Since the early thirteenth century, *commandments* has also been used in an explicitly religious sense, as shorthand for the Ten Commandments given to Moses on Mount Sinai (Harper). This is, indeed, what immediately springs to mind when we hear or read that term, which Orwell surely intended. In Exodus, as in *Animal Farm*, the commandments serve as a means for governing how the faithful should think and behave. There are laws that encourage or forbid certain actions ("You shall not bear false witness against your neighbor"), as well as those that determine correct attitudes and beliefs ("You shall have no other gods before me") (Exod. 20:1-13). As important as the Ten Commandments are for the ancient Israelites, their influence on contemporary Western society can hardly be measured. Even in countries with an explicitly atheistic legal framework, such as the United States, they are still a "fundamental part" of our lives, acting as both "a guide to personal morality" and the "glue that holds us together" (Osler 695).

Orwell would likely have viewed this influence as a negative one, well suited to parody and subversion. Having the animals draw up their own list of rules provides him with the perfect opportunity to comment upon the negative influence of the Ten Commandments on ancient and modern society. After being written down, the laws of the Israelites and of the animals are immediately placed under the supervision of a priestly class, as represented by the Levites and the pigs, respectively. It has long been recognized that the Levites, who by God's express command are given a central role in the "process of creating and establishing law," may have been responsible for writing most of the books in the Hebrew Bible that concern the law, providing them with a double opportunity to promote their own interests against those of the other tribes (Leuchter 422). Likewise, the pigs assume responsibility for revising the commandments and explaining them to others. In both cases, there is a danger that the priestly class will bemore concerned with preserving its own power and prestige than on faithfully interpreting the laws by which they insist the others must abide, which is exactly what happens in *Animal Farm*.

The animals' first two commandments seem intended to provide guidelines for distinguishing between friends and enemies. "Whatever goes upon two legs" should count as the former, and "Whatever goes upon four legs" as the latter (Orwell 43). Almost immediately, questions arise over how much any of this makes sense. Do not some animals, including birds, go about primarily on two legs? Not so, according to Snowball, for a wing is merely "an organ of propulsion and not of manipulation. It should therefore be regarded as a leg" (51). But even Squealer would be hard pressed to reconcile the second law with the fact that the farm's primary nemesis throughout most of the novel is a fellow four-legged creature. Even if he tried, it would hardly matter, since enemies can come on two, four, or no legs. The whole discussion may be intended to parody the endless squabbling over doctrinal matters among the various tribes of Israel or the denominations of Christianity, such as those involving, for instance, transubstantiation or creation *ex nihilo* (Bauerschmidt 32-33). Despite the contemporary reader's inclination to regard such debates as trivial, Orwell reminds us of the deadly consequences they have often had for those on the "losing" side of the battle over interpretation. The Church, after all, burned those it regarded as heretics; the pigs will show no less compulsion in punishing those who deviate from their law.

The Ten Commandments are given directly to Moses by God. This lends them an unmistakable aura of authority that is reinforced by their status as imperatives: "Thou shalt not . . ." The people play no role either in creating or in transcribing the rules by which they must agree to live; they are merely expected to receive them from the priests in a passive and uncritical manner. Orwell highlights some of the dangers of such an attitude in the scene depicting the creation of the Seven Commandments. One day, shortly after the revolution, the pigs call everyone together and proclaim a new and "unalterable law by which all the animals on Animal Farm must live for ever after" (Orwell 42). Somewhat gracelessly, Snowball is able to clamber up to the top of one of the farm buildings, where he writes them out "in great white letters that could be read thirty yards away" (43). Though they are written "very neatly," there are several mistakes, a reminder of their flawed conception, and the dangerous ease with which they will be subverted. But none of the animals think to question whether the rules make any sense, or are truly designed with their best, collective interests in mind. Like the ancient Israelites, they accept the laws as given, trusting that the pigs will be able to guide them in how to understand and follow them correctly.

We know now that a variety of authors, with different and sometimes conflicting motivations, must have contributed to the writing of the Pentateuch, which had been, in the past, attributed solely to Moses. Writers often "revised" earlier accounts of individuals and situations mentioned in other books, in order to portray their own faction more favorably (Propp 24). In *Animal Farm*, the pigs show a similar tendency to revise commandments that have become inconvenient to them, and are able to get away with it even after being caught in the act (Orwell 112). Finally, only one remains unbroken: "All animals are created equal." This simple maxim seems to represent the true spirit of Animalism, which has not been extinguished in the majority of the animals despite the unrelenting brutality of life after the revolution:

> And yet the animals never gave up hope. . . . It might be that their lives were hard and that not all of their hopes had been fulfilled; but they were conscious that they were not as other animals. If they were hungry, it was not from feeding tyrannical human beings; if they worked hard, at least they worked for themselves. No creature among them went upon two legs. No creature called any other "Master." All animals were equal. (130-31)

Of course, the pigs are soon walking around on two legs. Shortly after, they decide to alter even that last, sacrosanct commandment, though their control over the others is by now so absolute that it hardly matters one way or the other whether they are exposed as hypocrites. This last addendum allows Orwell to highlight the absurdity of the whole doomed endeavor in the form of the rewritten law: "But some animals are more equal than others" (133). Having set out to establish a perfectly just society, the animals instead find themselves living under the worst kind of tyranny. After being slaughtered by the Levites following the debacle with the golden calf, many of the Israelites might have felt the same way.

One difference worth noting between the Seven and the Ten Commandments is that, while the former are ostensibly intended to ensure equality between believers, the latter serve instead to reinforce a "strong tradition with an authoritarian and hierarchical base" that was a "common characteristic" of ancient societies like that of the Israelites (Shulman 171). The Ten Commandments have little to say about most of the things we expect from a modern-day legal code, such as personal freedom, happiness, or individuality. In a way, the complete failure of the animals' revolution suggests the danger of attempting to transform society through legislation alone. Despite their lofty rhetoric, most of the animals do not change much from how they were before the revolution: some, like Mollie, make only the most half-hearted attempt to play along, whereas others, like Boxer, would presumably work as hard for one regime as for the next. One cannot simply flip a switch and change human (or animal) nature. Of course, this is exactly the sort of criticism often heard regarding the ambitious social programs initiated by the Russian and the Chinese communists, which allows Orwell the opportunity to combine his interest in religious criticism with one of the larger themes of the book.

The Prodigal Son Returns?

In the final years of his life, Orwell often attended mass in Sutton Courtenay, a small village in Oxfordshire. He supposedly received Holy Communion on a regular basis; in the final will he drew up before his death in January of 1950, he requested an Anglican burial (Bowker 415). Perhaps there is no more meaning to these events than there is to Moses' fanciful stories about Sugarcandy Mountain. "Up there, comrades . . . just on the other side of that dark cloud that you can see—there it lies, Sugarcandy Mountain, that happy country where we poor animals shall rest for ever from our labours!" (119). Or perhaps this staunch and lifelong opponent of religion was not as confident in what he would discover in the afterlife as he would have liked to believe. In either case, he has left behind, in *Animal Farm*, some intriguing ideas about religious belief and law that deserve further attention.

Works Cited

Bauerschmidt, Frederick Christian. "'The Body of Christ is Made from Bread': Transubstantiation and the Grammar of Creation." *International Journal of Systematic Theology*, vol. 18, no. 1, Jan. 2016, pp. 30-46. EBSCO*host*, doi:10.1111/ijst.12137.

Bowker, Gordon. *Inside George Orwell: A Biography*. Palgrave Macmillan, 2003.

Brennan, Michael G. *George Orwell and Religion*. Bloomsbury, 2017.

"Commandment." *The American Heritage Dictionary of the English Language*, Houghton Mifflin, 6th edition, 2016. *Credo Reference*, ezproxy.indycc.edu/login?url=https://search.credoreference.com/

content/entry/hmdictenglang/commandment/0?institutionId=6445. Accessed 23 Feb. 2018.

Dugan, Lawrence. "Orwell and Catholicism." *Modern Age*, vol. 48, no. 3, Summer 2006, pp. 226-40. *Intercollegiate Studies Institute*, home.isi. org/taxonomy/term/117.

Gravett, Emily O. "'Who Am I?' The Biblical Moses as a Metaphor for Teaching." *Teaching Theology & Religion*, vol. 18, no. 2, Apr. 2015, pp. 159-69. EBSCO*host*, doi:10.1111/teth.12276.

Harper, Douglas. "Commandment." *The Online Etymology Dictionary*, www.etymonline.com/word/command?ref=etymonline_ crossreference.

The Bible. English Standard Version. Crossway, 2007.

Kirschner, Paul. "The Dual Purpose of 'Animal Farm.'" *Review of English Studies*, vol. 55, no. 222, Nov. 2004, pp. 759-86. *JSTOR*, www.jstor. org/stable/3661599.

Langston, Scott M. *Exodus: Through the Centuries (Blackwell Bible Commentaries)*. Wiley-Blackwell, 2005.

Leuchter, Mark. "'The Levite in your Gates': The Deuteronomic Redefinition of Levitical Authority." *Journal of Biblical Literature*, vol. 126, no. 3, Fall 2007, pp. 417-36. *Religion and Philosophy Collection*, EBSCO*host*.

Levering, Matthew. "God and Natural Law: Reflections on Genesis 22." *Modern Theology*, vol. 24, no. 2, Apr. 2008, pp. 151-77. EBSCO*host*, doi:10.1111/j.1468-0025.2007.00440.x.

Orwell, George. *Animal Farm*. Signet, 1996.

_____. "Lear, Tolstoy and the Fool." *Fifty Essays*. Oxford Press, 2010.

_____. "Such, Such Were the Joys." *George Orwell: A Collection of Essays*. Mariner, 1970.

Osler, Mark. "'AseretHad'Varim' in Tension: The Ten Commandments and the Bill of Rights." *Journal of Church & State*, vol. 49, no. 4, 2007, pp. 683-96. *MasterFILE Premier*, EBSCO*host*.

Propp, William H. "The Rod of Aaron and the Sin of Moses." *Journal of Biblical Literature*, vol. 107, no. 1, Mar. 1988, pp. 19-26. *Academic Search Premier*, EBSCO*host*.

Rodden, John, and John Rossi. "A Book More Equal Than Others: Orwell, *Animal Farm*, and the *Commonweal* Catholic." *Commonweal*, vol. 143, no. 15, 23 Sept. 2016, pp. 16-21. *Literary Reference Center*, EBSCO*host*.

Schulman, Bernard. "The Political Science of the Ten Commandments." *Journal of Individual Psychology*, vol. 59, no. 2, Summer 2003, pp. 166-75. *Academic Search Premier*, EBSCO*host*.

Smith, Mark S. "Remembering God: Collective Memory in Israelite Religion." *Catholic Biblical Quarterly*, vol. 64, no. 4, Oct. 2002, pp. 631-52. *Religion and Philosophy Collection*, EBSCO*host*.

Watts, James W. "Aaron and the Golden Calf in the Rhetoric of the Pentateuch." *Journal of Biblical Literature*, vol. 130, no. 3, Fall 2011, pp. 417-30. *JSTOR*, www.jstor.org/stable/41304211.

"Just Smile and Nod": The Absent Malcontent in *Animal Farm*

Charity Gibson

Unlike virtually every other dystopian novel, George Orwell's *Animal Farm* does not include a malcontent who opposes and fights against the system. Malcontents cause readers to question how such characters have managed to transcend the false consciousness (the belief system that obscures the truth of the oppressive and unjust situation) that most everyone else remains inundated beneath. The malcontent is typically a rebel. In some works, the malcontent, though correct in his rejection of society's values and mores, is a dark and even sinister character.

Traditional malcontents are often unlikable characters, due to a melancholic and taciturn disposition. However, despite a lackluster disposition, they serve an important role. Julia Lacey Brooke says of a malcontent, "Outsider he may be, yet this 'outside' mentality possibly permits him a truer judgement of the world, and to be more acutely tuned to the moral status quo than other, more 'engaged' individuals" (5). Modern classic dystopian novels that include malcontents range from John the Savage in Aldous Huxley's *Brave New World* (1933) to Winston Smith in Orwell's *Nineteen Eighty-Four* (1949) to Guy Montag in Ray Bradbury's *Fahrenheit 451* (1953). In such works, although the malcontents are commendable and certainly function as the protagonists of the story, none of them are heroes. John commits suicide after participating in a drug-induced orgy; Winston is tortured and brainwashed until he succumbs to the authority; and Montag becomes a worn exile, optimistic but unsure of the future. Though each of these malcontents experiences personal growth in his pursuit of truth, culminating in his stance against society's corruption, none is able to defeat the oppressive system he detests. As Chris Ferns argues, "Thus, while the provision of an [o]ppositional presence in dystopian fiction is clearly one of its most significant features, equally significant is the fact that in every case the defeat of the opposition is shown as virtually inevitable" (374).

The downfall of malcontents who attempt to resist governmental control may suggest a pessimistic view from authors. At the very least, this outlook is realistic rather than idealistic. Yet, this defeat does not mean that authors are without hope. Rather, they use literature as a scare tactic of sorts, showing a dire situation as a means of prompting readers to change before society reaches the point of no return. Amid their human frailties, readers are drawn to malcontents because they recognize that the malcontents are willing to take a stand and have a conviction of purpose, regardless of the result.

In most dystopian works, the totalitarian regime is already established at the beginning of the narrative. As the malcontent character is introduced and developed, it is in contrast with a society that has already been established. Yet *Animal Farm* is the story of Manor Farm being transformed into Animal Farm with its system of Animalism. The pig Napoleon is a dynamic character who morphs from a capable leader intent on following Old Major's directives to a tyrant, uninterested in anything aside from his own agenda. It is perhaps understandable why the malcontent is missing from this story when the difference of a society in flux versus an established one (which coincides with Napoleon's role from a neutral to a villainous character) is considered. It is hard to critique a system that has not yet fully manifested itself. Some may wonder whether Orwell himself as narrator fodders the malcontent's perspective. However, Orwell's narrative tone, though wry, is removed. He gives the facts but offers no evaluation of the pigs' actions. Samir Elbarbary argues, "We should not be at all astonished to see that the narrator is coldly uncritical where tragic happenings take place" (37). Just as Orwell does not include a malcontent character, neither does he write in a didactic manner in which the narrative itself subjectively criticizes the antagonistic forces. "Orwell's silence mirrors the animals' inability to discern the truth" (Elbarbary 38). Orwell's desire may have been for readers to appropriately discern for themselves, rather than rely on the narrator. The result is little to no challenging of corrupt authority from either the narrator or the characters.

While it would have been difficult for Orwell to begin his narrative with a malcontent, as do many other dystopian stories in which the government is already well established as the antagonistic force, it would have been possible to include what Brooke calls a "made" malcontent, one who becomes alienated during the course of the narrative as the plot develops (38-9), as does, for example, John the Savage in *Brave New World*. This kind of malcontent, Brooke argues, is relatable for audiences as they imagine what they would do in a similar situation: "[T]he average guy, as it were, [is] lugged into extraordinary circumstances and emotional exigencies [and] is forced to exceed certain bounds of moral convention and decency and is, potentially, any one of us, 'everyman'" (39). An animal who becomes a dissenter as Napoleon's plan becomes clearer could have been a fitting usage of a made malcontent in Orwell's work.

The Implications of an Absent Malcontent on the Story Line

The inclusion of a malcontent is important because in a story in which the government and its leaders constitute a collective antagonist, the malcontented protagonist's resistance gives the story an engaging plotline. Martha Alderson explains the need for this tension in a successful dystopian story: "Imagine a story as a conflict between energies of light and dark. . . . The antagonists represent darkness as they strive to keep the protagonist as she currently exists. The protagonist represents the light in the struggle to evolve" (101). Applying this concept of light and dark energy to *Animal Farm*, Napoleon and his regime are the darkness, but the question then becomes, who is the light? Old Major's dream, "Remove Man from the scene, and the root cause of hunger and overwork is abolished for ever," is not one meant to create a hierarchy of dominion among the animals (4): "And among us animals let there be perfect unity, perfect comradeship in the struggle" (6). Old Major's dream is essentially the age-old concept of the oppressed desiring to rise above their oppression and reestablish a productive social order. It is only as Napoleon's acquisition of power serves as an impetus for a dictatorship that he solidifies his role as an antagonist. Orwell focuses so much on the antagonism within the plotline because Napoleon's rise to power satirically parallels Joseph Stalin's establishment of the USSR. Orwell's primary focus appears to have been on constructing a political fable, resulting in an unbalanced plotline in which the audience is left not only without a character to serve as a moral compass but also with no one to connect with or cheer for. Neither is *Animal Farm* an exploration of the villain in which the goal is to humanize and understand the antagonist's motivation.

In *Animal Farm*, readers do not strongly identify with any one character's particular loss amid a hard-fought struggle. The novel's ending sentence focuses on the animals as a whole, rather than on any individual: "The creatures outside looked from pig to man, and from man to pig, and from pig to man again; but already it was impossible to say which was which" (93). Readers see the injustice in the animals' situation (and by association that of the people of Russia); however, readers may not be intrigued to pursue continued thinking about the characters, who by the end have been reduced to the collective category of unnamed "creatures," more types than well-rounded entities in and of themselves.

The characters seem like types because, of course, they are. Every animal represents a historical figure or group, and most of the occurrences in the story mirror historical happenings connected to Stalin's rise to power. While dystopian writers are usually inspired by their present to write a fictionalized warning of what could happen in the future if current paths are not altered, Orwell's work carefully parallels recent historical events of his time in order to serve as a warning against history repeating itself. Efraim Sicher and Natalia Skradol point out dystopian literature's tendency to draw fodder from what is conceivable, though not yet actualized, "Literary dystopia gives a negative appraisal of the here-and-now, a satire of what is already possible but not desirable" (7). Though Orwell was certainly influenced by the here and now of contemporary culture, most of his attention was spent looking at what had already been actualized in Soviet Russia. However, once the parallels between the animals' farmstead and Stalin's Russia are realized, there must be additional ways to interact with the story and its characters in order for scholars and students to regularly analyze and write about the work beyond identifying similarities.

Animal Farm is a secular allegory, as Jeremy Tambling notes. An allegory is a simple story that references a deeper meaning. As James Arnt Aune notes, "Part of the pleasure in reading the story, as well as educational usefulness, lies in the reader's detective work in tracking down the allegorical correspondences" (5). However, once this has been accomplished, there is little motivation to interact with the animal characters beyond identifying whom they represent historically. Tambling states that deep analysis of allegorical works has previously been uncommon: "Until recently, modern study of literature paid little attention to allegory unless specialist work was being done on a religious 'serious' writer" (1). While allegories have their merit, contemporary readers want a character with whom to connect. It is less important whether the character is or was real than it is that the character feels real to the reader. Whereas classic dystopian works show humanity's limitations in presenting characters unable to evoke change, contemporary dystopian literature suggests that one person—typically a malcontent—can change the world. Dave Astor discusses why contemporary audiences are so drawn to current dystopian fiction. Interestingly, he addresses exactly what is missing in *Animal Farm*: relatable characters and a malcontent: "We admire the best dystopian novels because they're written well and depict people we can relate to. . . . And we're compelled to turn the pages as we wonder if rebels and other members of the populace can somehow remake a wretched society into something more positive" (Astor). Though the role of the malcontent has changed over the years in dystopian literature, with the exception of *Animal Farm*, its presence has been a constant. The public is currently drawn to dystopian literature because, as individuals search for ways to demonstrate autonomy, they connect with the few literary outliers brave enough to question the corrupt system. As Melissa Ames observes, "Most authors set up dystopian worlds in order for their characters to have a hand in dismantling them" (16). In *Animal Farm*,

---

contrastingly, the animals are slowly duped. The pigs take over with very little resistance because of the missing malcontent(s). People do not want to imagine themselves as capable of being hoodwinked like the barnyard animals, and the lack of scholarship on *Animal Farm* may suggest this.

Some may argue that Orwell does give readers a character worthy of emulation, someone to connect with and care about, in Boxer the workhorse, who some might say serves as the hero of the story. He is indeed one of the most sympathetic characters, working his hardest for the good of the farm only to be betrayed by Napoleon. Boxer represents the exploited working class with his unrelenting mantra "I will work harder" (40). Some may even argue that Boxer is a tragic hero, with his naïveté serving as his hamartia, a classical term first used by Aristotle meaning the fatal flaw that brings about the undoing of a mostly positive character.

While it is true that Boxer is a mostly positive character with a fatal flaw, he is neither a malcontent nor a hero because he does not have the sense of awareness necessary for this position. Malcontents are able to intuitively recognize the gravity of their situation and work against its maintenance. Boxer, though good, is not heroic because his work is foolhardy. Boxer blindly works alongside the pigs, furthering their agenda, though with none of their sinister goals. He is equally worthy of reproof for his gullibility as he is commendable for his work ethic. He has not bettered anyone's situation or purposed to stand up for injustice. Even calling him a martyr may be a stretch, for he does not willingly take a stance against the pigs; going along with Napoleon is the safe choice, rather than a risky one. Boxer does not die for his beliefs; his ineffectual attempts to escape from the knacker's van indicate that he discovers too late that the pigs do not share his beliefs.

The Implication of an Absent Malcontent on Historical Integrity

Not including a malcontent protagonist hurts the story in terms of a compelling plotline with character development essential for reader buy-in. This omission also hurts the credibility of the historical narrative Orwell references. Orwell presents Stalin's rise to power as something that occurred with very little opposition. The idea of an authoritarian government ruling without any serious opposition from at least a few malcontents is not only atypical in dystopian stories but also contrary to reality. After publishing *Animal Farm,* Orwell wrote a letter to a friend in which he references the "intellectual honesty" of his work (*As I Please* 203). Yet there is irony in this, as *Animal Farm* is simultaneously factual and inaccurate. Throughout history, although the masses tend to act as sheep, passively doing as they are told, there have always been malcontents who have had the courage to stand up for liberty. Indeed, it is because this concept rings true that audiences love it; the malcontent is almost archetypal in scope. Brooke claims, "Malcontents came to represent a more contemporary *social* archetype: alienated, destructive, anarchic, a character-type with a real-life model" (7).

Classical dystopian malcontents are not always successful in defeating the system the way, for example, Suzanne Collins's *Hunger Games* trilogy allows Katniss Everdeen to function as a "girl on fire," capable of providing strong leadership to inspire revolution, but they contribute nonetheless. The often unsung malcontents who fought against Stalinism are what Orwell overlooked; presenting Stalin's rise to power as occurring without dissenting voices is historically inaccurate. Historian Juliane Fürst claims that this oversight is typical, "[L]ittle attention has been paid to the small groups of people who overtly resisted in word and deed" (354). Though overlooking malcontents amid Stalinism has been common, this omission in *Animal Farm* results not only in a less captivating story but also in historical revisionism.

Orwell fails to include the stories of those who were wary of Stalin and enacted resistance in various ways. Some may wonder whether Snowball serves as a malcontent: after they no longer agree, Snowball initially deters Napoleon, which is representative of Stalin's disassociation from Trotsky. However, Snowball is not opposed to the concept of a dictatorship; he simply wants to hold the authoritative position himself. Snowball agrees with the direction the government is taking but differs on who should lead and what direction that leadership should take. Napoleon and Snowball "disagreed at every point where disagreement was possible" (Orwell 30). In the end, Napoleon's dogs chase off Snowball, "He was running as only a pig can run, but the dogs were close on his heels. . . . Then he put on an extra spurt and, with a few inches to spare, slipped through a hole in the hedge and was seen no more" (35). "Snowball's expulsion," as Orwell calls it, represents Trotsky's exile (35). Snowball is far from a malcontent; he is a disposed political leader who paves the way for Napoleon's sovereign rule.

Interpreting Snowball as an enabler to Napoleon's rule coincides with the common understanding of Trotsky's role in Stalin's acquisition of power. Historian Robert Daniels explains that Trotsky was an assister rather than a deterrent to Stalinism, "Western historians, like Soviet writers during the first years of glasnost, have often looked on Trotsky and Trotskyism not as an alternative to Stalinism but as the forerunner of it" (277). Orwell could have included those who disagreed with Napoleon and went on to resist. Instead he presents the animals as passive and befuddled by Snowball's expulsion: "Several of them would have protested if they could have found the right arguments" (Orwell 36). Orwell acknowledges that the animals at times question the tide of change but shows them doing nothing, suggesting that Stalin was able to banish Trotsky and continue with his plans without any concerted resistance from the public.

The closest that Orwell comes to referencing historical malcontents is his inclusion of the hens' resistance to giving up their eggs, which Napoleon has required in order to fulfill his agreement to exchange 400 eggs a week for grain and meal. The hens refuse to give up their eggs for five days, instead laying them from the rafters where they fall onto the hard ground and break. After nine hens die from starvation, as Napoleon orders that they receive no food rations, the remaining hens relinquish their eggs. The event is covered up, and regarding the hens' corpses, "Their bodies were buried in the orchard, and it was given out that they had died of coccidiosis" (50). This event parallels the Kronstadt rebellion and Stalin's Great Purge that occurred from 1936 to 1938. However, this episode only takes up three paragraphs and includes no major characters. While typical malcontents in dystopian literature are well-rounded characters that readers come to know personally, gaining sympathy for their cause and actions, readers of *Animal Farm* have no connection to the hens, and, therefore, little reason to deeply explore this temporary rebellion. The hens' rebellion is the only possible malcontent activity in the book, suggesting that resistance against Stalin was attempted only once for a short period of time.

Orwell later mentions that three "ringleaders" headed the hens' rebellion (55). He delves no deeper into this, other than to say that they are executed. This reference could have provided a perfect entrance for several of the key players in the Kronstadt rebellion, such as Afanasi Matushenko, the leader of the crew of the ship *Petropavlovsk* that mutinied because of poor food rations and quality, or Stepan Maximovich Petrichenko, leader of the Kronstadt Commune as well as the leader of the revolutionary committee that headed the Kronstadt rebellion. The current information Orwell gives about the hens leading the rebellion actually differs from the reality of the rebellion, which did not have three connected figureheads. According to historian Lynne Thorndycraft, thirty sailors from Kronstadt did travel to Petrograd to try to negotiate with the Soviet leaders, though it resulted in their arrest. Perhaps the three hens are symbolic of these thirty. However, as information about specific malcontents involved in the Kronstadt rebellion is difficult to obtain, Orwell's lack of depth regarding this episode likely reflects his own ignorance of the details.

Allusions to Stalin's Great Purge continue in the episode about animals who come forward and confess crimes: "Then a goose came forward and confessed to having secreted six ears of corn during the last year's harvest and eaten them in the night . . . and two other sheep confessed to having murdered an old ram, an especially devoted follower of Napoleon, by chasing him round and round a bonfire when he was suffering from a cold. They were all slain on the spot" (Orwell 55). The crimes the animals claim to have committed are ludicrous, illustrating Orwell's point that Stalin murdered countless who were innocent of having participated in any anarchical activity. These episodes in the text are useful in showcasing that people innocent of insurrection were murdered. Yet since a few brief accounts are offered in lieu of many accounts of actual resistance efforts, *Animal Farm* also erroneously implies that such efforts were rare.

Because Stalinists fabricated putative resistance groups in order to punish scapegoats to illustrate the price of disloyalty, it is difficult for historians to know which groups were authentic and which were fictitious. Historian Kevin Murphy admits, "Source problems have, until recently, limited the investigation of opposition groups" (329). Therefore, Orwell's failure to address resistance groups may have stemmed from lack of awareness. Contemporary scholarship is divided in deciding how imperative it is to focus on resistance groups. Historian Lynne Viola acknowledges the potential of focusing too much on the subgroups, saying that there are "ahistorical pitfalls of either valorizing resistance or focusing on resistance to the exclusion of the rest of the historical record" (*Contending* 17). Orwell avoids these pitfalls, but because his work is perceived as an almost point-by-point chronicle of Stalin's rise to power, including as insignificant an amount of resistance as he does sends the message to readers that people did not resist. Part of the reason that Orwell did not include Russian malcontents in his story may be that many of them were communists, an ideology Orwell denounced. The United Kingdom's security service noted in a report of Orwell, "It is evident . . . that he does not hold with the Communist Party nor they with him" ("MI5 Confused by Orwell's Politics"). Furthermore, Elbarbary calls Orwell an "outspoken critic of communism" (36). However, even if Orwell was not keen on glorifying some historical malcontents on account of their communist leanings, there are also recorded stories of malcontents without overt political affiliations.

Several scholarly works acknowledge how the poor specifically fought against Stalinism. Viola's book *Peasant Rebels under Stalin* explores the everyday valor of commonplace people: "When peasants engage in acts of resistance, they 'speak out loud'... providing the historian with an otherwise often inaccessible sector of society. Resistance serves as a prism, distilling aspects of peasant culture, politics, and community" (5). Another work that explores malcontents under Stalinism is historian Sheila Fitzpatrick's *Stalin's Peasants*. Fitzpatrick unearths the ways in which subjected people resisted the government and the status quo: "These strategies may be called 'subaltern' because they were inextricably linked with the peasants' subordinate status in society and their position as objects of aggression and exploitation by superordinate institutions and individuals" (4-5). Examining actions ranging from violent uprisings to fleeing the regime, Fitzpatrick clarifies what resistance from the common people looked like.These occurrences challenged Stalinism, not because the dissenters were successful but because they dared to take a stand.

Successful dystopian literature generally includes malcontents. In earlier instances, these malcontents are defeated, and in more recent literature, they are victorious or at least unconquered. Regardless, they exist because they must in order for a strong plotline to develop and for society to keep believing that ordinary people can do extraordinary things. Not every attempt at resistance culminates in success for the individual malcontent, but these attempts can inspire others, be they other characters or engaged readers. If literature reflects life, malcontents within totalitarian societies must exist because historically this has always been the case. Unless the love for liberty is quenched within the human spirit, this will always be so. Orwell's *Animal Farm*, though successful as a warning against dictatorship, is untrue even while paralleling a true story. Orwell's focus was to represent mainstream Russia. In a letter to Dwight McDonald, he wrote, "I meant the moral to be that revolutions only effect a radical improvement when the masses are alert. . ." (qtd. in Rodden 134). However, it is not just the masses we should be concerned about. It is often the minority willing to contradict the masses who make all the difference. Though scholars are probably not consciously making a political statement when they shy away from *Animal Farm*, if and when more scholars look more closely at this work, the significance of the absent malcontent should be appreciated.

Works Cited

Alderson, Martha. *The Plot Whisperer: Secrets of Story Structure Any Writer Can Master*. Adams Media, 2011.

Ames, Melissa. "Engaging 'Apolitical' Adolescents: Analyzing the Popularity and Educational Potential of Dystopian Literature Post-9/11." *High School Journal,* vol. 97, no. 1, 2013, pp. 3-20. *JSTOR,* www.jstor.org/stable/43281204.

Astor, Dave. "Why Do We Like Dystopian Novels?" *Huffington Post.* 19 Dec. 2012. www.huffingtonpost.com/dave-astor/why-do-we-like-dystopian-novels_b_1979301.html.

Aune, James Arnt. "Literary Analysis of Animal Farm" *Understanding Animal Farm: A Student Casebook to Issues, Sources, and Historical Documents.* Edited by John Rodden, Greenwood, pp. 1-20.

Brooke, Julia Lacey. *The Stoic, the Weal and the Malcontent.* Tiger of the Stripe, 2013.

Daniels, Robert V. "The Left Opposition as an Alternative to Stalinism." *Slavic Review,* vol. 50, no. 2, 1991, pp. 277-85. *JSTOR,* www.jstor.org/stable/2500203.

Elbarbary, Samir. "Language as Theme in Animal Farm." *International Fiction Review*, vol. 19, no. 1, 1992, pp. 31-38.

Ferns, Chris. "The Value/s of Dystopia: The Handmaid's Tale and the Anti-Utopian Tradition." *Dalhousie Review*, vol. 69, no. 3, 1989. pp. 373-82. dalspace.library.dal.ca/bitstream/handle/10222/61007/dalrev_vol69_iss3_pp373_382.pdf?sequence=1).

Fitzpatrick, Sheila. *Stalin's Peasants: Resistance and Survival in the Russian Village after Collectivization.* Oxford UP, 1996.

Fürst, Juliane. "Prisoners of the Soviet Self? Political Youth Opposition in Late Stalinism." *Europe-Asia Studies*, vol. 54, no. 3, 2002, pp. 353-75. *JSTOR,* www.jstor.org/stable/826481.

"MI5 Confused by Orwell's Politics."*BBC News.* 4 Sept. 2007, news.bbc.co.uk/2/hi/uk_news/6976576.stm. Accessed 1 June 2018.

Murphy, Kevin. "Opposition at the Local Level: A Case Study of the Hammer and Sickle Factory." *Europe-Asia Studies*, vol. 53, no. 2, 2001, pp. 329-50. *JSTOR,* www.jstor.org/stable/826351.

Orwell, George. *Animal Farm.* Everyman's Library. 1993.

_____. *George Orwell: As I Please, 1943-1945. The Collected Essays, Journalism and Letters of George Orwell, Volume 3.* Harcourt, 1968.

Rodden, John. "Animal Farm and the Early Cold War." *Understanding Animal Farm: A Student Casebook to Issues, Sources, and Historical Documents.* Edited by John Rodden, Greenwood, 1999, pp. 117-58.

Sicher, Efraim, and Natalia Skradol. AWorld Neither Brave Nor New: Reading Dystopian Fiction after 9/11." *Partial Answers: Journal of Literature and the History of Ideas,* vol. 4, no. 1, 2006, pp. 151-79. *Project Muse,* doi.org/10.1353/pan.0.0057.

Soukhanov, Anne H., and Kaethe Ellis. *Websters II New Riverside University Dictionary.* Houghton Mifflin, 1984.

Tambling, Jeremy. *Allegory.* Routledge, 2009.

Thorndycraft, Lynne. "The Kronstadt Uprising of 1921." Left Bank Books, 1975.

Viola, Lynne. *Contending with Stalinism: Soviet Power and Popular Resistance in the 1930s.* Cornell UP, 2002.

_____. *Peasant Rebels Under Stalin: Collectivization and the Culture of Peasant Resistance.* Oxford UP, 1999.

been raised to the peerage in 1941, having served as Permanent Under Secretary to the Foreign Office for almost a decade. In the late 1930s he had been one of the most prominent advocates of a muscular line against Hitler's regime in Germany and was against totalitarianism in all its forms. For Vansittart, *Animal Farm* was a salutary tale given the current postwar picture—an example of his Commu-Nazi view of the world where dictatorship of both left and right was to be opposed at all costs. As he told the Lords in November 1947, with Stalin seemingly set on replacing democratically elected administrations behind the Iron Curtain with Soviet-approved puppets, the Labour Government should be considering "whether they are resigned to seeing their [socialist] colleagues gradually blotted out in Eastern Europe, or whether they think there is something further which they could do" (Hansard, col. 470)

Animal Farm laid out the future for these newly communist states. In Vansittart's mind, Orwell's text was "the story of a farm that was only too anxious to be socialized, but the animals had reckoned without 'Old Squealer,' the great hog, the commissar who hogged everything when he got on top and divided up the pie with his henchmen" (Hansard, col. 470). In doing so, Orwell had provided "a very admirable definition of the Communist hierarchy in a society that professes to be classless and of the Communist tyranny such as is being exercised in Europe now" (Hansard, col. 470). For Vansittart, the British government should have been standing up to the Soviets on the diplomatic sphere, largely through economic means. But there was a more direct question as to whether Clement Attlee's government itself was sleepwalking into Sovietism at home. This was particularly if, as Orwell believed, the group of "underground Communist MPs—that is, MPs elected as Labour men but secretly members of the C[ommunist] P[arty]" could steer the government even further to the left (*CEJL* 4:187). Such types would certainly, as Friedrich von Hayek concurrently argued from the right, lead Britain down *The Road to Serfdom* (1944) given half a chance.

For sure, Britain's first majority Labour Government had swiftly legislated to bring under state control vast tranches of the

British economy from the Bank of England to the railway system. The creation of the National Health Service in 1948 by Orwell's former associate Bevan would soon socialize medicine too. Orwell himself did not believe these measures should have been the chief priority for a government of the left, arguing instead for the abolition of private schools, titles, and the House of Lords (Davison 104). In a sense, this rather neatly portrays the differences between frontline politicians and literary figures such as Orwell. While Orwell could obsess about the symbolism of a few hundred Lords or even twenty thousand public school pupils, Labour's 1945 government was rooted in the day-to-day problems of the masses: health and work. As Orwell wrote in early 1946, "in a purely economic sense, I suppose, the drift is towards Socialism, or at least state ownership. . . . But in the social set-up there is no symptom by which one could infer that we are not living under a Conservative government" (*CEJL* 4:186). This verdict was pushing things.

But Orwell's political radar was far more perceptive in another manner: the contemporary growth of consumerism and the problems it would soon cause a Labour government continuing state-led rationing of food and clothing. As Orwell wrote, within a year of the end of the war "everyone is intent on having a good time, so far as our reduced circumstances permit. Football matches are attended by enormous crowds, pubs and picture houses are always packed, and motoring has revived to a surprising extent considered that petrol is still theoretically rationed" (*CEJL* 4:188). Yet, as he also noted, "life since the armistice has been physically as unpleasant as it was during the war, perhaps more so, because the effects of certain shortages are cumulative. The clothing shortage, for instance, becomes less and tolerable [and]. . . . Food is dull as ever, the queues do not get any shorter" (*CEJL* 4:185). In continuing rationing Labour was attempting to spread the burden of the conflict's aftereffects (principally the collapse of British industry) evenly. But as that conflict receded into the past, support for rationing, particularly among the middle class, began to decline sharply. Conservative claims about "state interference" and "bureaucracy" that Orwell had found unconvincing in 1946 began to cut through, and Labour was out of office by 1951 (*CEJL* 4:186). There were electoral as well as moral dangers for the heavy-handed socialist state in a parliamentary democracy.

The character of Mollie (the mare) in *Animal Farm* can be read two ways in this regard. Certainly there is the view that Mollie is either a traitor to the revolution or just intellectually limited. Her desire for ribbons and sugar in the face of epoch-defining changes on the farm can be rendered somewhat unsympathetic. But in another sense she is the most sensible creature of the lot. Her apolitical views see her leave the farm, having been neither obediently loyal to Mr. Jones nor to the revolution. In Britain the middle class, having given Labour a shot in 1945, were fast jettisoning the party in the late 1940s. The character has other parallels, most obviously with the Russian petit bourgeoisie, but there was an English dimension there—albeit one that took place a few years after *Animal Farm* was published. Just as Mollie would go on to enjoy a happy life on another farm, so too would 1950s middle-class Britain benefit through a booming private sector presided over (at arm's length) by a Conservative government. Unlike some of the working class, of course, the Mollies had the ability to risk the potentially lower provision of social services that a Tory government might also deliver. But, as Tony Blair remarked in a rather more modern context, until the left reached out to "the people listening to Duran Duran and Madonna" its electoral prospects were always limited (91).

Orwell's book was thus published at a particular juncture in both British and global history. Famously, it arrived barely a week after the dropping of the atomic bombs on Hiroshima and Nagasaki. But, albeit less dramatically, it also came between two periods where government was perceived to be doing alternatively too little and then, for some, too much. In *The Road to Wigan Pier* and *Down and Out in Paris and London* Orwell chronicled the "hungry thirties"—an age where the National Government in Britain had chosen to pursue a laissez-faire solution to the economic meltdown then gripping the West. In a sense, Farmer Jones represents Prime Ministers Stanley Baldwin and Neville Chamberlain as much as he did Tsar Nicholas II—an indolent leader asleep (or drunk) at the wheel while his farm careens toward mass poverty. The revolution that does take place was therefore initially attractive—a leap into the unknown from a previous form of economic tyranny. The increased encroachment of the state thereafter, be it Snowball's windmill or Attlee's nationalizations, may have ended in a less free individual, but its intent cannot be condemned out of hand.

The issue, of course, was where the masses could be taken, and here the legacy of the 1930s weighed heavy. The character of Boxer—loyal, hard-working but unquestioning of the world around him—was both a tribute to and a condemnation of the working class that Orwell felt could be led into tyrannical directions. This came from his interpretations of the rise of both the radical left *and* the radical right. Attending a meeting of the British Union of Fascists in 1936, Orwell heard their leader Oswald Mosley deliver "the usual clap trap—Empire free trade, down with the Jew and the foreigner, higher wages and shorter hours all round" (*CEJL* 1:203). The crowd did not share Orwell's negative verdict however: "after the preliminary booing the (mainly) working-class audience was easily bamboozled by M[osley] speaking from as it were a Socialist angle, condemning the treachery of successive governments towards the workers" (*CEJL* 1:203). He was "loudly clapped at the end" (*CEJL* 1:203). Orwell's belief in education for the masses was about their liberation but likewise born of the sort of noblesse oblige he sometimes criticized.

Orwell was also writing at a time when many on the British left remained impressed by Stalin. Future Labour Cabinet Minister Barbara Castle had found visiting the Soviet Union in 1937 a positive experience. Meanwhile, the Fabian thinkers Beatrice and Sidney Webb had asked whether the USSR, after their own visit in 1932, could even be called a *New Civilisation* (1). Even Alice Bacon, redoubtable figure of the postwar Labour right, found Stalin "considerate, friendly [and] polite" on her own visit to Moscow in 1946 (Reeves and Carr 74). For Orwell, in writing *Animal Farm*, it was therefore "of the utmost importance . . . that people in Western Europe should see the Soviet regime for what it really was." And "since 1930" he had "seen little evidence that the USSR was progressing towards anything that one could truly call Socialism" (*CEJL* 3:404). As Labour moved toward a more moderate, market-friendly position in the 1950s, the chance of communistic sleeper cells taking over the party and leading Britain into Stalinism receded, but Orwell's contempt for the USSR's useful idiots would likely have continued into the era of Tony Benn and Militant had he lived long enough.

As it was, though references to *Animal Farm* continued after Orwell's death in 1950, the period of postwar consensus in British politics kept them generally limited. One example occurred in 1960 when Fenner Brockway, the leftist Labour MP, took a trip to Malta where he witnessed the annual May Day parade of school children. When Brockway saw Maltese government officials remove Labour Party ties from some boys on account of their political overtones he became incensed. As the Conservative parliamentary benches laughed off the incident, he asked the House of Commons, "is it not time that these *Animal Farm* stupidities were ended under the dictatorship in Malta, where they bring ridicule on the Government even in the minds of the children?" (Hansard, col. 210). The Conservative minister charged with answering agreed that applying any ban on political uniforms to the ties of children "would be taking it a little far" (Hansard, col. 210). Yet, while no doubt interesting, this was hardly grandiose stuff. Indeed, moving into the 1980s, the future Labour shadow foreign secretary Gerald Kaufman later used Orwell's story to denounce the then Thatcher government's crude approach to state spending. As he told the Commons in 1983, "the Government have now divided local government expenditure into two distinct categories. Capital spending—as we are insistently told—is virtuous, and every council should do as much capital spending as possible. Current expenditure, however, is wicked, and only the most depraved councils will indulge in that forbidden vice. Such a crude categorisation is as unthinking and therefore as totalitarian as Snowball's slogan in *Animal Farm*: Four legs good, two legs bad." (Hansard, col. 739). Again, then, *Animal Farm*'s political use in the period up to the toppling of the Berlin Wall was as a useful retort on some issue of the day, rather than to score a meaningful ideological hit. Politicians had read the book and were quite prepared to misapply it. Its relevance seemed on the wane.

The 1990s, however, saw something of a serious return to political discourse for *Animal Farm*, no doubt partly inspired by Britain being governed by a prime minister called Old Major. In this case however, Old Major was the successor to the old prophet Thatcher. Famously, John Major's Conservative premiership would be riven with difficulties: a small and decreasing parliamentary majority on the one hand, a noisy and growing argument within the party on Britain's role within the European Union on the other. When asked what the mood was like in 1995, one anonymous Tory MP told the *Observer* newspaper that "it's like *Animal Farm*. They're all in the truck on the way to the knacker's yard—and the pigs are squealing" (Wheen 7). This metaphor of course fell down since the only creature who ended up in the knacker's yard was Boxer the horse, and the pigs did not squeal since they had condemned him to this fate. But around the fiftieth anniversary of Orwell's book his work demonstrably came back into fashion.

Still, whatever its then problems, at least the right was complaining from a position of power. The post-Cold War debate over what left-wing parties should do in an age where they had so often lost (four successive elections from 1979 to 1992 in the UK, three from 1980 to 1988 in the US), and where the Soviet Union had collapsed under its own contradictions, reignited interest in Orwell too. With Bill Clinton finally taking the Democrats to victory on a moderate platform in the US in 1992, and Tony Blair doing something similar in the UK, questions over ideology erupted in the mid-1990s. Much of this played out in the factionalism of the British left. As the *Guardian* reported in March 1995, an assistant of the veteran left-wing Labour MP Tony Benn had drawn up a list of policies where there was supposedly little difference between Blair's New Labour (a term redolent with Orwellian ambiguity) and various Conservative manifestos issued since the war (26). *The Guardian* article began with a riff on the end of *Animal Farm* where the creatures looked from "pig to man, and man to pig and pig to man again; but already it was impossible to say which was which."

As the *Guardian* slyly remarked, however, "if only the parallel from *Animal Farm* applied. In fact, those Tory manifestos from the fifties look rather radical by comparison with the new socialist vision" (26).

By whatever means Tony Blair was indeed rekindling an interest in Eric Blair. In 2000 various Labour MPs were asked what books they would recommend reading. Bob Marshall Andrews, whom we shall turn to shortly, eschewed Orwell in choosing Francis Wheen's (then recent) biography of Karl Marx. But another Labour MP, David Kidney, did choose *Animal Farm*. On March 9, 2000, the *Guardian* noted that its portrayal of a "hated *ancien* regime [being] overthrown—but the new bosses adopt the ways of the old masters" had something of a parallel to the way the Blair government had co-opted aspects of the conservatism of Margaret Thatcher and John Major (12). Kidney, however, thought otherwise: "I don't think it has any particular lessons for the Labour party now" (12). In any event, as the same article observed, Labour MPs were by then "falling over themselves to endorse a public schoolboy called Harry Potter" (12).

For Conservative MPs after Blair won power in 1997, *Animal Farm* remained useful as a way to indicate the Labour government's real agenda—generally felt to be cloaking old Labour solutions of nationalization in a fig leaf of new market-friendly language. For Howard Flight, the Blair government's willingness to interfere in nominally independent transport delivery agencies indicated "another case of *Animal Farm* language" (Hansard, col. 590). Equally, when it came to the appropriate relationship between the government and the private sector as to the running of Britain's railways, Blair's Third Way had produced a situation where the future Cabinet Minister Eric Pickles felt he was "living on the last page of George Orwell's *Animal Farm*, when it was no longer possible to tell the pigs from the people" (Hansard, col. 441). Since it was no longer possible to portray Labour, as Vansittart had hinted at in the 1940s, as truly on the path to Napoleon's dictatorship, *Animal Farm* had been reduced to its most famous lines.

Intriguingly, of course, Orwell's initial path to socialism somewhat mirrored Blair's. As he wrote in the Ukrainian preface to

Animal Farm, "up to 1930 I did not on the whole look upon myself as a socialist. In fact I had as yet no clearly defined political views" (*CEJL* 3:403). Instead, he became a socialist "more out of disgust with the way the poorer section of the industrial workers were oppressed and neglected than out of any theoretical admiration for a planned society" (*CEJL* 3:403). It is true that Orwell had immersed himself in the world of *Wigan Pier* to a degree that exceeded Tony Blair, but the two also had much of their worldview framed by exposure to the hard left. Blair's brief flirtation while a student at Oxford in the 1970s (a time when he spouted "the usual Marxist line" on the state taking over from the interests of a capitalism "which cared only about profit") had shown him that sections of the hard left preferred ideological purity to actually gaining power and effecting change (Blair 79).

Blair's centrism aside, the second launching pad to a reconsideration of Orwell in British politics was the attack on the Twin Towers by al-Qaeda. In the post-9/11 climate, many British MPs began to use *Animal Farm* as an allegory not just for the misuse of state power but for the repressive nature of this power being justified by some external threat. As Bob Marshall Andrews noted in 2004, "terrorism has two weapons. The first is the wanton, atrocious infliction of violence." The second was to use the fear of such violence "to make [Western governments] react by passing legislation that attacks the very values and principles that are the basis of those democratic societies" (Hansard, col. 1134). The contemporary example he had in mind here was "Guantanamo Bay . . . an institution in which al-Qaeda must glory and rejoice every single day, for the effortless recruitment—and in many ways, the legitimate recruitment—that it brings about to the ranks of those who protest" (Hansard, col. 1134). Here he utilized two of Orwell's publications. As he told the House of Commons, "it is not new that politicians should use fear of outside forces to pass draconian legislation or to enjoy abuse of power. In *Animal Farm* the pigs maintained order not by brute force, but by the persistent fear of the return of the farmer" (Hansard, col. 1134). Equally, "in *1984* Big Brother maintained his power not by brute force, but because of the unspecified fear of other, countervailing forces in the world—unspecified and probably non-existent" (Hansard, col. 1134).

Orwell's work, like any other, is ripe for reinterpretation. Its revisiting in the 1990s and 2000s reflects in part, of course, the "end of history" as chronicled by Francis Fukuyamain 1992. After the collapse of the Cold War, Western democracy had won the big arguments over a now almost defunct global communism and certainly defeated European fascism. Thus the only threats were in the imagined future.Yet such a position overlooks the fact that Jones had indeed *been* a threat, and the other farmers were a *current* threat. The Hitler-like Mr Frederick would likely have installed a dictatorship worse than even Jones—proactively cruel rather than lazy. Working out whom to empower, amid this atmosphere, is not easy.

We have thus arrived at a politics where the dreams of the early revolution seem impossible, and where the battles for freedom are as remote as the Cowshed skirmish that cemented the new regime of *Animal Farm*. Likewise, the horrors of Napoleon's imposed dictatorship on the one hand and Snowball's state-directed quackery on the other are deemed beyond the pale. So, what comes next? The closest we may aim for, arguably, is a coalition of the Mollies and the Boxers. This may be imperfect. It may on occasion reward frippery and lead to an imbalance of resource. But the alternatives—Jones on the one hand, the pigs on the other—are not worth thinking about. New Labour and the New Democrats were often criticized for Orwellian doublespeak, not least by the right, but this was a divide they more or less managed to bridge.

Works Cited

Anonymous, "Smallweed," *The Guardian* [London], 25 March 1995, p. 26.

Blair, Tony. *A Journey*. Arrow Books, 2011.

Carr, Richard. *Charlie Chaplin: A Political Biography from Victorian Britain to Modern America*. Routledge, 2017.

Claeys, Gregory. "The Lion and the Unicorn: Patriotism and Orwell's Politics," *Review of Politics*, vol. 47, no. 2, April 1985, pp.186-211.

Davison, Peter. *George Orwell: A Literary Life*. Palgrave Macmillan, 1996.

Denham, Jess. "George Orwell's Animal Farm Tops List of the Nation's Favourite Books." *The Independent* [London], 21 April 2016, p.36.

Fukuyama, Francis. *The End of History and the Last Man*. Free Press, 1992.

Hansard. *House of Commons Parliamentary Debates*. vol. 152, col. 470. 5 Nov. 1947.

_____. *House of Commons Parliamentary Debates*. vol. 624, col. 210, 24 May 1960.

_____. *House of Commons Parliamentary Debates*. vol. 41, col. 739. 26 1983.

_____. *House of Commons Parliamentary Debates*. vol. 309, col. 441. 25 March 1998.

_____. *House of Commons Parliamentary Debates*, vol. 382, col. 590. 25 March 2002.

_____. *House of Commons Parliamentary Debates*. vol. 416, col. 1134. 19 Jan. 2004.

Hayek, Friedrich von. *The Road to Serfdom*. Routledge, 1944.

Gibbons, Fiachra. "Potter Mania Grips New Labour." *The Guardian* [London], 9 March 2000, p.12.

Letemendia, Clare. "Revolution on Animal Farm: Orwell's Neglected Commentary," *Journal of Modern Literature*, vol. 18, no. 1, Winter 1992, pp. 127-37.

Orwell, Sonia, and Ian Angus, editors. *The Collected Essays, Journalism and Letters of George Orwell*, four volumes. Secker & Warburg, 1970.

Reeves, Rachel, and Richard Carr. *Alice in Westminster: The Political Life of Alice Bacon*. Tauris. 2018.

Scheall, Scott. "Hayek's Epistemic Theory of Industrial Fluctuation." *History of Economic Ideas*, vol. 23, no. 1, 2015, pp. 101-24.

Skidelsky, Robert, *Keynes: The Return of the Master*. Allen Lane, 2009.

Webb, Beatrice, and Sidney Webb. *Soviet Communism: A New Civilisation?* Fabian Society, 1935.

Wheen, Francis. "Major Example of Pig's Will." *The Observer* [London]. 21 June 1995, p. 7.

The Typecasting of Female Characters in George Orwell's *Animal Farm* and Disney's *Zootopia*

Melanie A. Marotta

In his beast fables, Aesop tells stories of animals that behave as humans; ultimately, the purpose of the works is to send Aesop's listeners (before being transcribed, Aesop's fables were told through oral narration) lessons regarding communal conduct, thereby ending with the moral. In *Animal Farm*, George Orwell follows the route Aesop takes by creating a farm run by animals in order to highlight the ills of Marxism-Leninism and elitism. Notably, Orwell uses this structure to comment on the roles of women. Included within Orwell's postmodern novel are the horses Mollie and Clover, the sheep, the cat, the hens, and Muriel the goat. While the male characters stand in the forefront as the leaders, it is the female members of the community who defy typecasting and rebel against the ideology set in place by Napoleon. This essay examines *Animal Farm* in conjunction with Disney's *Zootopia* (2016) to highlight Orwell's protofeminism. Like *Animal* Farm, *Zootopia* offers a beast fable set in what is supposed to be a utopian space. Like Orwell's animals, the *Zootopia* characters soon discover that their perception of the idyllic space is incorrect. In both works it is the female characters that ensure that flawed utopian spaces are exposed and that stereotypes regarding women are defied. Since both Orwell's novel and Pixar's film channel Aesop's animal creations, the Aesop construction must be examined.

Unfortunately, not a great deal about Aesop can be authenticated. Much of what has been ascertained comes from the biography *The Life of Aesop* (ca. first century BCE). It contains a glorified story of the exploits of Aesop, a Greek slave, portrayed heroically until betrayed by a group of Grecians and sent to his death. According to legend, Aesop was framed for theft by Delphinians after he obtained the favor of the court. Ironically, one of the reasons that Aesop dies is because of jealousy over his expertise in giving advice. In reference to the beast fable popularized by Aesop, Joseph Jacobs offers the following assertion: "The Fable is most effective as a literary or oratorical weapon under despotic governments allowing no free speech. A tyrant cannot take notice of a Fable without putting on the cap that fits" (qtd. in Patterson 17). Jacobs's observation regarding the fable as a tool for detractors explains why Aesop became legendary.

Although Aesop's precise ethnicity cannot be verified, readers of his biographical details often infer that he was black and is an early version of the so-called Magical Negro. In reference to this character construct, Afrofuturist Nnedi Okorafor-Mbachu documents a conversation she had with science fiction writer Steven Barnes: "He [Barnes] explained that a Magical Negro was a black character—usually depicted as wiser and spiritually deeper than the white protagonist—whose purpose in the plot was to help the protagonist get out of trouble, to help the protagonist realize his own faults and overcome them." Annabel Patterson delineates the source material regarding Aesop's life, observing that academics are divided with regard to "Aesop's ugliness—a mixture of actual deformity and racial stereotypification" (21). Maria Tatar comments on the place of Aesop's origin, whether it be Phrygia, Thrace, or Libya: "Aesop . . . remains something of an enigma. We know very little about the man and do not have a single tale written in his hand. The name, in fact, may be nothing more than a construct, much like Mother Goose." Whether authentic or formulated, Aesop appears as the storyteller figure, one who imparts wisdom to his adult audience.

As with other famed figures such as Richard III, Aesop was marked by disability, both physical and verbal. Rosemarie Garland Thomson, a prominent disability studies theorist, presents theories as to why people stare in *Staring: How We Look*. Thomson proposes that people stare because they are inquisitive, specifically seeking knowledge. Thomson states that people with disabilities have been concealed as many do not wish to look upon them, but others cannot help but to stare: "The visibly disabled body intrudes on our routine visual landscape and compels our attention, often obscuring the personhood of its bearer" (ch. 1). Thomson continues by noting that concealment may also happen when individuals undergo "normalizing medical procedures that erase disability" (ch. 1). In traditional Grecian style, a deity rewards the verbally impaired Aesop with the ability to speak, "the mute Aesop treated a priestess of the goddess Isis with such kindness that he was rewarded with the gift of speech" (Gibbs ix). However, this ability becomes problematic in the long run. As the gods are famed for assisting humans while also causing them problems, once Aesop obtains speech he is sold because he dared to criticize the slaves' overseer (Gibbs ix).

Aesop has been othered from the beginning and remains so for the rest of his life. He stands as a symbol of morality but, as one of the marginalized, from the periphery. Concerning his enslavement, Patterson writes that "he is sold as a slave to a renowned philosopher, Xanthus of Samos, whom he entertains with his witty tricks, solutions to problems, and general one-upmanship" (16). Once he gains his voice—his ability to verbally articulate and to impart wisdom—he is symbolically "concealed" by a stereotype (Thomson ch. 1). Sold to the philosopher, Aesop is regarded as a Magical Negro because of his role as advisor to the higher-ranking philosopher, who also has a lighter complexion. "The Magical Negro has great power and wisdom, yet he or she only uses it to help the white main character; he or she is not threatening because he or she only seeks to help, never hurt" (Okorafor-Mbachu). Even though Aesop stands for wisdom and acts as the voice of morality for others, he is oppressed and held against his will. If examined through the lens of Thomson's theory and the Magical Negro construct, Aesop is only permitted to reach a larger audience when he may assist authoritative Grecians. As Patterson points out, "Aesop quickly acquires an international reputation as a counselor to kings and city states, which eventually becomes his undoing" (16). If Aesop is seen as a quasi-historical figure, it is plausible that he is meant to represent the disadvantaged, to become a voice for those oppressed as in Orwell's anti-utopian *Animal Farm*.

Lyman Tower Sargent defines the utopia as "a non-existent society described in considerable detail and normally located in time and space" ("Three Faces" 9). Thomas More's *Utopia* (1516) is the most famed of the utopian literary creations. Sargent asserts that More "invented the genre," and that this creation offered his audience an alternative to sixteenth-century England ("Three Faces" 9). Famously critiqued, Orwell formats his novel as an allusion to Marxism-Leninism to suggest the detrimental effects that this political system could have if instituted in Britain. Peter Fitting connects the Soviet Union to the anti-utopia: it "was the Russian Revolution of 1917, which produced a living and breathing alternative to capitalism" and offers *Nineteen Eighty-Four* (1949), another of Orwell's texts, as a noteworthy example of the anti-utopian genre (139). Fitting emphasizes that while "The critique of contemporary society expressed in the dystopia implies (or asserts) the need for change; the anti-utopia is, on the other hand, explicitly or implicitly a defense of the status quo" (141). If *Animal Farm* may be seen as an anti-utopia, then Orwell is channeling Aesop, imparting through his "fairy story" wisdom regarding the implementation of Soviet-style communism in Britain. Calling Orwell's work "An attack on the myth of the nobility of Soviet communism," Russell Baker asserts that "*Animal Farm* became one of the century's most devastating literary acts of political destruction" (vi).

C. M. Woodhouse questions Orwell's reasoning for the subtitle's inclusion and debates whether the text may be considered a fairy story or even a fable. Woodhouse offers the following observation regarding the fairy story: "It is a transcription of a view of life into terms of highly simplified symbols; and when it succeeds in its literary purpose, it leaves us with a deep indefinable sense of truth; and, if it succeeds also, as Orwell set out to do, in a political as well as an artistic purpose, it leaves us also with a feeling of rebelliousness against the truth revealed" (xxiii-xxiv). According to Woodhouse, since no moral is imparted to the audience, Orwell's work leans away from the fable and more toward the fairy story (xxii). Yet Orwell does offer his readers a moral. Orwell's anti-utopian novel is a diatribe implicitly deconstructing the Stalinist system, which is hidden behind the farm renamed Animal Farm. The fairy story here is that Stalinism offers for its adherents Sargent's definition of a utopia as a myth, a "non-existent good place," that fools the animals of Manor Farm into believing that the pigs offer a preferable alternative to their current indentured servitude. According to Gibbs, "The encounters between the animals are not determined by any kind of rigid formula in Aesop: you can never be sure of what is going to happen when a wolf encounters a sheep, or when the donkey challenges the lion" (xix). As Snowball is a voice of reason and is martyred in Orwell's work, Orwell suggests the clichéd moral that appearances may be deceiving.

Kate Pollitt's concept of the Smurfette principle provides a useful way to understand gender politics in *Animal Farm*. According to Pollitt, "Contemporary shows are either essentially all-male, like "Garfield," or are organized on what I call the Smurfette principle: a group of male buddies will be accented by a lone female, stereotypically defined." The Smurfette principle applies both to Orwell's story and to *Zootopia*. Nevertheless, Orwell's portrayal of the female characters is more forward-thinking than that of Pixar.

This does not mean that Orwell was free of sexism. The female characters on Orwell's Manor Farm are outnumbered by the male characters, both animal and human, and not featured as prominently. As Pollitt explains, "The message is clear. Boys are the norm, *girls the variation*; boys are central, girls peripheral; boys are individuals, girls types. Boys define the group, its story and its code of values. Girls exist only in relation to boys" (emphasis added). As the farm's animals enter the barn, the narrator describes each, offering commentary regarding their physical appearance and mental acuity. Once again, the reader is reminded of Orwell's space as anti-utopian. Sargent observes that "Utopias are reflections of the issues that were important to the period in which their authors lived" (*Utopianism*). Orwell's satirical work regarding totalitarianism came early in the British postmodernist movement. While *Animal Farm* retains a traditional format, its narrator—like the author—is unreliable. In his analysis of a selection of Orwell's most influential essays peppered with anecdotes from Orwell's life, Louis Menard documents the lack of accuracy and the unpredictable nature of his views: "The point is not that Orwell made things up. The point is that he used writing in a literary, not a documentary way; he wrote in order to make you see what he wanted you to see, to persuade." The farm is shown as a false utopia for both human and animal, a representation of capitalism in the first and Stalinism in the second. Orwell shows readers why these political systems are so tempting and how they only offer objectification to women in particular.

While the females are typecast in the beginning of Orwell's morality tale, they, for the most part, are the ones who ultimately rebel against their anti-utopian society. Sargent notes that "When a convinced utopian tries to build a eutopia, conflict will arise because, failing to achieve eutopia, he or she will use force to achieve it" ("Three Faces" 24). For Mr. Jones, Manor Farm is a utopian space: he is the lord of the manor. Jones thinks that his position is secure through the threat and action of physical abuse. The theme of consumption appears throughout Orwell's text, showing its connection to Jones's corruption. He is a flawed leader, attributes that Napoleon takes on once he replaces Jones. As John Sutherland observes, "Manor Farm was once owned by aristocrats—lords of the manor. Hence its name. Before the 'Rebellion' it has become the property of a gentleman farmer, who is in fact, a drunken, philistine brute, lower, morally, than the animals he owns and exploits." Jones uses fear to enact control over his subjects—the animals—and in turn they scare him away to create their version of a utopian space.

Once the lights in the farmhouse are out, Orwell's cast of characters is introduced. Importantly, Orwell famously enjoyed the animals he had on his property, especially Muriel the goat. Orwell kept a diary, now a part of UCL library's special collections, in which he documented the happenings on his farm in Wallington, Britain. The entry from May 29, 1939, concerns Muriel's breeding and the animosity between the goat and a cow. Orwell used his experiences on this farm as the basis for his novel. When Orwell records Muriel's actions in the diary entry, he personifies her. Orwell anthropomorphizes his animals, utilizing them much in the same manner as Aesop to send a message to his readers about the objectification of animals for monetary gain. As the narrator relates the order in which the animals enter for their meeting, Old

Major is described in great detail; the narrator calls attention to his girth and intelligence. The female animals trail behind Old Major, receiving very little description. The description of Clover is telling as it shows a common attribute for almost all of the female animals: "Clover was a stout motherly mare approaching middle life, who had never quite got her figure back after her fourth foal" (Orwell 4). As Joan Gordon documents (331), Orwell expresses the capitalist relationship between Jones and the female animals. By this point in the novel, there are three female characters of note: Clover, Mollie, and the cat.

Clover represents the commodification of the female as the breeder, a fact that does not alter once Manor becomes Animal Farm. Here her body is deconstructed, making her a sum of her parts. Unlike Old Major who is also characterized as being "stout," the narrator criticizes Clover's shape, demeaning her. This description of Clover would resonate with female readers as this comment about her body shape after giving birth is one often levied at women. The female characters in this novel are primarily presented as breeders and mothers. In his speech to the animals, Old Major's rhetoric enables the reader to connect the animals' position on Manor Farm to enslavement. Since Aesop was a slave, it is fitting that Orwell approaches the capitalist section of the novel as an argument against slavery. In the twentieth and twenty-first centuries, many animal activists utilize language that connects the consumption of animals and animal testing to animal enslavement. During Old Major's speech, the animals verbally assert that their bodies have been commodified by Jones, which is one of the reasons for the Rebellion. Later, under Napoleon's rule, the bodies of the females in particular continue to be commodified, but more overtly so. It is these bodies that the female animals use to rebel against Napoleon's tyranny.

Moments before Old Major's speech, motherless ducklings enter the barn, confused as they have no guide (their mother died). Clover, the moral center of Orwell's novel, takes it upon herself to act as a surrogate mother for them. Daphne Patai compares the horses, Boxer and Clover, citing inequality in their portrayal (206).

Fundamental to Orwellian scholars is Patai's examination of the masculine and feminine in the author's body of work. Referencing Boxer first, Patai indicates that his superhuman physical feats as indicative of the masculine, citing his friendship with Benjamin integral to his patriarchal design (207, 215). Patai next examines Clover, pointing out that her commendable actions are those that are associated with femininity, citing the roles of mother and wife. Referring to the ducklings scene, Patai notes, "Orwell here attributes to the maternal female domination over the moral sphere but without any power to implement her values" (206). At the meeting in an action of protection for the ducklings, Clover uses her body both to shield them from harm and to offer them comfort. Notably, it is the horses who are described as "faithful disciples" of the pigs; they lack intelligence but not loyalty (18). Throughout the novel, Boxer suffers on account of his unfailing loyalty; he realizes too late that the pigs are having him carted away to the glue factory to die. Clover, on the other hand, identifies difficulties within the pigs' ideology, thereby suggesting to others that the system may be flawed and the animals may be exploited. While Patai may find Clover ineffective, in actuality Clover works to guarantee life to future generations. Clover's work on more than one occasion, including the communal gathering at the conclusion, serves to safeguard those who remain behind. *Animal Farm* ends with the pigs and man, but beforehand it is the community led by Clover that literally sees the truth behind Manor Farm and offers an inkling of hope for the future.

Alex Woloch points out that "[Orwell] casts himself, and his writing project, against the Soviet Union because it does *not* resemble 'anything that one can truly call Socialism' (88) but has, instead, contributed so much to the corruption of the original idea of Socialism' (88)" (Woloch 39). Orwell demonstrates the animalist community's lack of equality through his depiction of female animals taking on the position not only of provider but also of caregiver. Clover has had children under the capitalist system; their eventual whereabouts is unknown. The cows' milk is stolen by Napoleon immediately after the overthrow of Jones. Revealingly, a hen calls for the milk to be shared among the animals, equating the female perspective with egalitarianism, but Napoleon commandeers the milk for himself. Later, it is the hens who are portrayed as the dissenters. When Napoleon increases egg production to an astounding amount and is about to claim the fertilized eggs, the soon-to-be mothers are incensed: "For the first time since the expulsion of Jones, there was something resembling a rebellion" (Orwell 76). Napoleon's demands result in the hens laying their eggs in a space where they can be destroyed rather than stolen. Napoleon's response is to withhold food from the hens. After five days the hens' strike (during which nine hens died) ends. In order to be seen as more than a money-making machine and to save future children from death, the hens risked death themselves. Later, in a moment of shared trauma bonding, the hens that masterminded the plan "stated that Snowball had appeared to them in a dream and incited them to disobey Napoleon's orders" (Orwell 84). The hens martyr themselves for their cause as does a sheep that relates to Napoleon her defilement of his drinking water.

Ultimately, it is Clover who stands out for her defiant actions against Napoleon and his rule. The narrator describes Clover's advancing age near the close of the novel: "Clover was an old stout mare now, stiff in the joints and with a tendency to rheumy eyes" (127). As Animal Farm regresses to a capitalist state, Clover's sight fades. Orwell creates a Tiresias-like character with Clover; even though she is visually impaired, she is the only character that is able to see what is happening. When Boxer is overworking himself, thereby risking his health, Clover speaks to him about it. Later, when it is discovered that the pigs are living in the house and using the beds, an act expressly forbidden, Clover seeks further explanation from the animals' commandments. She asks for assistance from Muriel, since she is able to read but little and is confused when she does not recall the alteration made to the commandment. It is also Clover who attempts to warn Boxer that he is about to die, though regrettably her realization comes too late. In both *Animals Farm* and *Zootopia*, the female animals are responsible for unearthing corruption, thus becoming in their own way like Aesop.

Zootopia has been heralded in numerous reviews as a cinematic creation that asserts inclusivity for its young viewers. In fact, the film won an Oscar for the best animated film. Interestingly, for a film that garnered such interest from adults, there was little merchandizing for children, who should be Pixar's primary audience. While numerous reviews of the film contend that this Pixar product affirms twenty-first-century values for children, namely inclusive versus discriminatory actions, the viewer is unable to get past the stereotypes perpetuated. Pollitt indicates that "The sexism in preschool culture deforms both boys and girls. Little girls split their consciousness, filtering their dreams and ambitions through boy characters while admiring the clothes of the princess." The film begins with young bunny Judy Hopps and two classmates reenacting the unification of the animals in their supposedly utopian space. While Judy is the star of the show, it is problematic that when the predator and prey portion is discussed, the male tiger is the predator and Judy is the prey. In their review of the film, Gregory Beaudine, Oyemolade Osibodu, and Aliya Beavers note, much as David Crewe does, the purposeful inclusion of offensive constructs (230). Coincidently, both reviews are directed toward an audience of educators. Offering justification for the incorporation of this typecasting is deeply problematic, as this film is intended for children. Beaudine et al. state that Judy becomes a police officer because of the "Mammal Inclusion Initiative" and that she is "a creature of unassuming stature—physically cute, small, and youthful—and it is always a *bunny*, never a *rabbit*" (230). The writers highlight Judy's ability to excel in the police academy; they also label her an "underdog" and note her admission is due to a program that is meant to represent Affirmative Action (228). Judy spends the majority of the film looking foolish in her attire, which is a crop-top bulletproof vest, when she is not wearing her orange vest as a meter maid. In the elephant ice cream shop Judy defends Nick Wilde, a fox and predator, because she believes he is subject to discrimination. The female bunny appears as protector, but the moment is fleeting. Nick has duped her, giving the male a place of superiority over the ignorant-of-the-ways-the-world-works female bunny. Unlike Clover, who is able to ascertain the problematic system set in place by the pigs, Judy cannot solve the case of the missing animals without the help of her male predator counterpart.

In Orwell's creation and in the film, each space—the farm and Zootopia—exists as an anti-utopia. Despite the goal of a society based on equality, both Orwell and Pixar display that there are those within who render it an impossibility. When the pigs sup with the humans at the close of Orwell's novel, Clover leads the animals to observe the two groups together in a state of comradery. The future is ominous inside the farmhouse as the pigs, consumed by their own self-importance, change the name back to Manor Farm. Outside, with both Old Major and Boxer gone, Clover leads the group. Ultimately, Orwell's work offers criticism of political systems, but there is hope for gender equality. Judy is not so fortunate. While Judy and her new partner, Nick, are rewarded at the close of the film with an actual case and Judy gets to drive the police vehicle, Nick makes a joke about bunnies being "bad drivers." The derogatory comment precedes a moment of flirtation between the partners before they race off after a speeding car into the proverbial sunset. *Zootopia*'s demeaning portrayal of females offers a poor look at the twenty-first century whereas Orwell's twentieth-century novel is, fascinatingly, more forward-thinking.

Works Cited

Baker, Russell. Preface. *Animal Farm*. Signet, 1996.

Beaudine, Gregory, Oyemolade Osibodu, and Aliya Beavers. "Disney's Metaphorical Exploration of Racism and Stereotypes: A Review of *Zootopia*." *Comparative Education Review* vol. 61, no. 1, 2017, pp. 227-34. www.journals.uchicago.edu/t-and-c.

Crewe, David. Animal Harm: "Discrimination and Difference in *Zootopia*." *Screen Education*, no. 84, 2016, pp. 26-35.

Gibbs, Laura. Introduction. *Aesop's Fables*. Translated by Laura Gibbs, Oxford UP, 2002.

Gordon, Joan. "Animal Studies." *The Routledge Companion to Science Fiction*. Edited by Mark Bould et al., Routledge, 2009, pp. 331-40.

Fitting, Peter. "Utopia, Dystopia and Science Fiction." *The Cambridge Companion to Utopian Literature*. Edited by Gregory Claeys, Cambridge UP, 2010, pp. 135-53.

Menard, Louis. "Honest, Decent, Wrong: The Invention of George Orwell." *The New Yorker*, 27 Jan. 2003. www.newyorker.com/magazine/2003/01/27/honest-decent-wrong.

Okorafor-Mbachu, Nnedi. "Stephen King's Super-Duper Magical Negroes." *Strange Horizons*, 25 Oct. 2004. web.archive.org/web/20061114013842/http://ww.strangehorizons.com/2004/20041025/kinga.shtml.

Orwell, George. *Animal Farm*. 1945. Signet, 1996.

_____. Domestic Diary 1939-40. UCL Library Special Collections. www.bl.uk/collection-items/orwells-domestic-diary-1939-40.

Patai, Daphne. *The Orwell Mystique: A Study in Male Ideology*. U of Massachusetts P, 1984.

Patterson, Annabel. *Fables of Power: Aesopian Writing and Political History*. Duke UP, 1991.

Pollitt, Kate. "Hers; The Smurfette Principle." *New York Times Magazine*, 7 Apr. 1991. www.nytimes.com/1991/04/07/magazine/hers-the-smurfette-principle.html.

Sargent, Lyman Tower. "The Three Faces of Utopianism Revisited." *Utopian Studies*. vol. 5, no. 1, 1994, pp. 1-37.

_____. *Utopianism: A Very Short Introduction*, Oxford UP, 2010. Kindle.

Sutherland, John. "An Introduction to Animal Farm." *British Library*. www.bl.uk/20th-century-literature/articles/an-introduction-to-animal-farm.

Tatar, Maria. "All the Wiser." *New York Times*, 10 Nov. 2011. www.nytimes.com/2011/11/13/books/review/variations-on-aesops-fables.html.

Thomson, Rosemarie Garland. *Staring: How We Look*. Oxford UP, 2009. Kindle.

Woloch, Alex. *Or Orwell: Writing and Democratic Socialism*, Harvard UP, 2016.

Woodhouse, C. M. Introduction. *Animal Farm*. Signet, 1996, pp. xv-xxvii.

Tensions, Tenor, and Vehicle: *Animal Farm* and the Evolution of the Animal Fable_____

Josephine A. McQuail

Orwell's *Animal Farm* is one of the best-known animal stories or beast fables of the twentieth century. The ancient Greek Aesop (620-549 BCE) wrote—or maybe just collected—*Fables*, but they may be much older. In classical Greece and Rome, humans were generally thought to be superior to animals because humans possessed reason, so the popularity of Aesop's *Fables* was ironic. Perhaps because they were not considered cultured, Aesop's tales were passed down orally, many not written down until the Middle Ages. These tales are so pervasive in Western culture that many popular children's books, such as *Town Mouse Country Mouse* by Jan Brett, actually derive from Aesop. Almost every animal tale today in the Western world can be attributed in one way or another to Aesop, and Orwell's novella is no exception. Each of Aesop's fables comes with a moral at the end, but the morals of the different tales are sometimes contradictory and lack internal coherence, which may be because Aesop collected rather than authored them. Orwell's *Animal Farm* or, as he subtitled it, "A Fairy Story," has also provoked much critical controversy and debate. Most agree that Orwell's work is a satire that targets the Soviet Union and its inception via the Russian Revolution. There is disagreement about whether it is a masterpiece or a failure, yet the book has never been out of print since Orwell published it (after some difficulty) in 1945. As with Aesop's *Fables* the key motif that fascinates in *Animal Farm* is that of the humanized animals.

The Human Fascination with the Animal
The fascination with animals as a parallel to the human condition predates even Aesop and abides today. Animals are not just passively used as objects and symbols in human history to be literally or figuratively consumed by people but play a vital role in humanity's conception of itself. When one thinks of some of the earliest records

---

of humanity, such as Neolithic cave paintings where animals are depicted in living color, clearly human identification with animals goes back at least tens of thousands of years. With the animal rights movement stronger today than perhaps ever in human history, the anthropologist Claude Levi-Strauss's somewhat dismissive and oft-quoted observation that "animals are good to think [with]" (qtd. in Hill 118) has a different resonance today than it did when Orwell wrote his novel. We can trace the specific qualities of animals that are associated with certain human characteristics back to totemic beliefs of ancient peoples.

In his introduction to an edition of *Aesop's Fables*, G. K. Chesterton tries to get at how animal fables convey meaning: "They must be like abstractions in algebra, or like pieces in chess. The lion must always be stronger than the wolf, just as four is always the double of two. The fox in a fable must move crooked, just as the knight in chess must move crooked. The sheep in a fable must march on, just as the pawn in chess must march on." Chesterton points to exactly those aspects of animal symbolism that could be called cliché or maybe iconic. He goes on to say that in fables the sheep must stay sheepish and the lion strong. In their introduction to a collection of essays entitled *Thinking with Animals*, Lorraine Daston and Gregg Mitman call this "hyperhumanizing" animals through "caricature" (9). They theorize that if a human protagonist were used in a story to illustrate a certain point, that essential quality of the particular animal in a fable would be lost in the clutter of human attributes necessary to characterization in realistic fiction. Often animal protagonists serve to distance us from behaviors in humans that we have gotten too used to, an effect called defamiliarization, so that human behavior can be critiqued more easily. Thus, animal tales are often satirical.

The Beast Fable and the Rise of Children's Literature

Let's remember that Orwell included as a subtitle, "A Fairy Story," which adds to the irony of *Animal Farm*, for fairy stories were thought to be idle fantasy. Despite the tendency to think also of the beast fable as mere fantasy, as far back as Aesop animal stories served as allegory for human behavior and qualities, cautionary tales of what not to be. It was really in the beginning of the eighteenth century that the animal fable had a resurgence. This was no coincidence, for as children's literature as a genre had its birth, animal tales became something that children could easily identify with. However, the eighteenth century is known as the neoclassical period for the rebirth of classical values of reason and the rediscovery of the principles of science. The value that neoclassicism placed on logic was mocked by animal tales and fairy stories. A certain tension existed between the high culture values of society at large and the low culture folktales.

Orwell, by making his adult tale take the guise of a children's story, implicitly mocks the assumptions of eighteenth-century psychology: that children are primitive and irrational and adults are rational and logical. This same tension exists between the subject matter of animals and the depiction of human behavior in Orwell's allegory. Thus, René Descartes's elevation of human reason in his famous dictum "I think, therefore I am"—implicitly in praise of human rationality—is also shown up by Orwell's tale. Jonathan Swift's *Gulliver's Travels* (1726; 1735) puts a twist on this tendency that Aesop's *Fables* exploit: making us see negative human behaviors in a new way through defamiliarization. Swift makes rational animals of horses, the famous Houyhnhnms who recognize that humans are disgusting, bestial, and irrational. Similarly, Jones, the farmer who runs Manor Farm, is shown from the very beginning to be a worthless drunk, neglectful of his farm and his animals. Thus, in the beginning, the animals of *Animal Farm* are superior to the humans, as represented by the drunken Jones, and also his neighbors, who start the Rebellion by failing to feed the animals out of laziness.

Beast fables in the Victorian era were thought to be of more value and substance than "made up" fairy stories. Post-Darwin, many nineteenth-century animal stories were allegories of social evolution. Margaret Gatty's (1809-1873) *Parables of Nature* (1907) rejected evolution. Orwell was not the first to use clever pigs. Decades earlier, in "The Hogs' Court of Inquiry," sisters Ann (1782-1866) and Jane Taylor (1783-1824) in *Signor Topsy-Turvy's Wonderful*

Magic Lantern (1810) mocked Erasmus Darwin's notions of what his grandson would term "evolution": "Mere gluttons! —Contented to grovel in mire / To feast and to revel, to sleep and expire; / Say, citizen pigs, can it ever be true, / Such wretches were ever related to you?" (qtd. in Coslett 60). Their poem about hogs and humans certainly has something in common with *Animal Farm*, for the hogs point out to the pigs the animalistic, degraded state of humans.

The Rule of the Beasts (1925) by Violet T. Murray (1874-?) was a more benevolent take on the animal/human relationship than *Animal Farm*, for the animals help the humans after a devastating war. In Orwell's fable, evolution becomes devolution: when the pigs walk upright, the new, reformed society of animals has reached its nadir. The collective farm becomes a concentration camp. This should remind us that *Maus* (1980-1991) by Art Spiegelman (1948-) is heir to the beast fable. *Watership Down* (1972) by Richard Adams (1920-2016) is another in the genre of beast fable that treats the problem of political paranoia allegorically and allusively through rabbits. Putting *Animal Farm* in the continuum of the beast fable helps us see the ironies of Orwell's "fable," where a society founded on utopian principles all too quickly becomes a nightmarish dystopia, where "ALL ANIMALS ARE EQUAL" becomes "BUT SOME ANIMALS ARE MORE EQUAL THAN OTHERS" (Orwell 134). As Spiegelman illustrates in *Maus*, animal protagonists can help tell real stories of human horror with ironic distance.

Animal tales, especially in the nineteenth century, stressed cruelty to animals with an implicit or explicit desire to reform. In centuries where horses were used universally for transport and to power machinery, pull plows and carriages, and so on, cruelty to horses was often pointed out. In *Animal Farm*, the resilient Boxer, the hard-working cart horse, is central. In fact, Orwell had the germ of the idea for *Animal Farm* when he saw a massive horse being driven down the road by a small boy who was whipping it all the way (DeMello 2, Meyers 19, Rees 83). This is remarkably similar to an incident that Tolstoy (1828-1910) reported, which inspired his story "Strider," (1886) told from the perspective of a horse; it also recalls

Fyodor Dostoyevsky's (1821-1861) *Crime and Punishment*, (1866) wherein the main character, Raskolnikov, dreams of a horse being violently beaten. In *Animal Farm*, Boxer ultimately works himself so hard for the Animal Farm that he collapses while rebuilding the windmill. One of the saddest and most affecting passages in *Animal Farm* is when Boxer is transported to his death. Benjamin the donkey, who is Boxer's best friend, is able to read what is on the side of the van that carries Boxer from the farm: "Alfred Simmonds, Horse Slaughterer and Glue Boiler, Dealer in Hides and Bone-Meal, Kennels Supplied" (122).

This scene is very reminiscent of the moment in Chaucer's "Nun's Priest's Tale" when Reynard the fox takes Chaunticleer out of the barnyard in his mouth intending to eat him, for just as in that tale, the animals chase after the abductor of their friend, but, unlike in Chaucer's tale, the outcome in *Animal Farm* is not positive. In this tale, we see many plot features of *Animal Farm*: the setting is the barnyard or farm, and it is a dream that begins both tales. We might think of animal tales as far from human realities on first glance, but R. Howard Bloch calls the fabliaux the first example of realism in literature (534). Even the mock-heroic story of Chaunticleer—though about a rooster, a fox, and the other inhabitants of the barnyard—is very realistic in the way it assigns human characteristics, such as pride and greed, to animals.

Orwell invokes traditional representations of animals, which, like Aesop's hare, tortoise, and fox, conventionally exhibit specific characteristics. However, one must recognize the shifting nature of animal representation. For instance in Aesop's "The Eagle, the Sow, and the Cat," the cat outwits the eagle and the pig (sow) by telling them individually that both she and her respective audience are in danger from the scheming of the other: the sow is going to uproot the tree so that the eagle's and the cat's children will be in danger should they venture away from the tree; the eagle will swoop down and eat the sow's and the cat's children should either of them venture out. The cat sneaks out discreetly at night to get food while the other animals and their broods starve, which leaves the cat and her kittens plenty of food: the lesson is "foolish and gullible people" should know "that someone who speaks with a forked tongue often stirs up all kinds of trouble" (Aesop). Here we see the characteristics of the cat (so independent she is not even given a name) in Orwell's tale: crafty but lazy and self-involved. Yet in this tale by Aesop the pig is none too bright. Orwell plays on the more common perception of pigs—that they are "piggish" or greedy—and also one that is less frequently dwelt on, perhaps because so many people eat bacon and pork: that pigs are very intelligent!

Orwell skilfully uses the human perception of animal interactions and "barnyard hierarchies" just as Spiegelman uses the dynamic between cats and mice to allegorize the Nazis and their Jewish victims in *Maus*, his graphic narrative relating his father's experience in the Nazi era and how it affected the rest of his father's life and thus Spiegelman's own. By using animals in his graphic novel, Spiegelman exploits several traits associated with the various animals and also targets harmful stereotypes associated with racial and ethnic groups. In *Maus*, Spiegelman observes the animal archetypes: the cats are predatory and the mice are victimized. However, he also plays on the way the Nazis depicted Jews as vermin (rats or mice). In addition, Poles, whose country was invaded and occupied by the Nazis, were depicted as pigs. This is one of the most controversial aspects of *Maus*: its depiction of discrete groups of people as animals. The comparison between *Maus* and *Animal Farm* is an interesting one. It would be impossible to take *Maus* out of the context of the rise of National Socialism in Austria and Germany, and the consequent Holocaust in Europe. *Animal Farm*, on the other hand, while obviously lacking the autobiographical elements of *Maus*, also escapes a one-to-one identification that is unequivocally dictated by the story Orwell tells. The term *hypocatastasis*—which means *resemblance* or *substitution*—may be used for the sort of metaphorical meaning Orwell creates. A big difference between *Animal Farm* and *Maus* is that *Maus* includes some postmodern play of self-referentiality, with Spiegelman meditating on, for instance, what animal he should use to represent the French. The fact that Orwell employs hypocatastasis though, doesn't mean that at the time he wrote *Animal Farm* he didn't mean to convey the debacle that he perceived in Soviet Communism.

How Satire and Allegory Work: Tenor and Vehicle

One of the reasons *Animal Farm* has had such staying power is that by choosing animals as the vehicle for his message, Orwell gave universal appeal to his allegory of the Soviet Union and the gullible people—especially in England—who blindly swallowed the Stalinist message. Although many underscore the one-to-one relationship with the history of the formation of the Soviet Union to make the satire a fixed allegory, Orwell broadens the relationship between tenor (the meaning to be conveyed) and vehicle (what is used to convey that meaning) so that his satire applies equally to any failed revolutionary movement, from communism to Trumpism. As in the traditional beast fables it is human behavior broadly, and not any specific instance, that becomes the subject of Orwell's satire. *Animal Farm* resembles *Gulliver's Travels* in that both tales transcend a simple moral where the iconic quality of the animals serves to illustrate a cautionary tale. In *Gulliver's Travels*, through the fictional islands of Lilliput and Blefuscu, Swift satirizes the British political parties of the times, Whigs and Tories; but through the technique of defamiliarization the petty political squabbles of the eighteenth century are universalized in such a way that they apply to the political disputes of our own time, for instance between Democrats and Republicans. Similarly, though there is no doubt that Orwell had the history of the Soviet Union in mind in his depiction of the Animal Farm, the situation is universalized so that it applies to any revolutionary movement or class war. Ironically, the original message of the pig Old Major becomes distorted into just another movement that oppresses the worker animals in the same way that Farmer Jones's regime had. This makes the message of the novel even more ironic, since communism was supposed to be the alternative to the injustices caused by capitalism, where the goal is to amass as much capital as possible through exploiting workers.

Animal Farm shows the dangers of utopian thinking by critiquing the supposedly ideal system of communism and its ethos of collective ownership. That virtually all of the animals are deluded by the pigs shows that humans are also too credulous and follow the "herd," despite all of the warning signs. Denial is a powerful aspect of human psychology, and the animals of the Animal Farm show that all too clearly; their gullibility before the changing "commandments" of their existence reveals they are easily fooled. The seventh commandment, "All animals are equal" (25) becomes "All animals are equal but some animals are more equal than others" (134), which is now the only commandment; and the pigs start carrying whips.

The Political Background

The year 2017 was the hundredth anniversary of the Russian Revolution. The Russian government, led by Vladimir Putin, chose not to commemorate it. Fortunately, about 24 years after the Russian Revolution, George Orwell did commemorate it, and his allusive history of the USSR is sure to be forever remembered. *Animal Farm* uses the genre of the animal tale, usually associated with children's literature, for its allegory. Using Orwell's fable, Putin could be seen as the inevitable extension of the long line of leaders posing as advocates of the workers. Lenin, Stalin, and Trotsky, whose analogues in *Animal Farm* are Old Major, Napoleon, and Snowball, once they had gotten rid of the Tsar, symbolized by the farmer Jones, set themselves up to be the same despotic rulers. The logical culmination of the ruin of utopian hopes predicted in Orwell's *Animal Farm* is perhaps the Russia of today.

Yet Orwell believed in socialism; as he succinctly put it: "I want the existence of democratic socialism in the West to exert a regenerative influence upon Russia" (qtd. in Shelden 369). Orwell's spare animal tale is deceptively simple. Orwell wished to show that the brand of Soviet socialism or communism about which so many in England were enthusiastic was a lie. He explained to the American writer Dwight Macdonald that he "meant the moral to be that revolutions only effect a radical movement when the masses are alert and know how to chuck out their leaders as soon as the latter have done their job" (qtd. in Shelden 371).

Implications of the Animal Fable in the Anthropocene Era

Implications of the animal fable in our contemporary society are complex. We have seen that traditional animal fables and even great works of realistic fiction have implicitly or explicitly protested the exploitation of animals, particularly horses. Other works, such as *Maus*, have caused protestations over the depiction of Polish people as pigs and Jews as mice or "vermin." But what about the animals themselves, serving as vehicles for satire in beast fables and animal tales? In *Animal Rights and the Politics of Literary Representation*, John Simons writes,

> The role of animals in the fable is almost irrelevant. They are merely vehicles for the human and are not, in any way, presented as having physical or psychological existence in their own right. . . . The fable has little to offer and can teach us nothing about the deeper relationships between the human and the non-human. (119)

Harriett Ritvo, a historian who examines the relation between humans and animals, claims that the "animal fable has little connection to real creatures" (4). Nicolas Howe is even more censorious; he considers the use of nonhuman animals in fables as another form of their exploitation by humans:

> That we burden animals by asking them to teach us how to behave like human beings seems no more than yet another way of exploiting them. We force animals to do physical labor, we raise them under cruel conditions, we mistreat them in all sorts of ways, and then we domesticate them most fully by moralizing them. . . . better . . . [to] observe animals in their own environments to learn about the natural world . . . [and] resist treating animals as figures to be written into beast fables to confirm our moral categories. (231)

Today fewer and fewer people have contact with animals other than dogs, cats, and other pets or backyard animals such as squirrels. Certainly few people have contact with barnyard animals, and even fewer with horses. The only knowledge that many people have of animals comes from such books as *Animal Farm* and *Charlotte's Web*. Obviously, these are stereotypes of animals, not real ones. This is what makes animal rights advocates so angry.

Moreover, for some critics, the animal allegory is not at all effective. In *The Ends of Allegory* Sayre Greenfield asserts that satires such as *Animal Farm* that use animals

> employ the metaphoric axis of their allegorical structures to insult their victims with their bestial equivalents, the political attacks made by these tales pressure their allegories into collapse. The events depicted become direct examples of the events the texts criticize instead of metaphors for these abuses, and the vehicle of the allegory disappears into the tenor, as the animals become human. (19)

Greenfield suggests that the animal allegory fades away altogether in the political attack mounted by *Animal Farm*. No doubt Greenfield would say the same thing about *Maus*. But is the fault here the fault of the text or the fault of the reader? As Paul Ricouer points out, there is a sort of double vision involved in reading allegory, "a peculiar and rather sophisticated intellectual ability which W. Bedell Stanford metaphorically labels 'stereoscopic vision': the ability to entertain two different points of view at the same time. That is to say, the perspective prior to and subsequent to the transformation of the metaphor's principle subsidiary subjects must both be conjointly maintained" (154).

Also, defamiliarization helps underscore the satirical theme of works such as *Maus* and *Animal Farm*, which illustrate how people who gain power in oppressive political parties torture, abuse, deceive, and manipulate weaker people. The stereoscopic vision highlights the irony of animals acting out the horrors of human behavior. At the end of *Animal Farm*, when the pigs walk on two legs, readers get a sick thrill as we realize that the bestialization (or is it the humanization?) of the pigs is complete. This scene shows that there is now no difference between the leaders of the oppressed and the oppressors: pigs and humans are indistinguishable. The other animals watch the pigs play cards with humans and "already it was impossible to say which was which" (141). In "Why I

Write," Orwell says that in *Animal Farm* he consciously tried to "fuse political purpose and artistic purpose into one whole" (qtd. in Woodcock 192). He succeeded admirably by using the humble vehicle of the traditional beast fable for his political allegory.

Works Cited

Aesop. *Aesop's Fables*. Translated by Laura Gibbs, Oxford UP, 2002. www.mythfolklore.net/aesopica/oxford/128.htm.

Bloch, R. Howard. Postface, *Fabliaux Erotiques: Textes de jongleurs des XIIe et XIIIe siècles*. Rossi, Luciano; Richard Straub. Livre de Poche, 1992, pp. 531-45.

Brett, Jan. *Town Mouse Country Mouse*. Putnam, 1994, 2003.

Chaucer, Geoffrey. *Canterbury Tales* (c.1387-1400). Edited by Nevill Coghill, Penguin, 1951; 2003.

Chesterton, G. K. Introduction to *Aesop's Fables*. Classics of the Western World, 3. East West Studio. Google Books. 17 March 2018.

Coslett, Tess. *Talking Animals in British Children's Fiction, 1786-1914*. Ashgate, 2006.

Daston, Lorraine, and Gregg Mitman. *Thinking with Animals: New Perspectives on Anthropomorphism*. Columbia UP, 2005.

DeMello, Margo. *Speaking for Animals: Animal Autobiographical Writing*. Routledge, 2013.

Greenfield, Sayre N. *The Ends of Allegory*. U of Delaware P, 1998.

Hill, Erica. "Archaeology and Animal Persons: Toward a Prehistory of Human-Animal Relations." *Berghahn Journals*, 1 Sept. 2013, pp. 117-136. dx.doi.org/10.3167/ares.2013.040108.

Howe, Nicolas. "Fabling Beasts: Traces in Memory." *Humans and Other Animals*. Edited by Arien Mack. Ohio State U, 1999, pp. 229-47.

Meyers, Jeffrey. *George Orwell: The Critical Heritage*. Routledge, 1973.

Murray, Violet T. *The Rule of the Beasts*. Stanley Paul, 1925.

Orwell, George. *Animal Farm: A Fairy Story*. Preface by Russell Baker. Introduction by C. M. Woodhouse. Signet, 1946, 1977.

"Poles as Pigs in *Maus*: The Problems with Spiegelman's *Maus*. Why *Maus* Should Not Be Taught in High Schools or Elementary Schools." Canadian Polish Congress. 15 March 2018. kpk-toronto.org/wp-content/uploads/MAUSProblemsREVMarch2016-1.pdf.

Rees, Richard. *George Orwell: Fugitive from the Camp of Victory.* Preface by Harry T. Moore. Southern Illinois UP, 1962.

Ricouer, Paul. "The Metaphorical Process as Cognition, Imagination, Feeling." *Critical Inquiry,* vol. 5, no.1, 1978, pp. 143-59.

Ritvo, Harriet. *The Animal Estate: The English and Other Creatures in the Victorian Age.* Harvard UP, 1987.

Shelden, Michael. *Orwell: The Authorized Biography.* HarperCollins, 1991.

Simons, John. *Animal Rights and the Problem of Representation.* Palgrave Macmillan, 2002.

Spiegelman, Art. *The Complete Maus.* Pantheon, 1996.

Swift, Jonathan. *Gulliver's Travels.* 1726, 1735. Norton, 1996.

Taylor, Ann, and Jane Taylor. "The Hogs' Court of Inquiry," in *Signor Topsy-Turvy's Wonderful Magic Lantern.* Tabard, 1810.

White, E. B. *Charlotte's Web.* (1952). HarperCollins, 2012.

Woodcock, George. *The Crystal Spirit: A Study of George Orwell.* Little, Brown, 1966.

A Tale of Violence: *Animal Farm* as an Allegory of Social Order_____

Dario Altobelli

Animal Farm was the first book in which I tried, with full consciousness of what I was doing, to fuse political purpose and artistic purpose into one whole. (George Orwell, "Why I Write")

Any interpretation of *Animal Farm* must take into consideration the obvious but important fact that the work is a fairy story. The fabulist style—defined by a tradition dating back thousands of years—permeates a work in which the moral, social, and political meanings as well as the aesthetic dimension exceed the historic event they deal with on a symbolic level. As Orwell himself stated at the end of the 1946, "though Animal Farm was 'primarily a satire on the Russian Revolution' it was intended to have wider application" (qtd. in Davison vii). Proof of this is the fact that, though memories of the Stalinist period have faded, *Animal Farm* continues to be read without reference to specific historical events by virtue of its remarkable narrative strength, dealing with themes related to the human condition and social dynamics.

The Double Narrative Paradigm of the *Fabula*
This short novel's expressive power stems primarily from its being a fable (in Latin, *fabula*): a narrative form with specific traits, where the characters are played by talking animals, a style that can be traced to the origins of Western literature. The *fabula* leads the reader to a place where human facts are represented in an essential, figurative, *sub specie aeternitatis* manner, drawing upon "the readers' experience of tales told within an oral tradition" (Attebery 1991, Morse 85).

The *fabula* consists of stories of animals that embody vices, virtues, and human behavior; the "moral of the story" is a reflection or advice regarding the reader's habits and beliefs. Naturalizing the human allows the fabulist to portray the scene of our instinctual appetites with a cynical and disenchanted eye, often employing irony and sarcasm. Within this general framework, *Animal Farm* can be understood outside a specific historical timeline because it depicts a transtemporal and anthropological human condition. *Animal Farm* animalizes the human and humanizes the animal, building to the original and hallucinatory conclusion where the two worlds blend. A shocking and unsettling finale sets this *fabula* apart from many others, placing it within the realm of the horror genre: "Twelve voices were shouting in anger, and they were all alike. No question, now, what had happened to the faces of the pigs. The creatures outside looked from pig to man, and from man to pig, and from pig to man again; but already it was impossible to say which was which" (Orwell, *Animal Farm* 95).

This singular story must be read with reference to the fables by Aesop, Phaedrus, and Jean de La Fontaine, as the full expression of a noble and ancient tradition, weaving popular and high ingredients into the narrative. This literary tradition continues to exist in a form renewed in this book and in many others, such as the works of Luis Sepulveda, as well as in Walt Disney's animated drawings and films.

On the one hand, *Animal Farm* fits within the literary tradition of the fable. On the other hand, it displays differences such as the length of the story, which is typical of a novella—a literary form unknown to classical fabulists. Moreover, Orwell voices a clear political and social view that is generally not found in fables. Nevertheless, *Animal Farm* follows the path traced by Aesop and Phaedrus because it provides a "history of the oppressed." Indeed, Phaedrus is the author of the unique and remarkable statement that reads: "In a few words I now propose / To point from whence the Fable rose. / A servitude was all along / Exposed to most oppressive wrong, / The suff'rer therefore did not dare / His heart's true dictates to declare; / But couch'd his meaning in the veil / Of many an allegoric tale, / And jesting with a moral aim, / Eluded all offence and blame (Phaedrus, III, *Prologus*, vv. 33-37).

The playful inventions of Phaedrus and other fabulists portray and pass down a "minor" history, traditionally relegated to silence by official historiography, which is written by the "winners" and often enclosed in the shrines of "cultural heritage," where it can be neutralized and made harmless (Benjamin, *Theses* 256). The history of the losers, of the outcasts, the history of the masses, the history of "those with no history" is found in allegories and fiction, where it can be told, portrayed, and passed on without attracting the attention of the power establishment or succumbing to punishment and the violence of censorship.

This narrative tradition communicates, in this way, with the utopian tradition. In *Utopia* Thomas More presents the concept of *ductus obliquus* (leading indirectly). Caution guides *Utopia's* elaborate inventions in order to allow More to question the certainties of his time and criticize the living conditions of the masses and the issue of enclosures, while avoiding censorship.

The deeper contents of *Animal Farm* take shape following the dual direction of fabulist literature: one a timeless representation of human nature in animal guise, the other a literary form exploring relations of power, violence, and justice. This is the sophisticated structure—however simple and immediate it may appear to the reader—on which Orwell constructs his allegory of the sociopolitical dynamics at play in the revolutionary process.

Benjamin, Derrida, and the Problem of Violence

Animal Farm can be read in philosophical and political-sociological terms, with reference to the early essay *Zur Kritik der Gewalt* ("Critique of Violence") (1921) by Walter Benjamin. Written in the years following the October Revolution, Benjamin analyzes how a state's judicial system, which permeates the political and social order, attains and keeps power through violence. Through "justified means used for just ends," an ambiguous relationship with violence nurtures the newly established judicial order. The violence the state originates from becomes the means by which it is then protected:

> All violence as a means is either lawmaking or law-preserving. If it lays claim to neither of these predicates, it forfeits all validity. It follows, however, that all violence as a means, even in the most favorable case, is implicated in the problematic nature of law itself.

And if the importance of these problems cannot be assessed with certainty at this stage of the investigation, law nevertheless appears, from what has been said, in so ambiguous a moral light that the question poses itself whether there are no other than violent means for regulating conflicting human interests. ("Critique of Violence" 287)

The judicial creation, that is the ability to confer an effective and stable juridical form to social relations and to provide models of nonviolent solutions for conflicts between opposed interests, is the outcome of violence as the primary source of law, from which, throughout history, it never separates. From this perspective violence is an indispensable element within the political and social spheres to which the possibility of transforming, but also of conserving, the given order is paradoxically linked.

Considering the reality of his times, Benjamin brought to light the hypocrisy inherent in the critique of violence, acknowledging that violence is the main means of establishing and maintaining all forms of judicial and governmental order, even democratic order, as proven by the case of modern law enforcement, whose functions have increased disproportionately from surveillance to repression. The implicit reference was to Max Weber and his definition of the state as the "holder of legitimate violence" irrespective of the political form assumed:

In the past the most diverse kinds of associations—beginning with the clan—have regarded physical violence as a quite normal instrument. Nowadays, by contrast, we have to say that a state is that human community which (successfully) lays claim to the *monopoly of legitimate physical violence* within a certain territory, this "territory" being another of the defining characteristics of the state. For the specific feature of the present is that the right to use physical violence is attributed to any and all other associations or individuals only to the extent that the state for its part permits that to happen. The state is held to be the sole source of the "right" to use violence. (3-4)

Benjamin refers to the violence that establishes and maintains the law as "mythical violence"; to this he opposes the pure, divine violence ("divine power") that is present throughout religious traditions, for example in the Hebrew Bible:

> Just as in all spheres God opposes myth, mythical violence is confronted by the divine. And the latter constitutes its antithesis in all respects. If mythical violence is lawmaking, divine violence is law-destroying; if the former sets boundaries, the latter boundlessly destroys them; if mythical violence brings at once guilt and retribution, divine power only expiates; if the former threatens, the latter strikes; if the former is bloody, the latter is lethal without spilling blood. ("Critique of Violence" 297)

"Divine violence" is represented by the revolutionary violence that interrupts the "cycle maintained by mythical forms of law," and overthrows law and the state ("Critique of Violence" 300).

In recent years Jacques Derrida provided a detailed and fruitful critique of Benjamin's essay. Resuming some of Blaise Pascal's thoughts linking "justice and force," Derrida states the principle by which "there is no law without enforceability" (925): there is no law beyond an act of force or enforcement. The expression "force of law" is adequate for describing the meaning of the German term "Gewalt," employed by Benjamin because it covers both its main meanings: that of violence and that of legitimate power, authority, public force. Thus, like Benjamin, Derrida believes that law is a constitutional compromise with the sphere of violence. In addition, he considers the contradictory relationship between law and justice: "law is always an authorized force, a force that justifies itself or is justified in applying itself, even if this justification may be judged from elsewhere to be unjust or unjustifiable" (925). The legitimacy of a state's judicial order is separate from justice. This gap between law and justice cannot be breached: law refers to generality, while justice refers to singularity. The relationship between the two is aporetic: "Law (*droit*) is not justice. Law is the element of calculation, and it is just that there be law, but justice is incalculable; and aporetic experiences are the experiences, as improbable as they are necessary, of justice, that is to say moments in which the decision between just and unjust is never insured by a rule" (Derrida 947).

An interesting aspect of Derrida's thesis is that law—considered in its inaugural and original phase as a "new" judicial order compared to the predecessor it substitutes—establishes itself and emerges in a tear "in the homogeneous tissue of a history" in relation to the performative use of language: "The very emergence of justice and law, the founding and justifying moment that institutes law implies a performative force, which is always an interpretative force . . . the operation that consists of founding, inaugurating, justifying law (*droit*), making law, would consist of a *coup de force*, of a performative and therefore interpretative violence" (941). Here lies, following Michel de Montaigne and Pascal, the mystical foundation of authority. In its founding moment law is neither just nor unjust, legitimate nor illegitimate: it expresses the performative power of language that allows the establishment of law without a foundation: "since the origin of authority, the foundation or ground, the position of the law can't by definition rest on anything but themselves, they are themselves a violence without ground" (Derrida 943). It follows that law is "essentially deconstructible, whether because it is founded, constructed on interpretable and transformable textual strata (and that is the history of law (*droit*), its possible and necessary transformation, sometimes its amelioration), or because its ultimate foundation is by definition unfounded" (Derrida 943).

Violence, Power, and Justice in *Animal Farm*

The interpretative guidelines set by Benjamin and Derrida apply perfectly to *Animal Farm*, amplifying the book's range of meanings. In this fairy story the logical and dialectic sequence between different forms of violence (the "divine" and revolutionary violence at first, the "mythical" violence establishing and maintaining judicial order later) and the complicated historical path taken by a society undergoing a revolutionary process effectively converge. The "divine violence" that destroys the existing order is represented in the initial revolt of the animals against Jones and his helpers. The processes of foundation and legislation as well as political revolution are set in motion by a profound need for justice. This need is dictated by a new awareness of the life conditions of the animals on the farm. Following a dream—"a dream of the earth as it will be when Man has vanished" (Orwell, *Animal Farm* 6)—"old Major, the prize Middle White boar" summons all the animals to a meeting where he gives a revelatory speech:

> Is it not crystal clear, then, comrades, that all the evils of this life of ours spring from the tyranny of human beings? Only get rid of Man, and the produce of our labour would be our own. . . . That is my message to you, comrades: Rebellion! I do not know when that Rebellion will come, it might be in a week or in a hundred years, but I know, as surely as I see this straw beneath my feet, that *sooner or later justice will be done*. (5, emphasis added)

In the name of true and liberating justice and under the influence of the hunger suffered by the animals "the Rebellion was achieved much earlier and more easily than anyone had expected" (11). This is the explosion of a "divine violence" "that strikes without bloodshed" (Benjamin, "Critique of Violence" 297):

> [Jones's] men suddenly found themselves being butted and kicked from all sides. The situation was quite out of their control. . . . After only a moment or two they gave up trying to defend themselves and took to their heels. A minute later all five of them were in full flight down the cart-track that led to the main road, with the animals pursuing them in triumph. . . . And so, almost before they knew what was happening, the Rebellion had been successfully carried through: Jones was expelled, and the Manor Farm was theirs. (12)

The promise of a happy society of liberated animals, after the bloodless revolt against the human master, is followed by the slow and relentless establishment of a dictatorship by some of the animals, mostly by the pigs: this is the "mythical violence" that immediately establishes law.

A perfect example of this is the renaming of the master's farm as Animal Farm and the drafting of the Seven Commandments. The

---

violent nature of the foundation of law can be seen in the double action of renaming the community and writing its fundamental laws. The passage from an oral tradition to the use of writing marks the transition from a revolutionary moment to a constituent one. The precepts, handed down orally by Old Major in the speech that awakens the animals' consciences, through writing become the official idiom of society, the source legitimizing the newly established power, the boundaries within which relations between the animals must henceforth take place. The Seven Commandments provide the legal and moral standards for the new society. The fundamental law regulating this new social order is at the same time its foundation and its guarantee.

1. Whatever goes upon two legs is an enemy.
2. Whatever goes upon four legs, or has wings, is a friend.
3. No animal shall wear clothes.
4. No animal shall sleep in a bed.
5. No animal shall drink alcohol.
6. No animal shall kill any other animal.
7. All animals are equal. (15)

Orwell clearly shows the link between society, the founding nature of law, and the moral imperative at the moment of the establishment of a new social order:

At the beginning, rules are essentially imperative, either negative or positive, and they aim to establish desirable behavior or to avoid undesirable behavior by recourse to sanctions in this world or the next. The Ten Commandments immediately come to mind, and are just the most familiar example. . . . The moral world . . . is born with the formulation, imposition and application of commands and prohibitions . . . the primary function of the law is to constrict and not to liberate, to limit and not to open up areas of liberty, to straighten the twisted and not to allow it to grow wild. (Bobbio 37-38)

According to Norberto Bobbio, there is a precise tie between the moral sphere and the political one; it resides precisely in the original function of the rules of conduct: "to protect the group as a whole rather than the single individual" (38): "Originally the function of the precept 'thou shalt not kill' was not to protect the single member of the group so much as to remove one of the fundamental reasons for a group's disintegration. The best proof of this is that this precept, which is justifiably considered a moral cornerstone, was valid for members of the same group, but not of other groups" (38-39).

Law and Language between the Foundation and the Preservation of the Social Order

The Seven Commandments indicate that writing coincides with law and law coincides with writing: from this moment, the ability to master the tools for writing and reading become requisites for enjoying the right to citizenship in the new order. Only the pigs, however, fully understand the benefits of mastering these tools, and they use them to keep power and direct it toward different aims that are legitimate from a formal point of view—because they are supported by law—though not at all just.

Orwell's sensitivity toward the politics of language leads him to accentuate the disproportion between the animals with knowledge and power of language and those who remain unlettered and governed. The certainty of law in its written form reveals itself as the complete and coherent continuation of the mythical and original violence founding the "new" order. Orwell's attention to language ranges from general issues pertinent to cognitive processes— "if thought corrupts language, language can also corrupt thought" ("Politics and the English Language" 137)—to specifically political issues: "a society which cannot control its language is . . . doomed to be oppressed in terms which deny it the very most elemental aspects of humanity . . . those who control the means of communication have the most awful of powers—they literally can create the truth they choose" (Lee 127, qtd. in Hirvisaari 22).

Janne Hirvisaari observes that in relation to the ability to master language, "the pigs, who control the means of communication and have a far more advanced rhetoric, can thus persuade and govern the other animals according to their will" (43). In other terms, "linguistic oligarchy will sustain their exploitation of the animals through the monopoly of language" (Elbarbary 37). The manipulation of the commandments does not merely aim at taking control of language, but at manipulating the foundations of society. The Seven Commandments represent the "constitutional charter" of the Animal Farm, the modification of which reveals an agenda of ruthless constitutional engineering affecting the overall political and social organization, interfering with the basic shape of social relations.

Even before using the dogs' repressive and policing violence, the pigs employ an astute and subtle form of violence by modifying the fundamental judicial body at their own pleasure. Orwell shows that the manipulation of the judicial and legal (constitutional) sphere coincides with the manipulation of memory, since the Seven Commandments are also—especially on an interpretative level—the source of social memory. The inability to read the commandments provokes a sense of absolute existential bewilderment in the farm animals. The violent act of foundation of law and state remains unexplained to them. They have no key to access the memory of the original facts through which the legitimization of the "new" order takes place and is perpetuated: the return to the past can only happen through written law. The written law establishes which principles and vision inspired the achieved political and social revolution. The repressive and mystifying violence exerted on the past is even more terrible for those who, suffering it, do not have the cultural and cognitive resources to grasp the outcomes in the *present day* of what they themselves had participated in creating in the not-so-distant *yesterday* (Derrida 991).

Violence establishes the judicial relations within society, that is the political and social form of a society in its founding moment. In *Animal Farm* we see how the expression of the "force of law," as Derrida characterizes it, links to what he calls the "mystical foundation of authority" that in *Animal Farm* recalls the central role of writing and knowledge as expression of "a performative and therefore interpretative violence" (Derrida 941). Derrida himself quotes La Fontaine's fable "The Wolf and the Sheep" to demonstrate how the principle "Might makes right" still lacks the full understanding of "force as an essential predicate of justice" (*droit*) because it remains within a conception of "a conventionalist or utilitarian relativism . . . that would make the law a 'masked power'" (941).

Animal Farm also provides a representation of "mythical violence" as a force that preserves the law, exemplified by the institution of a police force of dogs. The audacious and ferocious nature of their duty leads to the desired effects of terror and enslavement. By threatening to use them—following Snowball's escape from the farm—Napoleon establishes a dictatorship. Among the many passages where Orwell recounts the unsettling role of the canine police force, perhaps the most terrible one is when Napoleon orders the execution of the animals who displayed reservations about his decisions: "And so the tale of confessions and executions went on, until there was a pile of corpses lying before Napoleon's feet and the air was heavy with the smell of blood, which had been unknown there since the expulsion of Jones" (57). The sense of bewilderment that comes upon the surviving animals is due not only to the fear of becoming themselves the victims of this kind of "justice" but also to the inability to find a supporting clause within society's law: "some of the animals remembered—or thought they remembered—that the Sixth Commandment decreed "No animal shall kill any other animal" (61). The imperative principle among animals demanding reciprocal respect of each other's lives, which was crucial to the original formulation by Old Major, has been overturned with the addition of two simple words that "slipped out of the animals' memory" (61): "No animal shall kill any other animal *without cause*" (61). By dealing with the issue of absolute power in matters of life and death, Orwell's novel raises the irresolvable question of the legitimacy of violence as the means for obtaining results defined legally as just. The rephrased Sixth Commandment exemplifies the dramatic passage from the dimension of an ethical universal assumption "do not kill" to a law of convenience and calculation legitimizing an oppressive social order, "for in the exercise of violence over life and death, more than in any other legal act, law reaffirms itself" (Benjamin, "Critique of Violence" 286).

Animal Farm is a complex allegory of social order developed on multiple levels. It is a fairy tale in the sense of Phaedrus: a "slave's tale," we could say: a story written by the losers of history. It is a narrative representation of the "force of law" in Derrida's sense: "a performative and therefore interpretative violence" affirmed through writing and related to the "mystical foundation of authority" (941). And, lastly, following the thought of Walter Benjamin, it is a bitter apologue on the distance that always separates justice from law, a consideration of law as an instrument of power, domination, and oppression.

Works Cited

Attebery, Brian. "Fantasy's Reconstruction of Narrative Conventions." *Journal of the Fantastic in the Arts*, vol. 1, no. 1, 1988, pp. 85-98.

_____. "Fantasy and the Narrative Transaction." *Style*, vol. 25, n. 1, 1991, pp. 28-41.

Benjamin, Walter. "Theses on the Philosophy of History." 1950. *Illuminations*. Edited and with an Introduction by H. Arendt, Schocken, 1969, pp. 253-64.

_____. "Critique of Violence." 1921. *Reflections, Essay, Aphorisms, Autobiographical Writing*. Translated by E. Jephcott; edited and with an introduction by P. Demetz, Schocken, 1996, pp. 277-300.

Bobbio, Norberto. *The Age of Rights*. 1990. Translated by A. Cameron, Polity, 1996.

Davison, Peter. "A Note on the Text." *Animal Farm*. By George Orwell. 1945. Penguin, 2008, pp. v-viii.

Derrida, Jacques. *Force of Law: The "Mystical Foundation of Authority."* *Cardozo Law Review*, vol. 11, no. 5-6, Jul.-Aug. 1990, pp. 919-1046.

Elbarbary, Samir. "Language as Theme in Animal Farm." *The International Fiction Review*, vol. 19, no. 1, 1992, pp. 31-38.

Hirvisaari, Janne. "Some animals are more equal than others"—A posthumanist reading of George Orwell's Animal Farm." Pro GraduThesis. University of Tampere, 2016, tampub.uta.fi/bitstream/handle/10024/99006/GRADU-1463652373.pdf?sequence=1. Accessed 5 July 2018.

Lee, Robert A. *Orwell's Fiction*. 1969. U of Notre Dame P, 1970.

More, Thomas. "Utopia" (1514). *Works of Sir Thomas More*, vol. IX. Hilliard, Gray, 1884.

Morse, Donald E. "'A Blatancy of Untruth': George Orwell's Uses of the Fantastic in 'Animal Farm.'" *Hungarian Journal of English and American Studies (HJEAS)*, vol. 1, no. 2, 1995, pp. 85-92.

Orwell, George. *Animal Farm*. 1945. Penguin, 2008.

_____. "Politics and the English Language." *The Collected Essays, Journalism & Letters of George Orwell*, vol. IV: *In Front of Your Nose 1945-1950*, pp. 127-40. Edited by S. Orwell and I. Angus, Secker &Warburg, 1969.

_____. "Why I Write." *England Your England and Other Essays*. Secker & and Warburg, 1954, pp. 7-16.

The Comedies of Terence and the Fables of Phædrus. Literally translated into English prose with notes by H. T. Riley, George Bell, 1887. www.gutenberg.org/files/25512/25512-h/25512-h.htm#smart_III_pro. Accessed 31 March 2018.

Weber, Max. *Politics as a Vocation*. Reprinted from *Essays in Sociology*. Translated, edited, and with an introduction by H. H. Gerth and C. Wright Mills. Oxford UP, 1946. archive.org/stream/weber_max_1864_1920_politics_as_a_vocation#page/n1/mode/2up/search/The+state+. Accessed 7 Jul. 2018.

The Biopolitics of Totalitarianism in Orwell's *Animal Farm*

Andrew Byers

In the wake of Chinese President Xi Jinping's move in February 2018 to abolish presidential term limits—which some fear means that Xi will remain ruler of China for the rest of his life—the Chinese government also cracked down on internal dissent, which included bans on two of George Orwell's books: *Nineteen Eighty-Four* and *Animal Farm* (Phillips). This is no accident. Both books depict life inside dystopian, totalitarian societies and retain enormous resonance in the twenty-first century for all observers and critics of totalitarianism. One of the chief continuities between real-life totalitarian societies—Nazi Germany, Stalinist Russia, China under Mao (and perhaps later), North Korea—and Orwell's allegorical one in *Animal Farm* is the desire by totalitarian states to control virtually all aspects of everyday life within their societies, down to the most innocuous, as a means of implementing sweeping political change and then cementing and maintaining their rule. It is this attempt to control individual actions, bodies, and entire bodies politic that Michel Foucault described as "biopolitics," arguing that it is a fundamental element of governance. Biopolitics is certainly in evidence throughout *Animal Farm*; by controlling the animals' daily lives and bodies, first with small interventions in their everyday activities and eventually by totally dominating every animal's waking moment, the pigs come to transform the bodies and lives of all the animals on Animal Farm, creating loyal and obedient slave laborers, ensuring their own dominance.

This essay will explore how biopolitics works within the context of *Animal Farm* and will use the intensely biopolitical reign of the pigs as an avenue for exploring how other totalitarian societies likewise employ biopolitics.

Biopolitics and Totalitarianism

At its most literal, biopolitics is the merger of life and biology with politics. Though the term *biopolitics* dates to the early decades of the twentieth century, it was only in the 1970s that Foucault explicitly articulated the idea that biopolitics, or "biopower" as he often described it, is a fundamental and constitutive aspect of governance. Foucault defined biopower as the "explosion of numerous and diverse techniques for achieving the subjugations of bodies and the control of populations" (*History* 140) as well as the set of mechanisms through which "the basic biological features of the human species became the object of a political strategy" (*Security* 1). Most obviously this would refer to the literal power over life and death possessed by the state (Foucault, *Discipline* 48-49), with sociologist Max Weber's discussion of the state as holding a monopoly on the legitimate use of physical force (129-98) and Foucault's descriptions of the disciplining of individual human bodies as a means of disciplining the body politic as important components. The seemingly less overtly violent activities of entire governmental bureaucracies that create and use highly politicized bodies of knowledge related to statistics, demography, epidemiology, and public health, among other disciplines, to exercise control over the bodies and lives of their subjects are likewise key elements of biopolitics.

It is worth taking some time to note what is so radically different about totalitarian societies from others as a means of exploring the linkage between state control and biopolitics. Totalitarian states recognize no limits to their authority; all rival institutions are either destroyed or co-opted. They strive to regulate not only all aspects of public life, but private life as well. Indeed, given the surveillance and disciplinary regimes that totalitarian states establish, there is little meaningful distinction between the public and the private. Central features of totalitarian states include dictatorial rule by a single leader or oligarchy, an overriding ideology that is used to unify the nation and demonize its enemies, heavy reliance on propaganda and state-run media and educational systems, intensive restrictions on personal freedoms, and the coupling of surveillance regimes with violence and terror as means of enforcing compliance (Arendt 301-

428). Of course, all states—totalitarian or otherwise, including modern liberal democracies—seek to regulate and manage the biopolitics of their citizens, but it is in totalitarian societies that these efforts are married most commonly with overt forms of violence and surveillance, and so are made much more legible than in other societies that have a softer touch or that may even attempt to conceal their interest in biopolitics.

Questions of the body and whether and how it may be regulated by the state have dominated modern politics. Foucault argued that "The disciplines of the body and the regulation of the population constitute the two poles around which the organization of power over life was deployed" (*History* 139). For Foucault, discipline is a mechanism of power that regulates the behavior—and the bodies—of individuals within the social or political spheres through the regulation of space, time, and activities, enforced through a complex, almost ubiquitous system of surveillance. Ultimately this creates bodies that are at once docile, disciplined, and productive. This disciplinary power is part of what Foucault describes as "governmentality," in which officials and various "experts" monitor, measure, and normalize individuals and entire populations through a variety of means—to include formal education, media campaigns, propaganda, and public discourse—with an eye toward promoting particular models of personal behavior (Turner 3-4). Governmentality encompasses the ways and means by which states attempt to produce the kinds of citizens (or subjects) that are best suited to the state's own interests. In the case of totalitarian states, such individuals are loyal, obedient, open to being propagandized, indoctrinated, and militarized, and, perhaps above all, are malleable and responsive to the state's ideology. In many ways, governmentality is the key expression of biopolitics as it is enforced and enacted by states as public policy, "the ensemble formed by institutions, procedures, analyses and reflections, the calculations and tactics that allow the exercise of this very specific, albeit very complex power, which has as its target the population, as its major form of knowledge political economy, and as its essential technical means apparatuses of security" (Foucault, "Governmentality" 102).

Surveillance and disciplinary techniques have been developed for regulating the behaviors and bodies of ever-larger populations with the goal of transforming them into "manageable subjects" (Crary 15). It is easy to perceive the disciplinary and surveillant nature of the modern state at work within the institutions of society where these are most explicit—prisons, schools, the military, for example—though as Gilles Deleuze pointed out, "societies of control" operate not simply by confining citizens in carceral institutions (though they do that too), but also through mechanisms of control permeated throughout society (3-7). Control over bodies, and therefore behaviors and lives, is the means to a utopian end, in which these created "manageable subjects" will be cooperative, productive, and reproductive. Orwell himself focused a great deal on the foundational importance of surveillance to totalitarian rule in *Nineteen Eighty-Four*; in Oceania, the Party's rule hinges on maintaining continual surveillance over all its subjects and then using the surveillance data it collects to enforce discipline and punish deviants (Byers 199-212). State interventions into the body (both individually and collectively), discipline, and surveillance are all key aspects for control of a populace and management of society as a whole. For states that seek wholesale transformation of a society, as clearly totalitarian states do, biopolitics is the means by which such states can achieve their ends and maintain their desired practices of governance.

The biological aspects of society, and the biology of the individual members of society, have become carefully managed by states for their own ends. Areas of biopolitical concern by states are expansive—and totalitarian states seem to be even more aggressive in this regard than other kinds of states—covering virtually the entirety of human existence, including reproduction, sexuality, physical and mental health, food consumption, appearance, and day-to-day activities. Indeed, biopolitics and biopolitical concerns play into all aspects of the functions of a state, from state formation to state maintenance and expansion; states have been and remain concerned with the management of populations to produce order and stability as well as an expanding population base from which state power can grow. There are clear parallels to each of these areas of biopolitical interest in *Animal Farm*, with their growth over time paralleling that of the growth (and power) of the pigs' state apparatus—and the concomitant domination of all aspects of life on the farm.

The Biopolitics of *Animal Farm*

Orwell was one of the keenest and most prescient observers of totalitarianism, so it is no surprise that *Animal Farm*, ostensibly an allegory of Stalinism but having much broader applicability, would have much to say regarding state interventions into the body and totalitarian embrace of biopolitics. *Animal Farm* is a classic example—alongside *Nineteen Eighty-Four*—of the uses to which a totalitarian state employs biopolitics to secure and maintain control over an entire population. Indeed, *Animal Farm* is practically a primer for instituting such a system. Chief among the many biopolitical developments in *Animal Farm* are the creation of a profoundly hierarchical society comprised of elites, enforcers, and workers; constant emphasis on labor as the highest attainment and sole focus for the majority of the population; control of everyday aspects of life, even minor and seemingly inconsequential ones, which steadily grows over time; control over the means of education and indoctrination; and the militarization of society, with the state freely exercising its control over the lives and bodies of each individual through the continual use or threat of violence, leading to the creation of a fear-based society that relies not only on discipline from the pigs and their dog enforcers, but on *self*-discipline by all the animals. Ultimately, *Animal Farm* represents the creation of a total institution that not only uses biopolitics as a means of control but has biopower interwoven into its very fabric, which is used to cement the pigs' rule across an entire society.

The first and perhaps most obvious biopolitical intervention in life on the farm is the conscious creation of a socially, politically, and economically stratified society, with basic and fundamental rights structured around the individual's place within this hierarchy. Note that one's position within the hierarchy is a product of genetic lineage, mirroring the creation of the *nomenklatura* and *apparatchik* classes of managers and functionaries that arose in the Soviet Union, whose positions were typically distributed to other members of these social groups, with relatively limited possibilities for political and social mobility. In *Animal Farm*, power is held chiefly by the pigs, who arise as a revolutionary vanguard but quickly evolve into a self-aggrandizing oligarchy that rules despotically and controls every aspect of life on the farm as well as the bodies and day-to-day activities of its inhabitants. The pigs seize control of census and demographic data on the farm, along with production statistics, which they use to change historical narratives and even collective memory as a means of reinforcing and maintaining their rule (Orwell 112-13). The pigs' rule is reinforced by their creation of the elite caste of dog enforcers/shock troopers, who provide a continual threat of violence and carry out these threats directly when commanded to do so by their pig masters (Orwell 52-53). The remainder of the animals, of varying species, are used as laborers, with their bodies conceived of as commodities, to be used and expended as needed by the pigs for their own purposes.

The pigs establish a society that revolves around work, with labor as the highest goal of each member of society (the pigs tasked with intellectual labor, the other animals assigned to menial chores). Elaborate and reinforcing structures are put in place to convince each animal to dedicate nearly every waking hour to its assigned work tasks. Boxer, the old farm horse, is the ideal worker, continually demonstrating his zeal and dedication to working harder and harder for the good of the society (or, rather, the pigs), though all of the farm's workers are increasingly asked to sacrifice their lives and health for the good of the state and its ruling elite. The animals are required to plant and harvest crops, performing even more agricultural labor than they had under the rule of Mr. Jones, and they are increasingly asked to expend more and more backbreaking effort to build (and then rebuild) the windmill. Not only is labor extracted from the animals, but their access to food is increasingly tied to their labor. Perform heroic amounts of labor and receive a barely adequate food ration; fail to do so and receive inadequate rations or no food at all. The promise of an end to these unceasing manual labors is held out via the (mythical) retirement and old age pension programs that are theoretically created, though no animal is ever actually allowed to retire (Orwell 112).

The tragic fate of Boxer—undoubtedly the hardest working, most self-sacrificing, and most loyal of all the animals on the farm—may have the clearest implications for how totalitarian states think about their subjects as commodities to be exploited; it also illustrates the role that biopolitics play in how these states conceptualize the utility of the bodies and lives of the individuals who live under their control. When Boxer can provide no more work for the state, he is sold to the knacker to have his body converted into glue, hides, bone meal, and meat for kennels, so that the last remaining bit of value can be literally extracted from his body (Orwell 121-24). That the pigs then use the proceeds to buy alcohol demonstrates just how cynically the elites view their most loyal follower. Boxer's fate is, of course, similar to the ultimate fate of the inmates of the Soviet gulags, whose manual labor was exploited while their bodies were worn down and abused until they were no longer capable of providing any additional labor. At which point they were simply murdered.

One of the seemingly innocuous elements of *Animal Farm*, but one that is central to the pigs' interest in biopower, is their attempt to control the various everyday aspects of the other animals' daily lives. These are initially expressed via several of the Seven Commandments, including "No animal shall wear clothes," "No animal shall sleep in a bed," and "No animal shall drink alcohol" (Orwell 24-25). Eventually, these commandments and the others are modified and then done away with, after the pigs decide to violate them. A clear example of how the pigs attempt to regulate even the smallest aesthetic choices of the animals is the case of Mollie the horse. Mollie is continually chastised and harassed for attempting to wear ribbons in her mane. Why the emphasis on controlling something as inconsequential as wearing ribbons? This prohibition is partially about erasing differences and distinctions—ostensibly a question of equality among the animals, before it becomes clear that in fact not all the animals are equal. It is also an attempt to eliminate petty luxuries that could distract from the performance of labor and hard work. From a biopolitical perspective, however, it is primarily about conditioning each of the animals to accept control over all aspects of their lives by the state. By conditioning the animals to accept control over small things—such as an individual's choice to wear ribbons as a decoration—control over the larger, more fundamentally important aspects of life is more easily achieved.

Control of the minds of the animals on the farm is just as important as controlling their bodies. Indeed, the mind is the pathway to the body. To this end, the pigs immediately seize control of the equivalents of the media and educational systems on the farm in order to first deploy their propaganda as a means of reinforcing their rule and the new way of life, and eventually to control how the next generations of animals will be conditioned from birth. Accordingly, Napoleon "said that the education of the young was more important than anything else that could be done for those who were already grown up" (Orwell 34-35). The prime examples of this are the puppies Napoleon takes for indoctrination soon after their birth. When next the adult dogs are revealed to the farm's other inhabitants, they have been transformed into killer attack dogs trained to enforce Napoleon's will, provide the constant threat of violence for those who might dissent, and commit acts of violence according to Napoleon's commands. Two other examples are worth mentioning in brief: Squealer, as the pigs' chief propagandist, translates the pigs' commands into forms more palatable to the other animals, often convincing them that their own senses or memories are at fault when they begin to see through the pigs' propaganda; and Moses the raven, obvious symbol of organized religion on the farm, spins fanciful tales of Sugarcandy Mountain, the idyllic land of plenty that he claims had been promised to the animals as their heavenly reward. It is clear that these are essential mechanisms for intervening in biopolitics: control of information, conditioning of the young in order to create more pliable subjects as adults, and the placation of dissent and conditioning of acceptance of the status quo via religious ideology.

Over time, the farm becomes increasingly militarized, meaning that the animals' identification with and use of warlike images and thinking become the norm, as does a belief in the need for continual preparation for war with enemies, internal and external; the dogs and other military forces are needed to guarantee safety in a dangerous world (Gillis 1-10). Militarization requires an enemy not only to justify the costs of building and maintaining strong defense and intelligence capabilities, but also to provide the rhetorical means for mobilizing popular and political support for such a build-up. This mindset drives a host of other changes on the farm—political, social, and cultural—that are used to justify the surveillance, propaganda, indoctrination, and ever-present readiness for war. By creating the perfect enemies—Farmer Jones and his men lurking outside the farm, constantly seeking to reclaim what Jones once controlled, and Snowball and his subversives, saboteurs, and traitors within the farm's community—the pigs are able to justify a state of perpetual near-war, an emergency situation that makes almost any act acceptable, no matter how violent, repressive, or intrusive. This fear of military defeat and internal subversion affords a sustaining base of support and consensus for the creation of a surveillance and biopolitical apparatus necessary to guarantee public safety in the face of such existential threats.

The pigs of *Animal Farm* manage to create a closed, repressive society that employs biopolitical control as its chief focus. Their society is not just totalitarian; it is a "total institution." Noted sociologist Erving Goffman introduced the concept of the total institution, one that comes to dominate all or nearly all aspects of the lives of its members. Goffman defined total institutions broadly, and examples include such disparate organizations as orphanages, mental hospitals, carceral institutions, militaries, ships, work camps, boarding schools, and monastic orders, among others. By stretching Goffman's use of the term slightly, it is easy to see that total control over almost all aspects of the daily lives of individuals is precisely what totalitarian states attempt (Goffman, *Asylums* 3-12; Goffman, "Characteristics" 354-67). Goffman observes that total institutions tend to break down the barriers separating the three most basic spheres of human activity: sleep, work, and play ("Characteristics" 355-59). In total institutions, all three aspects of life are conducted largely under the authority of the institution, which takes over responsibility for the lives of all individuals under its control, erasing any division between the public and private spheres for members of the institution. Activities are closely regimented and scheduled and are generally conducted in the presence of a large number of other individuals. Likewise, all activities are governed by an elaborate set of rules that are designed to fulfill the goals of the institution rather than the personal fulfillment of individuals. This bureaucratic handling of basic human needs is the key facet of total institutions.

Another important aspect of total institutions is the divide between the largest class of individuals within the organization— whose activities are tightly regulated and who have limited contact with the outside world—and the smaller body of individuals who are more socially integrated into the outside world (i.e., the pigs). It is elites who enforce the rules of the institution, define rewards and privileges, and punish violators. Enforced discipline and obedience to the established rules are common. Indoctrination generally involves a mortification process, which can and often does involve physical, mental, and emotional components, wherein personal identity and any sense of self as a separate entity from the institution are systematically stripped away, broken down, and supplanted with a new identity provided by the institution (the ideology of Animalism in the case of *Animal Farm*). Practices, argot, and dress unique to the institution, among other mechanisms, are used to construct and reinforce the new sense of identity and behavior. Inmates of the institution react to the indoctrination process in varying ways; some may withdraw, rebel, cooperate, or actively convert. Surveillance within total institutions tends to be all-pervasive, as it is on the farm; it is obviously the foundation for control, though resistance is always possible. Thus, in the face of such resistance, "total" control of all individuals within the institution is aspirational rather than a reality. But the degree to which the total institution is able to dominate the lives of those under its authority marks its success. It is easy to see how this operates in *Animal Farm*, since the pigs establish a total institution founded on principles of surveillance and militarization with an eye toward achieving biopolitical control over all the animals on the farm in perpetuity.

Totalitarianism and Biopolitics after *Animal Farm*

Even though the totalitarian societies that Orwell knew are gone, the merger of totalitarianism and biopolitics has persisted in the twenty-first century, and indeed new possibilities for biopolitical control have emerged. North Korea, a nation of starving slave laborers under constant surveillance by the Kim family and its networks of spies and soldiers, is as totalitarian as any society that has ever existed. Even though the days of Mao and the worst excesses of the Cultural Revolution are over, in recent years China has rolled out a plan to marry its authoritarian government with big data to create a "social credit system" in which every Chinese citizen's activities would be monitored and "anything from defaulting on a loan to criticizing the ruling party, from running a red light to failing to care for your parents properly, could cause you to lose [social credit] points (Denyer, "China's plan")." Once implemented on a national scale, these scores would then be used to determine "whether you can borrow money, get your children into the best schools or travel abroad; whether you get a room in a fancy hotel, a seat in a top restaurant—or even just get a date" along with other, presumably even less savory purposes that have not yet been publicly detailed (Denyer "China's plan"). Perhaps even more alarmingly, China has been rolling out a national network of surveillance cameras integrated with sophisticated facial-recognition software—increasing numbers of Chinese police officers are being equipped with special glasses linked with these technologies as well—that will provide the ability to locate anyone inside China in near-real time on a continuous basis (Denyer, "China's watchful eye"). These developments represent nothing less than the marriage of totalitarianism with biopolitics on a mass scale, made possible with twenty-first-century technology.

But as *Animal Farm* has shown us, social media and technologically enabled mass surveillance are not needed to create such a society: the pigs of Animal Farm are able to do just fine without those things, though the impulse of totalitarian governments to control virtually all aspects of life remains constant. While many twenty-first-century observations have focused on the role that technology plays in enabling the continued control of entire populations, making it possible for states—totalitarian or otherwise—and their corporate allies to engage in subtle forms of biopolitical control, *Animal Farm* is a reminder that advanced technologies are unnecessary for totalitarianism to function.

One of the key points regarding the linkages between biopolitics and totalitarianism is that while we can see biopolitics and governmentality at work most plainly in the extreme actions of totalitarian states, such as that of the Soviet Union under Stalin or the farm under Napoleon the pig, *all* states, even ostensibly democratic ones, employ biopolitics and governmentality for their own purposes to a greater or lesser degree. To be sure, nontotalitarian states are less overt and less physically destructive in their use of biopolitical measures, surveillance, and violence to control individuals and entire populations, but that may make nontotalitarian states even more insidious, since their purposes and means of oppression are much less obvious, making resistance that much more difficult. It is relatively easy to perceive Stalin, Mao, and Napoleon the pig's use of biopolitics as a tool of control and domination—and therefore resist such oppression—but much harder to observe these same biopolitical interventions in "enlightened" liberal democracies.

Works Cited

Arendt, Hannah. *The Origins of Totalitarianism.* Harcourt, Brace, 1951.

Byers, Andrew. "*Nineteen Eighty-Four*, Surveillance, and After: From Telescreens to the NSA." *Nineteen Eighty-Four: Critical Insights.* Edited by Thomas Horan, Salem, 2016, pp. 199-212.

Crary, Jonathan. *Techniques of the Observer: On Vision and Modernity in the Nineteenth Century.* MIT Press, 1990.

Deleuze, Gilles. "Postscript on the Societies of Control." *October,* vol. 59, Winter 1992, pp. 3-7.

Denyer, Simon. "China's plan to organize its society relies on 'big data' to rate everyone." *Washington Post*, 22 Oct. 2016, www.washingtonpost.

com/world/asia_pacific/chinas-plan-to-organize-its-whole-society-around-big-data-arating-for-everyone/2016/10/20/1cd0dd9c-9516-11e6-ae9d-0030ac1899cd_story.html. Accessed 19 May 2018.

_____. "China's watchful eye." *Washington Post*, 7 Jan. 7, 2018, www.washingtonpost.com/news/world/wp/2018/01/07/feature/in-china-facial-recognition-is-sharp-end-of-a-drive-for-total-surveillance/. Accessed 19 May 2018.

Foucault, Michel. *Discipline and Punish: The Birth of the Prison*, 2nd Vintage ed. Vintage, 1995.

_____. "Governmentality." *Understanding Foucault: A Critical Introduction*, 2nd ed. Edited by Tony Schirato, Geoff Danaher, and Jen Webb. SAGE Publications, 2012.

_____. *The History of Sexuality, Volume 1: An Introduction*. Vintage, 1990.

_____. *Security, Territory, Population: Lectures at the Collège de France, 1975-76*. Edited by François Ewald and Alessandro Fontana. Palgrave Macmillan, 2007.

Gillis, John R., editor. *The Militarization of the Western World*. Rutgers UP, 1989.

Goffman, Erving. *Asylums: Essays on the Social Situation of Mental Patients and Other Inmates*. Aldine, 1962.

_____. "Characteristics of Total Institutions." *Deviant Behavior: Readings in the Sociology of Deviance*. Edited by Delos H. Kelly, St. Martin's, 1979, pp. 354-67.

Orwell, George. *Animal Farm*. 1945. Signet, 1996.

Phillips, Tom. "Ce*sored! China bans letter N (briefly) from internet as Xi Jinping extends grip on power." *The Guardian*, February 28, 2018. www.theguardian.com/world/2018/feb/28/china-bans-the-letter-n-internet-xi-jinping-extends-power. Accessed 19 May 2018.

Turner, Bryan S. *The Body & Society: Explorations in Social Theory*, 3rd ed. SAGE, 2008.

Weber, Max. "Politics as Vocation." *Weber's Rationalism and Modern Society: New Translations on Politics, Bureaucracy, and Social Stratification*. Edited by Tony Waters and Dagmar Waters. Palgrave Macmillan, 2015.

The Function of Humor in George Orwell's *Animal Farm*

Robert C. Evans

Although George Orwell's *Animal Farm* is often praised for its wit, irony, and Swiftian satire, less attention has been paid to its frequent use of comedy and humor.[1] In places—especially in the novel's first half—the book is genuinely funny. Given the dark, grim, even brutal subject matter of Orwell's allegory, his use of humor in the first half is intriguing. Clearly he intended such comedy to help highlight, by contrast, the tragedies to come. By lulling both his readers and his characters into an often lighthearted beginning, he makes the ultimate catastrophe all the more emphatic and painful.

Pre-Revolutionary Comedy
Animal Farm is almost immediately funny. In the 1954 cartoon film based on the novel, Farmer Jones is presented as a menacing, violent figure—a mean drunk whose evil and viciousness are almost ridiculously obvious. But this is hardly the case in the novel itself. Instead, Orwell presents Jones as a drunken, comic buffoon, and Mrs. Jones (never shown in the film) is even funnier:

> Mr. Jones, of the Manor Farm, had locked the hen-houses for the night, but was too drunk to remember to shut the popholes. With the ring of light from his lantern dancing from side to side, he lurched across the yard, kicked off his boots at the back door, drew himself a last glass of beer from the barrel in the scullery, and made his way up to bed, where Mrs. Jones was already snoring. (3)

Orwell sets a comic tone, not only in the reference to the "dancing" lantern and the "last glass of beer" but especially in the indelicate reference to the "snoring" wife. Mrs. Jones, apparently, is no more dignified than her crude, boorish husband. Orwell presents his humans realistically, without attractive illusions. In fact, they are almost comically animalistic: Jones seems self-indulgent, undisciplined, and irrational, while his wife seems a comic lump of noisy flesh. It is hard to take either as worthy of respect or sympathy. The book opens on a deliberately comic note, making the ultimate tragedy—and then the return to comedy at the very end—all the more effective. As Patrick Reilly puts it, the "very style of the fable tames catastrophe through levity, resolves terror in comedy" (64).

Orwell, however, quickly shifts attention from the comical Joneses to the more dignified, respectable boar Old Major, who addresses the animals on a serious topic: "Old Major (so he was always called, though the name under which he had been exhibited was Willingdon Beauty) was so highly regarded on the farm that everyone was quite ready to lose an hour's sleep in order to hear what he had to say" (3). The contrast between Old Major's common name and his show name is variously funny: the show name doesn't fit him at all; it is hard to imagine any boar as a beauty; the name suggests the commercial interests of Farmer Jones. His most important motive in dealing with this prize boar is to market him most effectively. But the fake name also foreshadows later (and far more serious) examples of implausible, manipulative language.

As Orwell sketches the other animals' personalities, more humor arises. Benjamin, for instance, fits the stereotype of a stubborn, irascible donkey, just as he fits the stereotype of the bad-tempered old man (4). Since characters who humorlessly take themselves too seriously can potentially serve as butts of comic irony, Orwell initially suggests that Benjamin may be a target of humorous satire. (Of course, he will ultimately seem one of the more sensible and rational of the animals.) Meanwhile, Clover—a large, kindhearted mare—is more gently humorous: she is a "stout motherly mare approaching middle life, who had never quite got her figure back after her fourth foal" (4). Here as elsewhere, Orwell evokes smiles by comically comparing the predicaments of animals and humans: many middle-aged persons can "relate" to Clover's stoutness, and almost all readers will admire her gentleness: when some temporarily motherless ducklings enter the barn, Clover makes "a sort of wall around them with her great foreleg, and the ducklings [nestle] down inside it and promptly" fall asleep (4).

The makers of the 1954 film took this small, sweet, understated comic episode and ran with it: a single comic duckling appears repeatedly in the film, always getting into misadventures and always accompanied by blatantly "funny" music that ultimately seems manipulative and grating. Anyone who wants to appreciate the subtlety of Orwell's style need only watch the cartoon to see how cheap and cheesy his ideas can be when transferred from page to screen by filmmakers determined to make viewers laugh rather than allowing them to chuckle on their own. Clover is the ideal mother archetype; she is as kindhearted as old Benjamin is sober and irascible. In contrast to many of the animals, the humans seem almost uniformly unappealing (Reilly 82). They are motivated by greed and self-interest more than anything else, and indeed self-centeredness (rather than concern for others) is one of the novel's key themes.

But Orwell doesn't always treat self-centeredness seriously, especially when describing the superficial young mare Mollie, whose very name suggests a lightly comic tone. Imagine how different the effect would be if he had named her Elizabeth, Victoria, or even Mary (for which Mollie is a nickname). Mollie is a figure of fun throughout the book's first half, and it is significant that she disappears completely from the second. She is so completely a comic figure that Orwell dispenses with her entirely when things turn serious. But initially he uses her repeatedly to mock comically (rather than angrily satirize) such flaws as self-interest, vanity, and superficial materialism. She is the archetypal shallow-brained young female who cares more about looking good than about anything serious or substantial: "At the last moment Mollie, the foolish, pretty white mare who drew Mr. Jones's trap, came mincing daintily in, chewing at a lump of sugar. She took a place near the front and began flirting her white mane, hoping to draw attention to the red ribbons it was plaited with" (4). Her superficiality contrasts with (and thus helps emphasize) later, darkly serious developments (Reilly 67).

Orwell's skill at using ironic juxtaposition soon becomes clear. No sooner is the shallow Mollie described than Old Major begins to share his serious thoughts, thoughts that must make any moral human wince. Orwell felt real affection and sympathy for animals, so it is hard not to hear his own values expressed when Old Major shares thoughts that have come to him as he "lay alone in [his] stall":

> Now, comrades, what is the nature of this life of ours? Let us face it: our lives are miserable, laborious, and short. We are born, we are given just so much food as will keep the breath in our bodies, and those of us who are capable of it are forced to work to the last atom of our strength; and the very instant that our usefulness has come to an end we are slaughtered with hideous cruelty. No animal in England knows the meaning of happiness or leisure after he is a year old. No animal in England is free. The life of an animal is misery and slavery: that is the plain truth. (5)

Few readers, after finishing this paragraph, will be able to think of the animals in *Animal Farm* as figures of mere comedy. Whatever good humor they possess or evoke seems remarkable when one considers their inevitable fate, which includes not only their early deaths but exploitation in the meantime. Here is one function of the novel's comedy: Orwell wants to lull readers into a complacency that he then undercuts. He rubs our noses in the brutality farm animals suffer by having Old Major note that

> no animal escapes the cruel knife in the end. You young porkers who are sitting in front of me, every one of you will scream your lives out at the block within a year. To that horror we all must come—cows, pigs, hens, sheep, everyone. Even the horses and the dogs have no better fate. You, Boxer, the very day that those great muscles of yours lose their power, Jones will sell you to the knacker, who will cut your throat and boil you down for the foxhounds. As for the dogs, when they grow old and toothless, Jones ties a brick round their necks and drowns them in the nearest pond. (6-7)

Suddenly the tone of the book, which has heretofore been often comic, changes completely. Jones is no long a ridiculous old drunk;

he is a brutal butcher. The animals who have evoked smiles up to this point are headed for bloody slaughter. All of them will eventually be reduced to meat or raw materials. Even the dogs will be killed when they are no longer useful. Here, in miniature, is one key to the novel's whole design: it makes us smile or laugh and then makes us grimace.

But Orwell doesn't alter the book's comic tone entirely just yet. He describes, for instance, how, while "Major was speaking four large rats had crept out of their holes and were sitting on their hindquarters, listening to him. The dogs had suddenly caught sight of them, and it was only by a swift dash for their holes that the rats saved their lives" (7). In the midst of serious political discussion, the dogs unintentionally interject some madcap, farcical fun. They can't control their instincts, but since no one is hurt, we merely laugh. Later, of course, some specially trained dogs will be used to inflict cruel deaths on hapless victims. Dogs, who seem merely funny here, eventually become symbols of brutal tyranny.

Orwell also mocks the stereotypical conduct of cats. If dogs are often imagined to be enthusiastic, happy-go-lucky, and loyal, cats are typically seen as slyly self-centered and self-absorbed. Thus, it is not surprising, but is still very funny, when Orwell describes the behavior of a stereotypical cat when the animals are asked to decide whether rats can be true comrades: "The vote was taken at once, and it was agreed by an overwhelming majority that rats were comrades. There were only four dissentients, the three dogs and the cat, who was afterwards discovered to have voted on both sides" (7-8). Here, as so often, Orwell treats self-interest as funny—a technique that reinforces the change of tone when self-interest becomes a major theme associated with brutality and tyranny. Similarly, the comically hypocritical behavior of the cat foreshadows the darker, more dangerous hypocrisy that will later become an important issue.

Meanwhile, Orwell's jokes diversify the book's tone, keeping it from seeming relentlessly propagandistic. Paradoxically, the book is all the more effective as propaganda partly because it does not seem obsessed with manipulating our thoughts and feelings. Its comic touches imply that Orwell and the narrator are well-balanced, good-humored, likeable human beings, not narrow-minded anticommunist fanatics. They can see life in much of its fullness and real color rather than seeing only a simple, monochromatic picture. But after the revolution takes full effect, humor will almost seem impossible, if not in bad taste.

For the time being, however, humor of various kinds continues. Old Major, near death, nostalgically remembers not only a tune his mother taught him but, miraculously, words he never even heard before! Both the tune and the words are often silly. The narrator, for instance, reports that "it was a stirring tune, something between 'Clementine' and 'La Cucaracha'" (8). It is hard to imagine two tunes more different in meaning and tempo than these: the first is a slow, sentimental, romantic ballad from the American West; the second is a fast-paced, comic Spanish folk song about a handicapped cockroach. This joke characterizes the narrator as a person of sly wit with an eye for comic incongruities. The narrator's playfulness (at least in the novel's first half) is also evident when he later says of this difficult-to-imagine tune (with its miraculously "remembered" words) that the "cows lowed it, the dogs whined it, the sheep bleated it, the horses whinnied it, the ducks quacked it" (10). In Orwell's book, this is a brief, offhand, amusing comment, but in the 1954 cartoon, the corresponding moment is emphasized so strongly and at such length that it lacks much humor and quickly becomes annoying. Part of the appeal of Orwell's own humor is its subtlety.

Not long after mentioning the singing, Orwell abruptly shifts gears: Old Major, we are told, "died peacefully in his sleep" (10). Attention now turns to characters who dominate the action for the rest of the book: Napoleon, Snowball, and Squealer. These names already have a comic tinge—perhaps too comic in the case of Snowball and Squealer. The name Napoleon in some ways fits this pig's character: he fancies himself a great military leader and will soon prove a tyrant who betrays the hopes the animals place in him. These, of course, were all characteristics displayed by his famed French namesake. But this Napoleon is Orwell's version of Iosif Vissarionovich Dzhugashvili (1878-1953), the Soviet dictator who chose to call himself Stalin ("Steel") to suggest his supposedly unbending strength. Napoleon is an equally and appropriately pretentious name for Orwell's top pig.

Snowball is Orwell's version of Lev Davidovich Bronshtein (1879-1940), who called himself Trotsky and who became Stalin's major rival. The name Snowball seems somewhat too cute, contrasting almost too much with Snowball's later nature. On the other hand, the problem with Squealer is less his name (which in some ways seems very appropriate to his position as chief revolutionary propagandist) than his behavior. He is constantly described as "skipping from side to side and whisking his tail"—actions that were "somehow very persuasive" (11). This cute conduct, like Snowball's cute name, seems almost too obviously comical. In both cases, Orwell risks bathos.

More effective comedy returns when Orwell focuses again on the shallow Mollie. Her main interest, when the planned Rebellion is discussed, is whether she will still have access to sugar and ribbons after the revolution occurs (11-12). Here again, the key theme of narrow self-interest, so important to the whole novel, is raised in comic fashion. Later, when more brutal forms of selfishness appear, the early comedy highlights the striking contrast. Similarly clever are satirical references to the mythical "Sugarcandy Mountain" (12), which symbolizes religious notions of heaven used to pacify and distract the working class from earthly oppression. This shows that Orwell's satire often points in both directions: he not only mocks atheistic communists but also often mocks their ostensibly religious enemies. He never implies that life for the animals is ideal, nor does he make Jones seem anything less than a selfish, self-indulgent fool. Jones's laziness, neglect of the farm, and penchant for alcohol (12) help precipitate his fall: by forgetting to feed the animals, he provokes their Rebellion. And when he and his men try to put down the revolt by whipping the animals, the fact that the humans are "butted and kicked from all sides" (13) seems not only farcical but thoroughly justified. One of the book's best comic moments occurs when Jones's wife, seeing what is happening, deserts her husband and absconds with her own possessions, never to be heard from again (13). So much for "'til death do us part"! This is another example of the sort of throwaway comic moments that make this book sometimes laugh-out-loud funny.

Post-Revolutionary Comedy

Not long after the comic report about Mrs. Jones, Orwell reminds us of the grim reasons for the animals' behavior: the "harness-room at the end of the stables was broken open; the bits, the nose-rings, the dog-chains, the cruel knives with which Mr. Jones had been used to castrate the pigs and lambs, were all flung down the well" (14). Here, as so often, the narrator juxtaposes farcical comedy (Mrs. Jones' desertion) with evidence of sadistic brutality, so that the former tone emphasizes the latter by sheer contrast. Just when we have finished laughing we feel the need to grimace in guilt, especially since we realize that Jones is no different from almost all farmers in using such instruments of painful discipline and domination. The references to butchering are likely to disturb any meat eater with a conscience.

But right after Orwell makes us wince he makes us smile. When the animals are told that it is wrong to wear any kind of clothing (including ribbons), Boxer, in his typically self-sacrificing way, fetches "the small straw hat which he wore in summer to keep the flies out of his ears, and flung it on to the fire with the rest" (14). We smile because Boxer's decision is unwise: he would be an even better, more contented, more productive worker if had chosen to keep the hat, but his willingness to make common cause with the other animals is commendable. Mollie, after all, doesn't need her ribbons, but Boxer's hat served a practical purpose. His inability to see the distinction is part of Orwell's gentle satire of this gentle beast, whose motives are always good but whose intelligence is limited. Boxer, because he lacks intelligence, is partly a figure of fun, but his limited intellect also makes him easy for the pigs to manipulate. Orwell once more uses comedy to make subtle political points.

Just as Boxer's limited intelligence serves the interests of the increasingly dominant and domineering pigs, so Mollie's continual vanity comically symbolizes the kind of self-centeredness that will eventually pervert the original goals of the revolution. Joining a tour

---

of the now-vacated farmhouse, Mollie lags behind, having spotted "a piece of blue ribbon from Mrs. Jones's dressing-table." The other animals find her "holding it against her shoulder and admiring herself in the glass in a very foolish manner" (15). Mollie is a constant target of Orwell's mockery, but her superficial selfishness and vanity pale in comparison with the later behavior of the pigs, especially Napoleon. She, like the equally self-centered Mrs. Jones, soon disappears from the novel. There comes a point when joking about Mollie's taste for fancy ribbons seems too trivial and repetitive to be worth mentioning.

Sometimes, however, Orwell surprises readers with just a plain old laugh-out-loud funny comment. He mentions, for instance, that at the conclusion of the house tour some "hams hanging in the kitchen were taken out for burial" (15)—a report that reminds us not only how different the perspectives of humans and animals can be but also that the narrator has a sly sense of fun. With obviously comic evasiveness, the narrator reports that the pigs somehow "caused" a ladder "to be set" against the barn (16)—a nice instance of the passive voice being used to comic effect. Later we are explicitly told that "it is not easy for a pig to balance himself on a ladder,"(16) an admission that calls comic attention to the whole idea of the animals performing certain actions. By calling explicit attention to the liberties he is taking with literal realism, Orwell forestalls any criticism of those liberties: he is winking at the reader and saying, in essence, "I know this is implausible if not impossible, but play along with me. Let's have some fun." Orwell also provokes smiles by indicating that animals are not the world's best spellers, by suggesting that pigs are somehow capable of milking cows, and by noting that many of the animals look "with considerable interest" on the milk thus produced (16-17). The self-interest of the animals is only comic at this point, but it doesn't take long for Orwell to imply darker motives and actual deception. When the other animals (including Snowball) leave, Napoleon consumes the milk himself. Napoleon-as-Stalin has begun to emerge.

Comedy during the Dictatorship

Comedy is still a frequent presence in chapter 3. It is hard not to smile when the narrator reports that a pig walking behind two work horses shouts at them "'Gee up, comrade!' or "'Whoa back, comrade!'" as they perform their tasks (18). Here, the sheer incongruity between commands to animals and egalitarian Marxist jargon is amusing, but even this moment may comically foreshadow the much darker divergence between glib words and brutal exploitation later in the book. Orwell also mocks the communist tendency to bureaucratize everything in sight: Snowball (the more intellectual of the two leading pigs)

> formed the Egg Production Committee for the hens, the Clean Tails League for the cows, the Wild Comrades' Re-education Committee (the object of this was to tame the rats and rabbits), the Whiter Wool Movement for the sheep, and various others, besides instituting classes in reading and writing. On the whole, these projects were a failure. The attempt to tame the wild creatures, for instance, broke down almost immediately. They continued to behave very much as before, and when treated with generosity, simply took advantage of it. The cat joined the Re-education Committee and was very active in it for some days. She was seen one day sitting on a roof and talking to some sparrows who were just out of her reach. She was telling them that all animals were now comrades and that any sparrow who chose could come and perch on her paw; but the sparrows kept their distance. (20-21)

The first two committees mentioned are merely laughable, but the reference to the "Re-education Committee" is more ominous, reminding us that communists typically want to brainwash people rather than merely exploit their labor. The resistance of the wild animals to reeducation makes an effective comic point about the resilience of human nature and the practical wisdom of truly recognizing where one's real interests lie. Meanwhile, the humorous connivances of the cat imply that the "comrades" in charge of "re-education" efforts often have self-interested motives of their own.

Ensuing comic moments often illustrate the need to simplify propaganda by creating short slogans so that the farm's new values can be understood by the lowest common denominator of animal intelligence (21). Orwell continually stresses that the animals' intellectual limitations make them ripe for manipulation, satirizing the ways totalitarian regimes justify their conduct by alleging that it makes scientific sense (23). But Orwell's humor is occasionally purely slapstick, a fact that complicates and enriches the book's tones. For instance, as the revolutionary spirit begins to spread to other farms, some horses used for hunting refuse to jump obstacles and toss their humans onto the ground (25). Then, when the humans mount an armed attack on Animal Farm, they find themselves being shat upon by defiant pigeons (25). Jones himself gets tossed into a pile of dung (26). Thus, even the violence in this part of the book is comic: if any of the animals had seriously injured or killed a human, they might suddenly seem less sympathetic (Reilly 65). When Boxer fears that he may have unintentionally killed a person—a boy, no less—he is deeply distraught, once again illustrating his fundamental decency. Orwell flirts here with the possibility of tragedy only to dismiss it for the time being: the boy is not dead but merely stunned, so this incident, at least, has a happy ending (27). The book's actual violent deaths come later and will be suffered not by humans but by the animals themselves.

Meanwhile, Orwell continues to have fun with the animals' self-centeredness, such as their boasting about their military valor, Mollie's continuing vanity, and the comic parody of the "fallen woman": Mollie creates a minor scandal by letting a human stroke her nose (29). Various kinds of humor follow: the low comedy of dung-dropping (30), crude physical humor (although with ominous overtones) such as when Napoleon urinates on Snowball's careful, chalk-drawn architectural plans (31), Snowball's comic evasiveness (31), and the vivid comic imagery of a pig running at great speed, "as only a pig can run" (33). Menacing notes do occasionally appear, as when the dogs whom Napoleon has been secretly training growl "threateningly" (36), but for the most part the humor in this section of the book only hints at darker things to come. Thus, Napoleon commands Sunday work but, in classic doublespeak, calls it "strictly voluntary" (37); "even the pigs" sometimes perform such labor (already hinting at their special status and privileges); and humans draw diagrams to "prove to one another" that a construction project undertaken by the animals cannot succeed, parodying foolish optimism and self-deception (41).

Yet the examples of humor just cited deal increasingly with serious matters. Parallels between developments on the farm and the real-world history of the Soviet Union become more obvious. We are no longer laughing about buried hams or pigeon droppings. Instead, we begin to see an emerging satire of the development of a totalitarian state. Napoleon needs "a quiet place to work in"—Jones's farmhouse—a place that suits "the dignity of the Leader (for of late [Squealer] had taken to speaking of Napoleon under the title of 'Leader')" (41). This passage reminds us of a point too often forgotten: that the Nazis borrowed many of their own terms and practices from the Soviets. Likewise, when Boxer unthinkingly assumes that anything Napoleon declares "must be right," Orwell mocks the credulity of the unintelligent proletariat everywhere, who lack the capacity for (and perhaps even any interest in) critical thinking (50).

When Napoleon awards himself "Animal Hero, First Class," and—for good measure— "Animal Hero, Second Class" (50) we are at a far cry from Mollie's silly love of ribbons. But Orwell's point is precisely this contrast between superficial vanity and the all-encompassing pride of a dictator. Our earlier amusement at Mollie has been replaced by a growing recognition that Napoleon's hubris is infinite. It hardly seems surprising that the joke about his medals is followed by a reference to his "nine huge dogs frisking round him and uttering growls that sent shivers down all the animals' spines" (50). These are the dogs who subsequently attack Napoleon's enemies, tearing their throats out (50-51). The days of laughter are over.

Orwell's humor from this point forward becomes almost entirely satiric. A poet aptly named Minimus (partly because of his minimal literary talent) creates a fawning, pathetically inept song celebrating

---

Napoleon as (among other things) the *"Lord of the swill bucket"* (56). This phrase parodies the crudeness of much totalitarian "art" as well as the pure material self-interest that leads many people to support dictators: so long as one is well fed, nothing else matters. Through Minimus, Orwell skewers intellectuals who serve the interests of totalitarian regimes. So long as compliant artists kowtow to the all-powerful state and its "Leader," they can get away with songs as bad as this: *"Had I a sucking-pig, / Ere he had grown as big / Even as a pint bottle or as a rolling-pin, / He should have learned to be / Faithful and true to thee, / Yes, his first squeak should be /'Comrade Napoleon!'"* (56). These lines show that Orwell has not lost his touch for the absurd, but he soon mocks not only Napoleon's lackeys but the Great Pig himself. The dear Leader, afraid of being poisoned, appoints a young pig (comically named Pinkeye) as his food taster (57). Later, the great military hero directs defense of the farm against human attack, but he does so safely "from the rear" (62). Moreover, Orwell also notes that Squealer makes himself "absent during the fighting" (63). By now, any such comedy provokes only rueful sneers: Napoleon and Squealer may be cowardly, but somehow they remain firmly in control. No one dares mock them to their faces, if at all. No comedians or even licensed fools (of the sort famous from Shakespeare's *King Lear*) can exist in this brave new world of humorless tyranny.

But even as *Animal Farm* moves through its horrifying middle sections toward its ironic and absurd conclusion, Orwell pauses to include some farcical comedy. The episode involving the drunken pigs (64-65), in which Napoleon assumes that he is going to die because he has never suffered a severe hangover before, is one of the book's funniest moments. It is all the funnier because Orwell lets readers figure out for themselves why Napoleon and Squealer are feeling so sick. (Perhaps many readers can relate.) This episode not only shows the hypocrisy of the new regime but also associates its leaders, ironically, with Farmer Jones, whose alcoholism—the butt of previous humor—ultimately leads to his downfall. Orwell suggests that powerful figures, whether human or animal, capitalist or communist, will always overindulge their appetites. But here only the pigs are hypocritical about their drinking. Jones didn't care that he was a drunk, but Napoleon and Squealer mask or justify their taste for booze. The problem, they explain, isn't drinking per se but drinking "to excess" (66). Orwell thus parodies the constantly changing party line in communist dictatorships. (Fascist dictatorships rarely seem to feel the need to alter their rigid rules.)

As the book concludes, the humor darkens. The reference to "Spontaneous Demonstration[s]" (68), for instance, involves the kind of absurd oxymoron that Orwell would later lampoon so mercilessly in *Nineteen Eighty-Four*. Likewise, the claim that the animals are now "truly their own masters" is absurd (69). We may smile, but nothing suggests that this dictatorship is in danger of falling soon, if ever: Napoleon is far smarter (and more brutal) than Jones ever was. At least Jones would not have lied about Boxer's fate, as Napoleon's regime hypocritically does. It is hard to laugh any longer. Even Jones's death—in an "inebriates' home" (75)—seems pathetic; it is reported in passing, along with the deaths of various animals.

Conclusion

Humor emphasizes the contrast between the often comic opening chapters of *Animal Farm* and the brutal realities of the second half, keeping the book from seeming blatantly, narrowly, and darkly propagandistic. It thereby, ironically, makes the book more effective as propaganda. Orwell's humor implies that although some regimes are worse than others, self-centeredness and selfish motives afflict most societies. The satire is directed as much at human nature as at the flaws of any particular political system (Reilly 87-88). Orwell's dark humor frequently implies the sheer absurdity, ridiculousness, and hypocrisy of totalitarian regimes, especially the tendency of those regimes to corrupt not only thought but also language. From one perspective, such tyrannies are hard to take seriously; from another perspective, they must be taken very seriously indeed. Sometimes the parodic aspects of this book are laugh-out-loud funny; sometimes they are ominously dark. Each tone emphasizes the other. Orwell's use of humor displays his range as a writer, even as it implies that people who fall for foolish ideas are foolish themselves. Since the very essence of laughter implies a kind of freedom, a kind of letting go, and an ability to perceive irrationality, real humor is always a threat to totalitarianism. Dictators such as Hitler, Stalin, Mao, and Kim Il Jun know how to deal with direct challenges to their power. But they cannot stand the thought of being ridiculed.[2]

Notes

1. Humor *is* discussed extensively by Patrick Reilly, although he also emphasizes Swiftian satire.
2. As I finish this essay, the Communist Party of China has just announced that *Animal Farm* will be banned in that country. This decision coincides with President Xi Jinping's drive to abolish term limits and become president (i.e., dictator) for life. Another Napoleon is born.

Works Cited

Animal Farm. Directed by John Halas and Joy Batchelor, performances by Maurice Denham and Gordon Heath, de Rochemont Films, 1954.

Orwell, George. *Animal Farm / 1984*. Harcourt, 2003.

Reilly, Patrick. "The Utopian Shipwreck." In *George Orwell's* Animal Farm: *Modern Critical Interpretations*. Edited by Harold Bloom, Chelsea House, 199, pp. 61-89.

RESOURCES

Chronology of George Orwell's Life _____

1903	George Orwell was born Eric Arthur Blair on June 25 in Motihari, Bengal (now part of India), to Richard Walmesley Blair and Ida Mabel Blair (née Limouzin). His older sister, Marjorie Frances Blair, was born on April 21, 1898.
1904	Richard Blair settles his young family in England following an outbreak of plague.
1908	Avril Norah Blair, Orwell's younger sister, born on April 6.
1911-17	Orwell attends St. Cyprian's, a private boarding school in Eastbourne, Sussex, on partial scholarship; befriends Cyril Connolly, a fellow student.
1917	Attends spring term at Wellington College on scholarship.
1917-21	Attends Eton College, where Aldous Huxley is his French teacher, on scholarship as a King's Scholar.
1922-27	Works as a police officer in Burma.
1927-28	Returns to England, stays initially with family then settles in London, living intermittently among tramps.
1928-29	Moves to a working-class neighborhood in Paris and works as a journalist. Does various menial jobs to supplement his small income. Returns to England in December of 1929.

1930	Works in England over the next five years as a private tutor, a bookseller, and a teacher. Occasionally tramps under the assumed name P. S. Burton.
1933	*Down and Out in Paris and London* published under the pseudonym George Orwell.
1934	*Burmese Days* published.
1935	*A Clergyman's Daughter* published.
1935	Meets his future wife, Eileen O'Shaughnessy.
1936	Travels to north of England on assignment from his publisher Victor Gollancz to investigate living conditions among the poor. His experiences there provide material for *The Road to Wigan Pier*.
1936	*Keep the Aspidistra Flying* published.
1936	Marries Eileen O'Shaughnessy on June 9, 1936.
1936	Leaves for Spain in December to support Republican Cause.
1937	Serves in POUM Militia and is wounded in the throat by sniper fire on May 20. Flees Spain when POUM is outlawed by Spanish government. *Road to Wigan Pier* published while Orwell is in Spain.
1938	*Homage to Catalonia* published.
1939	*Coming Up for Air* published.
1939	Richard Blair dies.
1940	*Inside the Whale and Other Essays* published.

1941	"The Lion and the Unicorn: Socialism and the English Genius" published.
1941-43	Works as English language producer for the Indian Section of the BBC.
1943	Ida Blair dies.
1943-45	Works as literary editor for *Tribune*.
1944	Orwell and his wife adopt a three-week-old baby, naming him Richard Horatio Blair.
1945	Eileen Blair dies.
1945	*Animal Farm* published.
1946	*Critical Essays* published.
1946	Marjorie Dakin (née Blair), Orwell's older sister, dies.
1946	Relocates to Jura.
1949	*Nineteen Eighty-Four* published.
1949	Marries Sonia Brownell on October 13.
1950	Dies of pulmonary tuberculosis on January 21.

Major Works by George Orwell_____

Novels

Burmese Days (1934)

A Clergyman's Daughter (1935)

Keep the Aspidistra Flying (1936)

Coming Up for Air (1939)

Animal Farm (1945)

Nineteen Eighty-Four (1949)

Nonfiction

Down and Out in Paris and London (1933)

The Road to Wigan Pier (1937)

Homage to Catalonia (1938)

Inside the Whale and Other Essays (1940)

"The Lion and the Unicorn: Socialism and the English Genius" (1941)

Critical Essays / US edition: *Dickens, Dali, and Others: Studies in Popular Culture* (1946)

Shooting an Elephant and Other Essays (1950)

"Such, Such Were the Joys" (1952)

The Collected Essays, Journalism, and Letters of George Orwell (four volumes, 1968)

Orwell: The War Broadcasts / US edition: *Orwell: The Lost Writings* (1985)

Orwell: The War Commentaries (1986)

Other

The Complete Works of George Orwell (twenty volumes, 1986-1998)

The Lost Orwell (2006)

Orwell: Diaries (2009)

Orwell: A Life in Letters (2010)

Bibliography

Baker, Russell. Preface. *Animal Farm*, by George Orwell. Signet Classics, 2015.

Bowker, Gordon. *George Orwell*. Abacus, 2004.

Bloom, Harold, editor. *Bloom's Modern Critical Interpretations: George Orwell's Animal Farm*. Chelsea House, 2009.

Carr, Craig L. *Orwell, Politics, and Power*. Bloomsbury, 2010.

Cole, Stewart. "'The True Struggle': Orwell and the Specter of the Animal." *Lit: Literature Interpretation Theory*, vol. 28, no. 4, 2017, pp. 335-53.

Cook, Timothy. "Upton Sinclair's *The Jungle* and Orwell's *Animal Farm*: A Relationship Explored." *Modern Fiction Studies*, vol. 30, no. 4, 1984, pp. 696-703.

Crick, Bernard. *George Orwell: A Life*. Penguin, 1982.

Dwan, David. "Orwell's Paradox: Equality in *Animal Farm*." *ELH*, vol. 79, no. 3, 2012, pp. 655-83.

Elbarbary, Samir. "Language as Theme in *Animal Farm*." *International Fiction Review*, vol. 19, no. 1, 1992, pp: 31-38.

Farrow, Stephen. "Debating in the Curriculum." *The Use of English*, vol. 58, no. 2, 2007, pp. 116-33.

Fergenson, Laraine. "George Orwell's *Animal Farm*: A Twentieth-Century Beast Fable." *Bestia*, vol. 2, 1990, pp. 109-18.

Fowler, Roger. *The Language of George Orwell*. St. Martin's, 1995.

Gottlieb, Erika. "George Orwell's Dystopias: *Animal Farm* and *Nineteen Eighty-Four*." *A Companion to the British and Irish Novel*, edited by Brian W. Shaffer, Wiley-Blackwell, 2004, pp. 241-53.

Grofman, Bernard. "Pig and Proletariat: *Animal Farm* as History." *San Jose Studies*, vol. 16, no. 2, 1990, pp. 5-39.

Gulbin, Suzanne. "Parallels and Contrasts in *Lord of the Flies* and *Animal Farm*. *English Journal,* vol. 55, no. 1, 1966, pp. 86-88, 92.

Harger-Grinling, Virginia, and Chantal Jordaan, "Fifty Years On: *Animal Farm* Gets Under the Skin Author(s)." *Journal of the Fantastic in the Arts*, vol. 14, no. 2, 2003, pp. 246-54.

Hollis, Christopher. *A Study of George Orwell*. Hollis and Carter, 1956.

Hunter, Lynette. "*Animal Farm*: Satire into Allegory." *George Orwell*, edited by Graham Holderness, Bryan Loughrey, Yousaf Nahem. St. Martin's, 1998, pp. 31-46.

Jones, Myrddin. "Orwell, Wells and the Animal Fable." *Journal of the English Association*, vol. 33, no. 146, 1984, pp. 127-36.

Kirschner, Paul. "The Dual Purpose of *Animal Farm*." *Review of English Studies*, vol. 55, no. 222, 2004, pp. 759-86.

Lee, Robert A. "The Uses of Form: A Rereading of *Animal Farm*." *Studies in Short Fiction*, vol. 6, no. 5, 1969, pp. 557-73.

Letemendia, V. C. "Revolution on *Animal Farm*: Orwell's Neglected Commentary." *George Orwell*, edited by Graham Holderness. St. Martin's, 1998, pp. 15-30.

Ligda, Kenneth. "Orwellian Comedy." *Twentieth-Century Literature*, vol. 60, no. 4, 2014, pp. 513-37.

Magráns, Ramón. "Anti-Totalitarianism in *Animal Farm* and *Time of the Hero*." *Maria Vargas Llosa: Opera Omnia*, edited by Ana María Hernández de López. Pliegos, 1994, pp. 393-400.

McHugh, Susan. "*Animal Farm*'s Lessons for Literary (and) Animal Studies." *Humanimalia*, vol. 1, no. 1, 2009, pp. 24-39.

Meyers, Jeffrey. "Orwell's Bestiary: The Political Allegory of *Animal Farm*." *Studies in the Twentieth Century*, vol. 8, 1971, pp. 65-84.

Morse, Donald E. "A Blatancy of Untruth: George Orwell's Uses of the Fantastic in *Animal Farm*." *Hungarian Journal of English and American Studies*, vol. 1, no. 2, 1995, pp. 85-92.

O'Neill, Terry, editor. *Readings on Animal Farm*. Greenhaven, 1998.

Patai, Daphne. *The Orwell Mystique*. U of Massachusetts P, 1984.

Pearce, Robert. "Orwell, Tolstoy, and *Animal Farm*." *Review of English Studies*, vol. 49, no. 193, pp. 64-69.

Popescu, Andreea. "Four Legs Good, Two Legs Bad: The Dystopia of Power in George Orwell's *Animal Farm*." *From Francis Bacon to William Golding: Utopias and Dystopias Today and of Yore*, edited by Ligia Tomoiagă, MinodoraBarbul, and Ramona Demarcsek. Cambridge Scholars, 2012, pp. 192-200.

Pyle, Steve. "George Orwell's *Animal Farm*: The Little Book That Could." *The Antigonish Review*, vol. 111, pp. 31-36.

Rodden, John. "Big Rock (Sugar)candy Mountain? How George Orwell Tramped toward *Animal Farm.*" *Papers on Language and Literature*, vol. 46, no. 3, 2010, pp. 315-41.

_____. *Cambridge Companion to George Orwell*, Cambridge UP, 2007.

_____. *Understanding Animal Farm*. Greenwood, 1999.

Rodden, John, and John Rossi. "A Book More Equal than Others: Orwell, *Animal Farm*, and the Commonweal Catholic." *Commonweal*, 2016, vol. 143, no. 15, pp. 16-21.

_____. "*Animal Farm* at 70." *Modern Age*, vol. 58, no. 4, 2016, pp. 19-27.

Savage, Robert. "Are Rats Comrades? Some Readings of a Question in Orwell." *Colloquy*, vol. 12, 2006, pp. 83-90.

Shelden, Michael. *Orwell: The Authorized Biography*, Harper Perennial, 1992.

Smyer, Richard I. "*Animal Farm*: The Burden of Consciousness." *English Language Notes*, vol. 9, no. 1, 1971, pp. 55-59.

_____. *Animal Farm: Pastoralism and Politics*. Twayne, 1988.

Spencer, Luke. "*Animal Farm* and *Nineteen Eighty-Four*." *George Orwell*, edited by J. A. Jowitt and Richard K. S. Taylor. U of Leeds P, 1981, pp. 67-83.

Thagard, Paul. "The Brain is Wider than the Sky: Analogy, Emotion, and Allegory. *Metaphor and Symbol*, vol. 26, 2011, pp. 131-42.

Woloch, Alex. *Or Orwell: Writing and Democratic Socialism*. Harvard UP, 2016.

Yoon, Haeryung. "On Purposeless Evil in George Orwell's *Animal Farm* and *1984*." *British and American Fiction*, vol. 21, no. 3, 2014, pp. 239-56.

Zwerdling, Alex. *Orwell and the Left*. Yale UP, 1974.

About the Editor

Thomas Horan is a professor of English at The Citadel. He holds an AB from Harvard University, a JD from Cornell University, and a PhD from the University of North Carolina. His teaching and research interests include dystopian literature, twentieth-century British and Commonwealth literature, and modern and contemporary drama. His monograph, *Desire and Empathy in Twentieth-Century Dystopian Fiction*, was published by Palgrave Macmillan in 2018. He edited *Critical Insights: Nineteen Eighty-Four*. His work appears in *Modern Drama, Extrapolation*, and *The Arthur Miller Journal*. He has also contributed chapters to *Critical Insights: Dystopia* and *Critical Insights: Brave New World*.

Contributors

Dario Altobelli holds a PhD in social and cultural anthropology and another PhD in sociology, both from Sapienza University of Rome, and a specialization in archival science from the State Archive in Rome. He teaches sociology of law at the University of Rome 3 and collaborates with the chairs of sociology in the department of political sciences in Sapienza University of Rome. He has published *L'utile e il ragionevole. Saggio su Cesare Lombroso* (2017); *I sogni della biologia. Utopia e ideologia delle scienze della vita del Novecento* (2012); *Il fondo archivistico Gaetano Mosca* (2010); *Indagine su un bandito. Il caso Musolino* (2006). He is also the author of various articles on utopia, science, and the history of the human and social sciences published in academic journals and in edited books, including "The Cold, White Reproduction of the Same: A New Hypothesis About John Carpenter's *The Thing*" in *Horror in Space: Critical Essays on a Film Subgenre*, (2017); "The 'reasonableness' of irrationality: A sociological reading of Cesare Lombroso and his Work" in *Between Rationality and Irrationality: Early Sociological Theory in Italy* (2017); "*Nineteen Eighty-Four* Today: The Impossible Desire to Archive as the Secret Core of Ideology" in *Critical Insights: Nineteen Eighty-Four* (2016); "Utopia and the Archive. Some Reflections on Archaeology of Knowledge and the Utopian Thought" in *Engaging Foucault*, (2015).

Gregory Brophy is chair of the English Department at Bishop's University in Sherbrooke, Quebec. He published "Gothic Optics and Impressionable Minds in Richard Marsh's *The Beetle*," as part of a collection of essays titled *Monstrous Media* (2012) and "The Sphygmograph: Pros-theses on the Body" in *Victorian Review* in the fall of 2009. His teaching and scholarship interests include Victorian and Modern British Literature as well and film and visual culture. He has studied at Trent and Queen's University (BEd), and earned his Masters and his PhD in English Literature at Western University.

Paige Busby is a PhD student at the Ohio State University. Her interests lie primarily in nineteenth-century transatlantic literature, where she studies the intersection of utopian and dystopian studies as philosophical concepts and literary genres.

Andrew Byers (PhD, Duke, 2012) served as visiting assistant professor in the department of history at Duke University. He researches the history of the regulation of the human body and the intersection of science, sexuality, and law in civilian and military contexts. He is coeditor of *Biopolitics and Utopia: An Interdisciplinary Reader* (2015) and author of the forthcoming monograph *The Sexual Economy of War: Discipline and Desire in the U.S. Army* (2019).

Richard Carr is senior lecturer in history and politics at Anglia Ruskin University, UK. He has published widely on twentieth-century history, including a political biography of *Charlie Chaplin* (2016), and the monograph *Veteran MPs and Conservative Politics in the Aftermath of the Great War* (2013). He is currently working on a history of The Third Way, provisionally entitled *March of the Moderates*.

Robert C. Evans is I. B. Young Professor of English at Auburn University at Montgomery. He earned his PhD from Princeton University in 1984. In 1982 he began teaching at AUM, where he has been named Distinguished Research Professor, Distinguished Teaching Professor, and University Alumni Professor. External awards include fellowships from the American Council of Learned Societies, the American Philosophical Society, the National Endowment for the Humanities, the UCLA Center for Medieval and Renaissance Studies, and the Folger, Huntington, and Newberry Libraries. He is the author or editor of roughly fifty books and of more than four hundred essays, including recent work on various American writers.

Charity Gibson received her MA in English literature from Missouri State University and her PhD in literature and criticism from Indiana University of Pennsylvania. Her dissertation focuses on twentieth-century American literature and includes a multidisciplinary approach, interweaving sociology and anthropology into literary analysis. She has also written in collections focusing on topics regarding modern American

---

literature. She is an assistant professor of English at College of the Ozarks, where she teaches literature, composition, and critical theory.

Bradley Hart is assistant professor at California State University, Fresno. He is the author of *George Pitt-Rivers and the Nazis*, a biography exploring the life of a major British anthropologist who turned to far-right politics in the 1930s. His forthcoming book, *Hitler's American Friends: The Third Reich's Supporters in the United States* will be published in October 2018.

Brian Ireland is originally from Belfast in Northern Ireland. He did his undergraduate degree at the University of Ulster and on exchange at the University of Wyoming. After completing an MA in American Studies at the University of Ulster, he moved to Honolulu, living there for five years while completing a PhD at the University of Hawaii, Manoa. He is the author of two books of modern history. He has written about such diverse topics as the US military in Hawaii, road narratives, horror and science fiction stories, and comic books. His latest book, published by Manchester University Press in 2017, is entitled *The Hippie Trail: A History*. He has received a number of awards, including a Centre for Asia-Pacific Exchange scholarship, an Access to College Excellence award, and a Carl Bode Journal Award.

Erik Jaccard is a lecturer in English at the University of Washington, Seattle. He completed his PhD in English in 2017, and his dissertation, "Speculative Fiction, Catastrophe, and the Devolutionary Imagination in Postwar Britain," explores how British speculative and science fiction novels written between 1945 and 2000 extend, challenge, and reimagine narratives of British imperial culture as post-British futures. His research focuses on the intersections between British devolutionary cultures, science fiction, and postcolonial theory, and he has secondary expertise in African literature and Scottish literature. In 2016, his essay "Not Death, But Annihilation: Orwell's *1984* and the Catastrophe of Englishness" appeared in *Critical Insights*: *Nineteen Eighty-Four*. He has also published in *Foundation* and *Studies in Scottish Literature*, and is currently at work on his first book, a study of British catastrophe narrative from H. G. Wells to the present.

Melanie A. Marotta received her PhD in English from Morgan State University, Baltimore, Maryland. She is a lecturer in the Department of English and Language Arts and an editor for the Museum of Science Fiction's *Journal of Science Fiction*. She is originally from Ontario, Canada, and received her BA in English from the University of Guelph. Her research focuses on science fiction, the American West, contemporary American literature (in particular African American), young adult literature, and ecocriticism. She is currently working on a collection about the science fiction Western.

Rafeeq O. McGiveron holds a BA with Honors in English and History from Michigan State University, an MA in English and History from MSU, and an MA in English from Western Michigan University. He has published several dozen articles, chapters, and reference entries on the works of authors ranging from Ray Bradbury and Robert A. Heinlein to Willa Cather and Shakespeare, including editing *Critical Insights: Fahrenheit 451* (2013), *Critical Insights: Robert A. Heinlein* (2015), and *Critical Insights: Ray Bradbury* (2017) for Salem Press. Currently he works in student services at Lansing Community College, where he has served since 1992. He also dabbles in fiction, occasionally poetry, and mobile art. His website, which includes huge galleries of Heinlein cover art, is www.rafeeqmcgiveron.com, and his novel *Student Body* was released in 2014.

Josephine A. McQuail is a professor of English at Tennessee Technological University. *Focus on Frame: Women Analyze the Works of the New Zealand Writer,* her edited collection of essays, was published in 2018 by McFarland Publishers. She is currently working on a project on James Joyce and William Blake. She also has an interest in utopian and dystopian communities, real and imagined, and serves on the board of directors of Historic Rugby, Tennessee.

Camilo Peralta is an associate professor of English at Independence Community College. His research interests include medieval literature and culture and the influence of religion on modern society. He is also a PhD student at Faulkner University in Montgomery, Alabama.

Index

Skradol, Natalia 108, 117
slaughterhouse 44
Smith, Adam xxii
Smith, Winston 49, 55, 105
Smyer, Richard I. xvi
Snowball xiii, 18, 24, 39, 40, 43,
    45, 51, 52, 64, 65, 69, 86,
    87, 88, 95, 97, 99, 100, 111,
    112, 123, 124, 128, 134,
    138, 149, 164, 175, 185,
    186, 188, 189, 190
Socialism vii, xii, xiii, xxvii,
    xxviii, 3, 4, 7, 8, 10, 11, 13,
    24, 27, 32, 64, 71, 73, 93,
    118, 126, 149
socialist revolution 8, 10
social order 69, 70, 107, 156, 161,
    164, 165
society 9, 17, 129, 179
Soule, George 7, 72
Soviet Communism 22, 28, 129,
    148
Soviet myth xi, xii, 4, 32, 64
Soviet socialism 149
Soviet Union xii, xxi, 5, 9, 12, 19,
    23, 26, 28, 29, 77, 123, 125,
    133, 137, 142, 148, 172,
    178, 191
Spanish Civil War xii
speciesism xix, 34
Spiegelman, Art 71, 145
Spiegelman, Vladek 71
Squealer xiii, 24, 40, 41, 42, 43,
    51, 83, 84, 85, 86, 87, 88,
    95, 96, 99, 120, 174, 185,
    186, 191, 192, 193
Stalinism xii, xxi, 4, 7, 28, 92,
    111, 112, 114, 115, 116, 117,
    124, 133, 135, 171

Stalinist socialism 10
Stalin, Joseph 64, 108
Stalin's Peasants 115, 116
Stanford, W. Bedell 151
state, the 123, 127, 156, 157, 158,
    168, 169, 171, 172, 173, 174
Sutherland, John 135
Swift, Jonathan vii, 65, 144
symbolism 121, 143
sympathy xvii, 113, 181, 183
synecdoche 45

Tambling, Jeremy 109
Tatar, Maria 131
Ten Commandments, the 100,
    101, 103, 161
tenor 142, 148
Thinking with Animals 143, 152
third-person limited POV 49, 56,
    57, 59
third-person omniscient POV 49
Thompson, E. P. 10
Thomson, Rosemarie Garland 131
Thorndycraft, Lynne 113
Tiffin, Helen 43
tone xvii, 45, 79, 86, 106, 180,
    182, 183, 184, 187, 193
total institution 171, 175, 176, 177
totalitarian communism 64, 118
totalitarian fascism 64
totalitarianism xiv, xxviii, xxix,
    9, 19, 27, 48, 57, 71, 77, 78,
    81, 82, 120, 134, 167, 171,
    177, 178, 194
tragedy 24, 40, 181, 190
Trilling, Lionel 8
Trotskyism 112
Trotsky, Leon 64
Trumpism ix, 148